STATE OF PLAY

Poets of East & Southeast Asian Heritage in Conversation

Edited by Eddie Tay & Jennifer Wong

Out-Spoken Press
London

Published by Out-Spoken Press,
PO Box 78744,
London, N11 9FG

First edition published 2023
ISBN: 978-1-7399021-4-8

Typeset in Adobe Caslon
Design by Patricia Ferguson
Printed and bound by Print Resources

Out-Spoken Press is supported using public funding by the National
Lottery through Arts Council England.

Supported using public funding by
ARTS COUNCIL
ENGLAND

CONTENTS

HOME

*

*

***

INTRODUCTION

It has been an inspiring journey editing this book of conversations among Asian poets. At the beginning of this project, we set out to ask what we think of ourselves as poets, and how do our race, our home(s), and cultural heritage, shape our sense of belonging, our ways of seeing or experiencing the world? How can we learn from and offer support to each other? These topics range from the sense of home, racialised expectations and community, to multilingualism as well as the process of writing poetry.

We are delighted by this book's exciting, international line-up of poets, showing us the ways a life lived in many places invigorates one's writing. Shirley Geok-lin Lim, the Asian American poet, novelist, critic, and winner of the Commonwealth Poetry Prize, chats with her longtime friend, Leong Liew Geok, author of *Love is Not Enough* and *Women without Men*.[1] Their conversation ranges from their shared sense of 'nomadism' that includes living in the US, Malaysia, Singapore, and elsewhere, to the very first time they wrote seriously. Yanyi, who wrote *Dream of the Divided Field* and Mary Jean Chan, author of *Bright Fear*, meanwhile, reflect on their personal beginnings as writers, the life-changing force in poetry, and the importance of trusting one's writing.[2]

As writers ourselves, we are thrilled by the rich insights into the creative process of these writers. Li-Young Lee, a leading Asian American poet, shares with us a new poem, telling us how he thinks of the act of writing as 'a spiritual practice', describing it as going from 'my-doing' to 'not-my-doing'. Born in eastern China and having moved to the US with her family as a child, Jenny Xie discusses with US-based Chinese-Scottish poet and author of *Imperium*, Jay Gao, her process of revision and publishing her work:[3] 'We're allowed gratitude, glee, pride, cheer, joy—all tempered, or

---

1 Leong Liew Geok, *Love is Not Enough* (Times Books International, 1991) and *Women without Men* (Times Books International, 2000).

2 Yanyi, *Dream of the Divided Field* (One World, 2022); Mary Jean Chan, *Bright Fear* (Faber, 2023).

3 Jay Gao, *Imperium* (Carcanet, 2022).

marbled, by some degree of modesty. What gets discussed far less, at least in public, is the private discomfort and alienation.'

We see how writing becomes a source of inner joy for the artist, a welcoming home. Kit Fan, Hong Kong-born and UK-based author of *The Ink Cloud Reader* and Winner of the Northern Writers' Award for Poetry, talks about how 'poetry is no fun without taking risks.'[4] Victoria Chang, author of the Griffin Poetry Prize-shortlisted *OBIT* and *The Trees Witness Everything*, and Nina Mingya Powles, author of *Magnolia*, 木蘭 and whose book *Small Bodies of Water* won the Nan Shepherd Prize, share with the reader their love for nature and thoughts on how birds inhabit their poetry.[5]

Pulitzer-finalist poet, translator, and professor, Arthur Sze, responds to notions of identity and language with a letter poem inspired by Tao Qian.

Many of the poets included in this anthology see the questioning of their racial identity and sense of belonging as an essential part of their everyday life and creative process. Romalyn Ante, a UK-based poet who grew up in the Philippines, and Louise Leung, a Hong Kong poet, discuss the colonial legacies of their respective home-lands, recognising both the 'sense of dread and hopelessness from the past' and how 'our reflection and imagination is rooted in the present position.'

Sarah Howe, whose T. S. Eliot Prize-winning collection *Loop of Jade* has inspired so many other Asian poets, and Monica Youn, with her latest collection *From From*—a powerful narrative that problematises race—deconstruct the stereotype of 'the Asian face as a mask', offering a close reading of their respective poetics, as they reflect on how their childhoods and heritage, as well as the socio-political events around them, have impacted their writing

---

4 Kit Fan, *The Ink Cloud Reader* (Carcanet, 2023).

5 Victoria Chang, *OBIT* (Copper Canyon Press, 2020; Corsair, 2022) and *The Trees Witness Everything* (Copper Canyon Press, 2022; Corsair, 2022); Nina Mingya Powles, Magnolia, 木蘭 (Nine Arches Press, 2020) and *Small Bodies of Water* (Canongate, 2021).

lives.[6] Alvin Pang, whose works have been translated into more than fifteen languages and Laura Jane Lee, whose book *flinch & air* explores identity through language(s) and stereotypes about Asian womanhood, talk about home 'not as a noun but as a verb.'[7]

The conversation between Marylyn Tan, author of *GAZE BACK*, and Mukahang Limbu, author of *Mother of Flip-Flops*, prompts us to think more deeply about the complexity of LGBTQ+ identities, expressed in such gloriously fiery language: 'to be a certain kind of queer in Singapore is to be consistently reminded that you're one fuck up away from everything shattering.'[8]

Meanwhile, Chen Chen, author of *Your Emergency Contact Has Experienced an Emergency*, and Lora Supandi write beautiful, lyrical letters on queer joy, pain, creativity, self-growth, friendship and love.[9]

The representation of 'Asia' in this book is certainly not encyclo-paedic, and our focus is on poets from East and Southeast Asia. Asian Americans are represented here, as are British Asians. So are Singaporeans, Hong Kongers, and Filipinos, among others. Some regard themselves as being part of a diasporic community, others not. Some Asian writers have lived in different Asian diasporas as well as outside Asia. We hope that the selection reflects the importance of accepting the complexity and diversity of these poets, of appreciating what they care about, write about, struggle with, or call out against.

Stuart Hall suggested that cultural identity is 'a matter of 'becoming' as well as of 'being'. It belongs to the future as much as to the past.[10] In these days of global citizenship and cultural diaspora, the Asian

6   Sarah Howe, *Loop of Jade* (Chatto & Windus, 2015); Monica Youn, *From From* (Carcanet, 2023).

7   Laura Jane Lee, *flinch & air* (Out-Spoken Press, 2021).

8   Marylyn Tan, *GAZE BACK* (Ethos Books, 2018; University of Georgia Press, 2022); Mukahang Limbu, *Mother of Flip-Flops* (Out-Spoken Press, 2022).

9   Chen Chen, Your Emergency Contact Has Experienced an Emergency (BOA Editions and Bloodaxe Books, 2022).

10 Stuart Hall, 'Cultural Identity and Diaspora' in Jonathan Rutherford (Ed.) *Identity: Community, Culture, Difference* (Laurence & Wishart, 1990).

identity is open-ended and subject to change. It is impossible to fully encompass the complexities of Asian identities, and this book does not pretend to do so. What it does, however, is initiate exchanges among poets who identify as Asians.

We see it as a beautiful beginning of more conversations and a deeper understanding into the worlds of these East and Southeast Asian poets across continents, as we read and are inspired by their poetry.

—Eddie Tay & Jennifer Wong[11]

---

11   Jennifer was born and grew up in Hong Kong and now lives in the UK. Eddie was born in Singapore and spends most of his time in Hong Kong.

HERITAGE

ON THE LYRIC SELF

Jennifer Lee Tsai and Dong Li

In this conversation, Jennifer Lee Tsai and Dong Li explore what it means to find one's own lyric voice in the language of poetry.

JENNIFER

I would like to start by asking what inspires and compels you to write? What does writing offer you? Could you tell me a bit also about the space that you are currently inhabiting (and please do interpret that as you wish), whether it relates physically, geographically, or metaphorically?

DONG

I was interested in foreign/translated literature in high school back in China and wanted to give it a try myself. That kind of creative writing was not encouraged in a more test-oriented environment. So I kept this mostly to myself and to my diary. After I started over in college in the Californian desert, the pent-up energy seemed to have found an outlet in the open space, but the language shifted. I was still improving my English through verbal community and was often forced to articulate myself in a way that was unfamiliar and nerve-racking. My frustrations took me on many walks. I think writing began for me when I was asked to give a speech about my family. I had to bring my faraway longing and a different cultural constellation into new linguistic structures and strictures. In the desert, I learned to listen. Writing seems to take me forward into the mess of my feelings and the desire to shape it toward something legible. It commands an articulated response from me. It teaches me to listen and be heard.

Having lived in the US for many years, I had to leave, because my visa ran out. American English has never left me though. I have been living in Germany for the past few years. So the language of my environment has shifted again. I have been doing translation work in various directions, for survival and as a way of bettering my language skills. The struggles and frustrations remain, but I have gained confidence in encountering and embracing them. Translation has allowed me to make a simple living and, more importantly, it offers new roads where my writing and being can take place. That's also how I can give back to the languages upon which I stumble and grow.

Your family's migrant history seems to be a wellspring of your work. What propels you to record and reassemble this history in English? Do you ever feel constrained by this obsession? Where is this obsession taking you? Where are you now?

JENNIFER

Your question invites me to reflect on the significance of migration, language, and the inspirations behind writing. Firstly, I write in English as it's my dominant language, the only language that I can fully write in. I'm second-generation British Chinese; I was born, grew up, and was educated in the UK within a Western tradition and literary canon, which radically differs from my cultural heritage and the experiences of my Chinese parents and grandparents. With regard to my family's migrant history as an inspiration for my work, I think when I first started writing seriously, I felt that the narratives and experiences of British Chinese immigrants were absent or invisible. I felt compelled to write about them in some way, complex and problematic though that may be. In 2022, I interviewed Valzhyna Mort for *The White Review*.[1] She spoke about notions of displacement and misplacement, that '[d]isplacement presupposes a place of belonging left behind, a source of nostalgia. A misplaced person doesn't have such a place. A misplaced person submits to the fact that she has no other country but herself.' Part of my impulse behind writing is to explore such concerns, and what they illuminate about the self and one's identity.

As for limitations to writing about one's family history, your question

---

1 'Interview with Valzhyna Mort', *The White Review*, November 2022, https://www.thewhitereview.org/feature/interview-with-valzhyna-mort/

prompted me to reflect on what Kayo Chingonyi terms 'the double bind' in which poets of colour often find themselves within the context of a majority white literary culture. Chingonyi writes that often 'either [poets of colour] imitate the—predominantly white—canonical writers of the literary establishment, doing violence to a part of themselves, or they write into or through their heritage and encourage a critical reading that privileges their identity.'[2]

From my own perspective, I would like to break free of such imposed constrictions, whether internal or external. This currently leads me to think about alternative ways of writing about or into the lyric 'I' in poetry. What new directions might there be for the lyric in contemporary poetry? What are the myriad ways in which migration acts upon and is affected by a body's language and cultural heritage? Over the last few years, I have been immersed in work by writers such as Theresa Hak Kyung Cha, Bhanu Kapil, Nuar Alsadir, Valzhyna Mort and Sandeep Parmar, as well as work by the so-called French feminists including Julia Kristeva, Catherine Clément, Hélène Cixous and Luce Irigaray on ideas of female divinity, spirituality and mysticism. They inspire me in my quest to re-imagine and re-envision ways to further explore my poetic obsessions, to reflect on theoretical and poetic considerations of language and otherness, the problematics of cultural and racial identity as well as their enriching possibilities. However, I do find myself at a transitional point now.

In the foreword to your debut, *The Orange Tree*, Srikanth Reddy refers to your book as 'a family history, which, we learn, is also a history of modern China. To write this history, the poet adopts the literary persona of a wise and innocent child exploring the memory palace of ancestry.'[3] I was wondering, therefore, if you could speak to this, and what the role of both personal and public history plays in your work. How do you reconcile or negotiate the two? Do you consider the use of persona important or necessary in your work and, if so, what strategies does it enable for you in writing? With

2   Kayo Chingonyi, 'Worrying the [Blood]line of British Poetry: Notes on Inheritence and Alterity', *Swimmers*, 1 (2016), 1–11.

3   Dong Li, *The Orange Tree* (University of Chicago Press, 2023), ix.

the publication of your first full length collection, where do you feel you are currently in your writing practice? Where do you hope to go next?

My debut *The Orange Tree* recounts many stories, myths, legends, and atrocities that I learned of mostly from my mother and the women in my extended family. As a child, I often had to stay with different relatives due to my parents' night shifts. It seemed easier for my aunts to open themselves up to a child. They would talk, mostly to themselves, as if I could understand. I remember little of what they had told me, but I know I listened and was fascinated by how alive their telling was. The women made me feel that their histories and hearsays were just another layer of the present, a layer perhaps more real to a child. In school, I often found history textbooks dry and the memorisation of historical dates tedious, but they did help me to situate these vaguely remembered fragments and to fill up the silences that were left unspoken. These personal histories were a potent source for this book, which turned the personal into public display. My maternal family poured all their resources into the wellbeing of their only son, and the women were never given opportunities to thrive. In a private moment of telling what was curdled inside them, the women perhaps saw themselves as authors, in dignity and glory, of this living that had been sharpened by all its rough edges. I wanted to convey my wonder by shaping these moments into a public record of its own.

As for persona, it was useful to be consistent with that child's voice for *The Orange Tree*. I wrote the eponymous poem first as a speech that I gave in college and later formed into poetry. As I was writing the other sections of the book, I never thought much of the persona, as I kept hearing that same voice in my head. I was just listening. As the title poem rippled out, an orbit came about quite naturally. Of course, I was not that child anymore and could never be, I refrained from using the 'I', but in writing out the histories, the voice of that listening child came alive to me, so did those of the women. That persona, which set the tone for the book, perhaps also provided a kind of distance that prevented the writing from falling into too much pathos. In a way, the material I was working with inspired a method that became the means of shaping this book. So the use of that particular persona, a part of my own history, was important for *The Orange Tree*, but I wouldn't say it is necessary for my other works.

It took me a long time to get this book published. I thought it would never go into print while my mother and many of the women are still alive. So I am happy that it is becoming a reality. I have been working on a quintet with themes related to China for the past decade. *The Orange Tree* is the first in that series. I would like to keep publishing and making my poetic experiments public and hope that the next few books won't take as long. Shortly before I moved to Europe, I started to write about Europe. Writing can be prophetic in that regard. In retrospect, it probably has more to do with the fact that I have been learning French and German and that my interest in translation has been deepening. Since moving to Europe and gaining more confidence in my language skills, especially German, I am interested in the practice of self-translation and writing in other foreign languages. I'd like to pursue whatever little space I am allowed to have and can carve out. Besides, I'll continue to translate between the languages I know and learn and to listen to the vitality of all that singing.

I am intrigued by Mort's differentiation of displacement and mis-placement. Personally, I feel neither displaced nor misplaced. I believe I must work with my condition and improve it so that I can do the things I am most interested in. I appreciate all the countries I have lived in or passed through. They all give me opportunities to learn and grow. Being somewhat a nomad due to circumstances perhaps helps in that regard. As a second-generation British Chinese person, you probably face a totally different set of challenges. In your poem 'Mystical Discourse', you cite Irigaray's notion of *la mystérique*: 'the way that subject and object can intermingle... an obliteration of... imperfect, personal identity.' I am fascinated by your exploration of the splintered self, but you seem to move toward an erasure of such an identity. You also mentioned that you are at a transitional stage in your poetics, could you speak more to this tug of war between identity and its obliteration? You are versed in

French feminist theories, and you also work as a critic. What role does criticism play in your poetry?

JENNIFER

I'm interested in exploring the subtleties and nuances of identity in my work, in how the construction of the racialised lyric self in poetry is not a fixed entity but one that is constantly involved in flux, multiplicity, reconfiguration and redemption. Recently, in relation to British Chinese and Asian American identity, I've been thinking about the concept of 'racial melancholia' and the complex processes of loss associated with assimilation, grief, immigration, displacement and diaspora, as discussed by the critic David L. Eng and psychotherapist Shinhee Han.[4] This condition of racial melancholia may manifest itself in fragmentation or psychic splitting. However, I am interested in the possibility of and movement towards healing and recuperation. Irigaray's notion of *la mystérique* suggests mysticism (*mysticism*), hysteria (*hystérie*) and mystery (*mystère*). The mystic desires to erase her personal identity to reflect the divine perfection of God. The process of mirroring the divinity both effaces and reaffirms the mystic's identity as distinctions between them are collapsed. Critically, I've also recently been engaged with the work of Anne Anlin Cheng and her brilliant but troubling theorisations of Asiatic femininity in the Western imagination, how she precisely pinpoints the ways in which the ideology of race renders the figure of the 'Asiatic yellow woman' as both highly visible and absent/unseen/erased as well as '*hybrid*: present/absent, organic/synthetic, a figure of civilizational value and a disposable object of decadence.'[5] Unravelling these contradictions and complexities is a personal, critical and creative quest, one that currently imbues me with a sense of subversive joy at pursuing these radical possibilities.

***

---

4   David L. Eng, Shinhee Han, *Racial Melancholia, Racial Dissociation: On the Social and Psychic Lives of Asian Americans* (Duke University Press, 2018).

5   Anne Anlin Cheng, *Ornamentalism* (Oxford University Press, 2018).

FILIPINO IDENTITY, URBAN LIFE, AND MOVING DIVERSITY FORWARD

Troy Cabida and Theresa Muñoz

Troy Cabida and Theresa Muñoz talk about negotiating between where they are from and where they are, and how the urban spaces of Edinburgh and London affect their senses of self.

TROY: How are you doing today?

THERESA: I'm good. Where are you? I'm in Edinburgh.

TROY: I'm in London, south west specifically. I've been living here since 2007. I was born and raised in the Philippines, then I moved to the UK in 2007 with my parents. I've been back to Manila twice so far, too. And yourself?

THERESA: Well, I was born in Vancouver, Canada. My parents are Filipino, but my grandfather was Spanish, so my dad is half-Filipino and I grew up with my Filipino culture kind of at a distance. You know how it is. Everyone moves with their family. My parents have six brothers and sisters each. They all moved with them, together. So I've never been to the Philippines. All of my Filipino family have been in Canada. I've always connected to my culture through my family in Vancouver. Then I moved to Scotland to do an MLitt and then a PhD, I met my husband, and now I'm here.

TROY: I've only been to Edinburgh once and it's such a beautiful city. It's very different from London because it feels so business-like here sometimes and the time I spent in Edinburgh felt very holistic, maybe being there on holiday played a huge part in that. As a comic book fan, I'll always remember Edinburgh for that pretty cool scene in the third *Avengers* film where Wanda and Vision fight Thanos' cronies.

THERESA: How do you find living in London?

TROY: I have a unique experience of living in the UK in the sense that I have a lot of family that were living here before we moved. My grandmother from my mother's side moved here in, I think, 1984, with three of my uncles. My mom is the oldest and couldn't come with them at the same time because she had just given birth to her first child. And then, in the nineties, members of my dad's family moved here. So I guess migrating and the idea of living abroad was inevitable and such a present image in my mind. I know a lot of Filipinos who move here for work and how they really have to start from scratch and make new friends and connections along the way. And it's not something I've explored yet in my writing because I feel like I don't have the initial language to explain that kind of dynamic yet.

How about you? How are you finding Edinburgh?

THERESA: I moved here when I was twenty-one. I came to do my Masters in Glasgow. And my husband is Scottish and Canadian—we actually met in Canada—so we have dual citizenship, which is good, because then you don't feel tied to one place. My friends and I are really close here, but, you know, you definitely feel the pull. I have three sisters and my parents back home.

TROY: How do you think the urban spaces you inhabit affect your relationship with your identity, and by proxy, your writing? Because from my experience, people normally don't expect poems that deal with urban life from me, or rather they're surprised when my poems aren't about beaches or farm life. I grew up in Manila, and saw the grime and cement of it all, and that has really informed not only how I understand home, but how I understand myself as a Filipino person. And the closer proximity I reach to that space in my writing, the more that I seem to contradict other people's expectations and perceptions of me as a Filipino, if that makes sense. I wonder if you feel the same way?

THERESA: In Canadian literature, it feels as though everyone writes about the environment. You've got the mountains and the sea, sometimes in your backyard. It's really beautiful. But I just never thought that was me. I never found myself in those spaces, and I never saw my culture in those spaces. Lately, I have been writing a lot about archives. My new book is all about archives and the relationship between paper and people and boxes. It's very tactile. But even still, I'm trying to put myself in there, as this Scottish-Canadian-Filipino migrant. I just try to always put myself in the poem. You can forget yourself trying to fit in.

It's weird, though, because my parents were born in big cities. They were born in…I think my dad's from Cebu, my mom from Mindanao. I find my heart in the urban landscapes because I like the way it changes. I like the way it makes me feel. I like how it makes me feel small. You know, I miss skyscrapers. Do you ever? Well, you live in London, so you always have big things.

TROY: Yeah, we have huge buildings: the Gherkin, the BT Tower and pretty much all of Liverpool Street is filled with skyscrapers.

THERESA: When I'm in London or big cities in North America… You walk around massive buildings or skyscrapers. I really miss feeling small in that way. Obviously I'm not very tall, but I really miss feeling anonymous.

TROY: Have you seen the movie *One Fine Day*? It's a super-cheesy 1990s romcom with Michelle Pfeiffer and George Clooney.

THERESA: Oh, yeah. That came out a long, long time ago.

TROY: I watched it for the first time the other day and I thought that's one of the best romcoms ever, because the plot of the film, as you may know, is about these two single parents who keep finding themselves in sticky situations where they end up throwing their children to one another. And it's set in the hustle and traffic of nineties New York, and of course by the end of it they fall in love. I find it a very accurate, if not saccharine, representation of city life because even if urban living is exhausting, they still really enjoy the rush of it, and part of the romance that builds up between them is because of the setting that they're in.

THERESA: Oh yeah. No, I think so. In my first collection, *Settle*, I wrote a lot about the city, but I find it hard to write about the city in relation to my emotions.[1] You know, when you're talking about yourself in relation to, like, the light in the building reminds you of something or maybe the marble on a statue is a metaphor for some part of you. I don't know how you feel about that.

TROY: I've never thought about personalising the city in that way, but the last poem in my own pamphlet *War Dove* talks about the city as this figure that looms over me.[2] It's titled, quite appropriately so, 'Not Dying for London'. It's written after another poem titled 'What Are We' by Jeremiah Brown, and a huge inspiration of it was the time it snowed so hard in April of 2017 and the weather was so brittle that I couldn't get to work on time; people were risking their lives at this random burst of cold weather during what should have been a warmer time.[3] I even read a headline somewhere that sheep couldn't give birth, something that stayed in my head for so long, I thought I was losing it. I spoke to a friend about this day a while after and we both joked about not letting London kill us, which then inspired me to write a poem about the idea that London is this villainous figure looming over us looking to devour us at any moment it can, like the alien in Jordan Peele's *NOPE*.[4]

THERESA: One thing I've been trying to do is write more about my heritage here. People here have said to me, you should write about, you know, your language and your history. It's taken me a long time to do that, because growing up I never had to do that. I never had to present myself in a way like, oh, I'm, you know, I'm Filipino. This is my Filipino poem.

TROY: I have yet to find my so-called Filipino poem, too.

---

1   Theresa Muñoz, *Settle* (Vagabond Voices, 2016).

2   Troy Cabida, *War Dove* (Bad Betty Press, 2020).

3   Jeremiah Brown, 'What Are We' in *Barbican Young Poets Anthology: For Those With Collages For Tongues* (2018), 12–13.

4   *Nope* (2022) directed by Jordan Peele.

THERESA: Yeah.

TROY: My Filipino poem will be primarily about pineapples, Theresa.

THERESA: Or the jackfruit, I miss the jackfruit.

TROY: And the dried mangoes!

THERESA: I have to find my Filipino food poem! I write a lot, though, about mixed race relationships. That's been a big obsession of mine…I got a grant to do a big sequence on that, which is coming in my next collection. Because it was the one thing that I thought was really different here. You know, in Vancouver, lots of people are mixed race, lots of people are in interracial relationships, and it's no big deal. But over here, it's like I think it was 20% in Vancouver and it's less than 4% in the UK.

So I've been writing a lot about that, and I was researching other mixed race relationships. I have found lots to write about, including Harry and Meghan, psychoanalyst Marie Battle Singer and the poet James Burns Singer, the story of Eliza Junor, a mixed-race free coloured woman, one of the first recorded in Scotland. I've interviewed couples therapists who have worked with interracial couples, as well as some local interracial couples who are also my friends. And I write about my own experiences, some of which have been positive while some negative, things like that. I do notice younger couples who are mixed race around the university where I live and they're always young students. You never see older ones and I'm always really curious about that. That is something that I write about. But I like my poetry to be situated in the *now*.

TROY: And I think there's something really important about exploring that relationality in your writing. Not only do you have your own experiences to root your perspective on, but your position also as someone in an interracial relationship can help you understand the narratives and challenges that come from these conversations.

THERESA: Totally. So another question: how do you feel Asians fit into the UK poetry scene? Or do we?

TROY: I think so. I think our space is getting bigger, though still far from the ideal. I work at the National Poetry Library in London, and for our open day in October, each librarian has to create a book display for patrons and guests to see around the Southbank Centre as a way of advertising the library to those who may not have heard of us yet. I remember mine was a huge focus on the theme of water as explored by Asian poets, and I remember including your book, as well.

THERESA: Oh, thank you!

TROY: Just to amplify the fact that, hey, at the National Poetry Library, the biggest public collection of contemporary poetry in the UK, we have so far collected a substantial amount of poetry written by Asian poets, that actually we do exist, and that we're still writing enough work today to make a substantial public display. So it's those little things that I feel like I should be doing, to help emphasise the fact that we are here and that poetry within the Asian community in the UK scene happens, and from so many different kinds of Asian voices. Not just East Asian, not just South Asian, not just Southeast Asian, but all of us.

I feel like it not only cements the fact that we are here, and that we are part of the general conversation, but it lets other Asian people know that reading and writing poetry isn't overly idealistic or esoteric or a waste of time, and that if they ever feel the desire to try it out, it wouldn't be so out of their reality despite what people may say.

THERESA: Yes, that's true.

TROY: How do you feel about the poetry scene there right now?

THERESA: I think it's getting better in terms of diversity and providing a platform for different voices. It's getting different, it's getting more inclusive. But that's only in the last few years. You know, Scotland has been slow to change. For a long time, there has been a predominately white narrative in the literature that comes up, so it's been hard trying to establish my career here. And for a long time, I felt like no one cared about my migration story but that's not true. That's not the way it is.

One thing I think about when it comes to my writing is…how can I maintain a grip on my true self? Because this is something that I find, if you're from a different country. I find the longer I stay here, the more my writing gets closer to UK literature, like my poems inch closer to the left margin and become more constrained.

TROY: I know what you mean. Like the general assumption of what a Filipino migration story consists of is so linear and individual to the point of it being almost like a prediction, when there's actually so many different experiences that all deserve their own story.

THERESA: I've been trying to get back to who I am. I read a lot of Canadian and American poetry to inform my voice. It's been a conscious thing, to keep a Canadian tone. I feel sometimes I have to record myself, just to remind myself of what I sound like. What do you do to possess your distinct voice?

TROY: You know what's so funny, Theresa? I've never written in Tagalog. I can't do it. I speak the language every day. I speak Tagalog to my friends and family every day. I speak Tagalog to my colleagues when it's 6pm and I'm running out of energy to carry on speaking in English, but I've always felt like it's a tool within my arsenal that I can't use or reach for when it comes to my writing practice.

THERESA: What do you mean?

TROY: I feel like it's one of those bilingual things where living in an English-speaking country has only made me more conscious of my relationship with Tagalog, and just how visceral that relationship actually has been. In the Philippines, our relationship with our mother tongue is interesting. English is seen as the more fashionable language, the language that you need to learn and master if you'd like to be employable or more socially accepted. And I know I've still got a lot of unlearning to do when it comes to that part of my brain, which may inform why I find it hard to write poetry in Tagalog.

When I read poems written in Tagalog and other Filipino languages, I can't help but recognise just how differently these poets use language in their work, and how that requires such technical skill and honing of the muscle that I know I don't have in me yet. To me, poetry has been a very English concept, even though poetry is such a substantial part of our culture and our artistic history, which I really want to work on unlearning.

THERESA: I tell you, I totally get that. I've been reflecting more on this, on being Asian, and on how people tend to lump all us Asians together. The number of times that people called me Thai, Chinese, Korean, Vietnamese, but never Filipino.

TROY: Yeah.

THERESA: So now in my poetry, I try to make my poems reflect who I am and what I look like. But, like, when I write about my body, would that mean I'm fetishising my own appearance? You know, if I want to point out that I am brown. Am I doing that? I wondered what you thought about that. If your appearance comes out in your poetry.

TROY: Yeah, I do. I feel like there's a fine line between providing space for who you are and the exploration you need to do in order to understand yourself more and just plain playing up to the stereotype because that's what we're told is considered art.

Though I feel that more with my sexuality as a queer person, I am really reconciling with the fact that, yeah, I have agency over my sexuality and I can write whatever I want. I can write about my experiences as a queer person in any way, shape or form. And in many ways, I have the ability to drive this conversation onward, however I need it to be. Whenever I write about intimate topics, I guess the sole purpose of this expression is to dictate the fact that this is my experience, first and foremost, and that I have the right and ability to write about it.

THERESA: I just wonder, you know, how far we can go in describing our own selves. And it's interesting, in terms of writing about your sexuality and your queerness and things that are integral to your identity—how do you do that in terms of your craft? How do you describe yourself? Because that's one thing I do worry about. Like, how am I describing myself? I want to make sure that people know I'm a third culture individual, as it affects everything I do.

TROY: I guess I am at the very core of what I write. And I just trust the fact that anything I write will always be a Filipino queer poem, it doesn't have to adhere to specific stereotypes or specific expectations that come from the outside. And that takes a lot of conviction, in my opinion.

I always go back to Rachel Long's debut collection, *My Darling from the Lions*, which I read in one sitting as soon as I received it in the post.[5] The way she writes about her lived experiences as a mixed race woman are always so quiet and often leaning towards the mundane and the individual, like the poem 'Car Sweetness', where she remembers a memory of being a child and sitting in the back seat of the car, watching her parents hold each other's hands while they drive. I really enjoy how she uses silences and objects around the space to do the talking for the people in that space, like how she writes 'their wedding rings glinting / like mouths not used to smiling', as if to say that even if something is undeclared, it still permeates and plays a formative part of one's experience, and of one's understanding of the self in relation to others. It can be a poem about childhood, it can be a poem about womanhood, it can be a poem about being a person carrying different racial backgrounds in you, and how navigating the spaces that you find yourself in affects that experience.

***

---

5   Rachel Long, *My Darling from the Lions* (Pan Macmillan, 2020).

ON EXPECTATIONS

Sarah Howe and Monica Youn

Sarah Howe and Monica Youn reflect on how their childhoods and heritage, as well as the socio-political events around them, have impacted their writing lives.

MONICA YOUN: How are you? What has your day been looking like?

SARAH HOWE: It's been a nice leisurely day until 5pm after-school pickup, then the house becomes a chaos of small tired people—who have just been dispatched to bed!

MONICA: And how old are your children? I don't actually know that—which isn't surprising, given we've never met in person, although I've long admired your work.

SARAH: They just turned three and five. Their birthdays are in January. Is your son still seven? I look forward to that day!

MONICA: He's just turned eight. And he's reached the age of at least a semblance of rationality. That proposition gets tested pretty often. I think that you're very much in the thick of things with two at that age, fully mobile. And very much their own people, I'm sure.

SARAH: Yeah, I guess it becomes very acutely apparent to me, having two: there's an awful lot that's already built in. They are their own people already.

MONICA: Yeah, you kind of learn the limits of parenting, like this person just came like this. And there's very little I can do to change it. I mean, I'm very lucky in that my son is healthy and happy and interested in things and not yet surly.

SARAH: In reading your long lyric essay piece, 'The Passive Voice', as well as the many other things I found wonderful in that poem, I was struck by the caterpillars in their jar, your son's birthday gift. I was horrified and fascinated by them because I have a bit of a phobia of caterpillars. Another version of that key image of containment that opens the book. There they are smearing their horrifying shit across the glass. Having started out with their feeding...?

MONICA: ...feeding medium...

SARAH: ...medium, yes!

MONICA: Yes, I didn't at the time have a phobia of caterpillars... yet. So I was unwise enough to put that thing on my dining table where I then just spent a lot of time looking at them in this kind of repulsed fascination. Part of that essay is that I was really trying to bring my dailiness into it in a way that I felt I hadn't previously in the book. It was one of the last things I had written for the book.[1] And one thing I thought was important for me to do, both ethically and aesthetically, was to make my own positionality with regard to what I had been talking about clear. I'm not usually a directly autobiographical poet, so I had to force myself to say: look, just write about how your day was. And there were quite a few things that were happening during that particular time period, including the pandemic, the BLM movement catching on worldwide, the beginnings of a surge in anti-Asian violence, which entered a new phase after the Atlanta shootings...

SARAH: Yeah, absolutely: well, almost in live action you record the Atlanta shooting taking place in that record of dailiness. So yeah, I guess a sense of the passage of time and *unextraordinariness*, yet also this sense of living through markers in history, and turning points when things seem to change. Was it living through these sorts of times that you think gave this book its character? Particularly the way that you seem to set yourself the task of writing more explicitly about race and racialised experiences than perhaps was the case in your previous books.

---

1   Monica Youn, *From From* (Carcanet, 2023).

MONICA: I think that's absolutely right. I feel that my last book, *Blackacre*, was a political book in the sense of being feminist, and some of the poems deal explicitly or less explicitly with race, but it was quite a personal book.[2] That book was published in fall 2016— and of course in fall 2016, Trump was elected; suddenly a lot of people were being moved to participate in a conversation more directly than they had previously and I thought to myself: 'Look, you don't just get to be a chin-stroking, vaguely academic poet anymore. To the extent that there is an urgent conversation that's going on, and some people are actually listening for the first time, and you feel you might have something to say, it's your job to put it out there, even though you don't really know how to do that yet.'

At the same time, I didn't feel that my own personal situation was really the point of what I wanted to say. I didn't feel the need or the desire to centre myself in what I was writing about. In fact, I thought it was important that I didn't. And so, I was intentionally absent for much of the book as a first person 'I'. But then, toward the end stages of the book, I thought, 'Well, you don't just get to come at this from this omniscient viewpoint, that seems above criticism, above the fray. You have to show where you are, what you know, what you don't know.' So for the last poems in the book, I had an all-caps exhortation to myself in my writing journal saying, SHOW YOUR WORK—show how hard it is for you to write about this, it's not as if I'm someone who comes out with pronouncements on race easily.

I had a very similar question, actually, about your work. You are someone who I think writes both more explicitly autobiographically and more explicitly politically about race and colonialism than I do. However, I think one of the things that struck me in particular about *Loop of Jade* is that it maintains its privacy and its intimacy: You are willing to turn your back on the larger part of the audience, and speak directly to an intimate 'You', or to a familiar 'You', or to a 'You' that remains relatively opaque.[3] And I know that you had described about your current projects that you were thinking of writing more directly about China's interaction with the West and the protests

2   Monica Youn, *Blackacre* (Graywolf Press, 2016).
3   Sarah Howe, *Loop of Jade* (Chatto & Windus, 2015).

in Hong Kong. And of course, that situation has both escalated in urgency and in the resulting crackdown. And I'm wondering whether you feel a tension between the personal or intimate, and the political in your own work, both in the past and now.

SARAH: Oh, what a beautiful series of thoughts, Monica. I am intrigued, and feel the inherent rightness of the idea, that *Loop of Jade* is a book wary of forgoing its privacy. I felt that coming through particularly in the way that the book deals with the narrative of my mother, and the difficulty I imagined readers must have had in working out the actual autobiographical-biographical picture there. There was some resistance and reluctance on my part in writing that strand of the book: a sense of not wanting to expose her or myself too much, and yet doing too much of both. But how that translates into my relationship with the political... Over the last few years I've been trying to gather myself towards a second book of poems, but that new project has been derailed by various things. First off, my attempts to write an erasure poem out of the text of the *Basic Law* in Hong Kong started out as an act of protest and defiance. But over the seven or so years I worked on that poem, on and off, the political situation in Hong Kong became so utterly hopeless that I no longer feel like I really have the heart or the stomach to write it. As well as feeling increasingly as if I didn't have the right to, or that I'm not the right person to write that work. Whether fragments or snippets of that poem do end up in my next book is still an open question for me.

I feel like I've been rebuilding myself and my ability to write poems from scratch. Part of me feels like I want to be writing about my dailiness too, and the experience of mothering very small children that I've been consumed by in the last few years. But yet not really knowing how to do that, and not feeling equal to the task. The poems have been dripping out very slowly. I feel like I'm still looking for the overarching concept or impetus that might link these various preoccupations with one another. I'm sure there'll be a way. But at the moment, all I have are disparate stars, rather than any sort of constellation. I'm pretty much messing around, seeing what happens, and where the pieces land.

Something that really interested me about this new book—well, all your books really—is the way that *From From* moves between its different component parts. Another thing that struck me is where the affect lies in these poems. There's such a stately analytical power of intellect here, which makes these poems hugely satisfying and suggestive to interact with as pieces of thought architecture—from the opening pages of your Pasiphaë/Sado double portrait onwards. But it did make me wonder if one of the things being contained in these poems is rage: that the recurring images of containment in these poems are not just about race, or thinking through divisions of race in the racial capitalist system, but also about feeling, and anger… This comes through so strikingly for me in that paragraph in 'In the Passive Voice', where suddenly this rage—which is fire and shit and excess—overflows, it bursts all the dams. That was such an interesting moment, thinking through these racialised ideas of containment and passivity, as you do in that poem. One stereotype sees the Asian face as a mask or a blankness, emotionally speaking.

MONICA: Yes, I think I backed into the affect of these poems. The Pasiphaë/Sado poem that you referenced was the first poem that I wrote for the book, because I spent so long trying to figure out a voice that would work for me. What I came up with is that this could not be my own voice. This could not be a personal voice, this really shouldn't be beautiful. What it should be is a voice that inspires resistance, a voice that is in some ways untrustworthy. I thought of the voice of many of the poems, particularly in the 'Study of Two Figures' series, as being in this kind of power language, which might be thought of as legal or academic. And those instances of power language are often saying things that are 70% wrong, the way that the 'beauty is truth, truth beauty' declaration is largely wrong. The way that so many legal analogies are wrong. And yet people build on them—'corporations are people', 'money is speech' has led to catastrophic consequences in the United States through the *Citizens United* decision.

I wanted to use that kind of an affect or tone, as a very rigid building material. I've also been writing these poems not knowing where they were going, I start with an initial tone and a starting point, which is: okay, there are these two figures that to me seem to have something in common, let's talk about what they have in common. Okay, they're both contained. What else? Oh, they're both Asian. Well, what does that do? Well, that creates a racial marker, well, what does that do? Well, that affects the relationship with the readership. Just to state what is happening on the particular rigid plank of affect that I am working with for that stair step. And then to see where the stair step leads, and then to watch this kind of double helix staircase start to collapse on its own, to become recursive, to start becoming self-referential, and to watch that rhythm develop. I don't know if you would call that a form in these poems, but it was what I was palpably doing at the level of craft. And I think that is itself another form of container. That is not my voice, that is the voice that as a person who is privileged to be fluent in both legal discourse and academic discourse, I can deploy, but it is not my voice, not a lyric voice.

I wanted to kick this back to your work because you are someone who was trained as an English literature academic. You have a fluency and malleability in the pentameter, which you inhabit with a confidence that enables you to make it your own. I always think of pentameter the way I think of a pentagram—it's a little house, and you've made a home of it.

And I'm wondering if you consider your home as a poet to be within the English literary tradition? You have talked in essays about whether you have the right to call yourself a Hong Kong poet and you've just referenced that now, at this remove where the situation in Hong Kong is at a crisis point, and there's all the uncertainty of what is going to happen next.

SARAH: It feels so perceptive to use the pentameter as a leaping-off point for the question of where one's literary home is: where one's formation as poet and ear and voice lies. I guess I wouldn't have thought of it like this, but I suppose that must be true—that my ear and my voice were formed, in some sense, by the pentameter, by spending so many years immersed in Shakespeare and his contemporaries and blank verse as a medium. And yet, I can't help but quarrel with the notions you sometimes encounter in academic discourse that pentameter is somehow the most 'natural' verse form, that it's inherently closest to speech, rather than struck through with acculturatedness...

MONICA: Yes, I think I noticed it so strongly in your work because there are what I think of as the macho pentameter dudes, and you are not one of those dudes. I mean, you make the pentameter uniquely your own. And I noticed that particularly because I personally have never felt at home in the pentameter.

SARAH: That's really very interesting. I do feel like it is probably a bit of a default I fall back into, despite myself. At the moment, I keep finding myself writing in rhyme. Even in rhyming couplets, which is unheard of for me. I wonder why that's the case—almost like a kind of survival mechanism. I find rhyme, its familiar pulses, working for me like a sort of crutch, as I scrabble for anything to get myself going again as a writer. And yet prose has been very important to me, too. I've been writing in prose recently: prose poems that aren't quite structured like yours in this book, but that are also interested in the relationship between the one-off sentence and longer chunks, and feeling the alternation in the rhythm between those. But even when I write in prose, I find that prose also ends up deeply patterned, sonically and maybe even metrically.

To come around to the other part of your question, my very early reading as a poet was overwhelmingly in the English tradition. And so discovering contemporary American poetry, which I didn't do until I went to the US to study as a graduate student in my early twenties, was a vital opening up. And then I've gone on to try to open myself up to other world poetries in more recent years. And yet I suppose the Chinese literary canon is not really accessible to me except through translation. I've never had the fluency of poets like Mary Jean Chan, for example, who genuinely has both of those traditions at their fingertips. But I think that this is something else that we have in common: you reflect quite self-consciously about this in *From From*. I was struck by the way you circle back to the rice chest in the last poem in the book, and talk about all the layers of mediation that you experienced in coming to that story, that emblem. The fact that that Korean story was mediated for you by this film, with its different titles in Korean and English translation, but also via the English novelist Margaret Drabble…

MONICA: …of all people…

SARAH: …at so many removes: you're exploding any notion that this Korean history-cum-myth was something easily inherited via your mother's milk.

MONICA: Yes. It's not the sort of thing that my mother told me as a bedtime story. In my book, one autobiographical fact is that I remember my mother reading a book to me—*Curious George* (which the poem goes on to criticise in hindsight)—when she was teaching me to read. That's actually my earliest memory. Since she had English as a fluent second language, my reading skills outpaced hers very early on. So yes, I think we do very much have that in common.

I wanted to give a shout-out to the thing that made me think that I had to know you as soon as I first encountered your work years ago, which was that I had used the 'certain Chinese encyclopedia' quotation from Borges, also via Foucault, as my college yearbook quote. I had come across it, and—like you—had been struck by the idea that this has nothing to do with China. This has to do with Westerners' ideas about China and the functions of China in the Western imagination. I have almost no Korean. And I, too, have Korean American friends who are truly bilingual—like you are in Cantonese and English—and I deeply envy their fluency. I think of all of my early exposures to Asia and Asian literary traditions as mediated largely by Westerners. Like I initially learned about Chinese poetry from Ezra Pound, for god's sake, like so many other Western readers. I started to learn about Korea from the accounts of Western missionaries who travelled there and hated the place. Because so many of the Korean texts are not translated, I had very little ability to access them until very recently.

My family's history was sufficiently political that they don't talk about Korea. My parents came over as teenagers. They were refugees during the Korean War but were relatively sheltered from the post-war fallout and then they left for the United States. I know that you had said in an article that your British-born father had encouraged you while you were growing up in Hong Kong to continue to think of England as a home and I did want to ask you a little bit about that. Was that something that you felt you resisted? Something that you feel now?

SARAH: At that age, I think I just took it as gospel. Looking back on that usage in both my parents' mouths—talking about England as 'home'—the strangest thing is the way my mum was buying into the colonial propaganda: she had never lived in England at that point, but she still copied him in talking about our moving here as 'going home'. She had lived her whole life in Hong Kong, but still presented her husband's country to her children as if that was our real origin and destination, that that's where we belonged. I guess there's pathos in that colonial trajectory too, thinking about my mum as someone who never quite fit in comfortably in her own culture, as an orphan and a bit of a loner. I guess her hope was that we would fit-in in this one, even if that meant her effectively erasing herself.

Where is home now? Unquestionably Britain. I suppose I've lived parts of my life in Hong Kong, even shorter parts in the US. And I've moved around different towns and cities in England, but am now settled in London, not so far from where I spent my later childhood in an outer-London satellite town. Having had that experience of arriving as an alien and being dropped into an English primary school at the age of seven, I found many of the aggressions and microaggressions explored in your central sequence in *From From*, with its wonderful play on the sonics of the word 'Deracination', both familiar and vivid. But after those childhood years, even if I continued to think of myself as a mixed-race person, I think I spent many years of my life in this country mostly 'passing', especially in my teens and early twenties. Probably partly because of the ways I sought to present myself, and partly because of my own racial ambiguity, that early experience of being constantly othered was one that mostly dropped away. The way it came back, or I came back to it, was through my engagement with poetry. As I started to find myself trying to make sense of various aspects of myself and my history, I found myself running up against this question of how—or whether—to use racial markers in a poem, and how that changed the poem. The question is one you place at the beginning of this book, in 'Pasiphaë/Sado': 'To mention the Asianness of the figures creates a "racial marker" in the poem. // This means that the poem can no longer pass as a White poem, that different people can be expected to read the poem, that they can be expected to read the poem in different ways.'

I remember discussions with well-meaning writer friends who would say, 'Aren't you lucky you have this interesting story to write about?', when they really meant, 'Aren't you lucky you can play the race card in this way?' But they would also question whether that was something I really wanted to do, as if marking myself in that way was something I was doing to myself, since I had the option of passing—and whether that was a good idea or not.

MONICA: There was a question as to whether someone with my level of privilege, having led a very comfortable existence here in the United States, having been treated to an absurdly elite education, whether I was entitled to talk about race. I spent so much of my poetic training at Princeton, at Oxford, and then at Stanford, with entirely White teachers with White models, but also I was very worried about 'doing race wrong.' I was very sensitive, for example, to Homi Bhabha's criticism of Salman Rushdie that in *Midnight's Children* he was packaging Asianness for Western consumption. That was something that I was trying so hard not to do for the last three books, and the result was a kind of paralysis—how to write in a way that wouldn't do that (not to say that I agree with Bhabha's criticism of Rushdie). I felt like I did not want to self-exploit, or exploit a culture that, (a) has been exploited enough and that (b) I, like you, didn't feel that I really had a right to claim myself.

A lot of the weird affect of the book was my attempt to say, 'Look, here are these figures, these stories, they have been exoticised by countless artists for Western consumption for centuries or millennia. And I do not want to continue doing that.' And so I put them in as figures in the beginning and ending poems just to say, 'These are outlines, but let's focus on yourself as the reader looking at these figures. And let's focus on me as the artist showing them to you. And let's focus on what allows us to do that, which is this container.' I had not articulated it to myself that consciously when I was writing the poems. I was just really groping my way from line to line. I have been trying so hard not to 'do race wrong' for such a long time that this was the only way that these thoughts could work their way out of the mind traps that I had constructed for them.

SARAH: I find that so interesting, and that is what I might have expected from reading these poems. They have this feeling, as you said, of progressing via logical arguments and rational propositions—in the opening poem, there's almost the sense of a philosophical text working through various hypotheses. And yet, they also seem to undermine their authority, through those moments of wonky reasoning or specious leaps. I'm interested in the way the rational and the intuitive collide in the book's images: one image I find myself drawn back to is the emblem of the magpie trapped by the human in the box, whose only job, it's slowly revealed, is to draw the other magpies to their doom. The trapped magpie chimes with Sado in his rice chest, or Pasiphaë in her cow: these resonant emblems that allow you to make arguments and connections, but via images that are so layered and complicated and ambivalent that they need us to return to them on multiple sweeps.

MONICA: I do like to return to these images and I think they need room. The same room that, for example, *Loop of Jade* required to give it some space to echo, to make it loop, so to speak. I think returning to our question of home, one of the very complicated and multi-layered images that I was struck by in your book is from 'Crossing from Guangdong'. In 'My heart is bounded by a scallop shell / this strange pilgrimage to home', the scallop shell I take as a reference to the Canterbury pilgrims, who—if I'm not wrong—would wear scallop shells in their hats. This idea of the pilgrimage to home being both English and Chinese really calls into question what direction this pilgrimage is going, what is considered home in a way that keeps resonating to the point of almost tearing itself apart in your work.

SARAH: Yes, definitely, and also I suppose this recursive sense of the 'point of origin' as a sort of mirage that endlessly recedes as you get nearer to it. That's there too in the playfulness of your title, *From From*, whose reduplication and tautology starts to sound a bit like wonderful nonsense. I love the way you've picked out that phrase for scrutiny from its usual place in 'But where are you *from* from?', and the way it becomes suddenly strange severed from the rest of the question. I presume it's that locution you're referencing here, with a bit of a chuckle. Can I turn the question about home back on you, Monica? What is the point of origin, the trajectory, the journey, that you're grappling with in that phrase, 'from from'?

MONICA: Yes—like you, I was raised by very assimilationist parents, but unlike you, I didn't spend time in the so-called homeland as a young child. My mother's parents had come over with her, and my father was alienated from his father, who had been part of the Syngman Rhee government, the first military dictatorship of Korea. And so we never went back to Korea. We never talked about it. My parents had come over at around age fifteen. So they spoke English quite fluently; they didn't usually speak very much Korean, particularly not to us kids. This idea that Korea should be my home was very alien to me. At the same time, I was growing up in Texas in the American South. I was constantly being told, 'You're not from around here, are you?' When I would be two blocks from my house. I know that you experienced similar feelings of alienation. I think that's all pretty standard with regard to the immigrant experience. I think what was so striking to me about the anti-Asian hate surge of the pandemic was that I had come to regard Brooklyn as my home. It was where I lived, it was where I had chosen to raise my son, and I had consciously chosen a neighbourhood that was very racially and economically diverse. I felt like I was part of the neighbourhood. Being harassed constantly in front of my own front door, or a block from my apartment, feeling like I couldn't go to my own subway station, was a feeling that was completely new to me. I had lived at that point in New York City for 21 years. I had always thought of it as the safest place I had ever lived and the place in which I felt most at home. So suddenly being uncomfortable in my own neighbourhood was part of what I was trying to get at in that long prose poem.

SARAH: It's quite a complex moment: there are a couple of different incidents of harassment explored up close in that poem, 'In the Passive Voice', aren't there? The first one you introduce via the experience of a neighbour who is harassed in the lift of the Brooklyn apartment block, who sends an email round to warn her fellow Asian American female neighbours. The speaker of the poem toys with whether or not to reply to her message, and whether it's appropriate to remind her neighbour of the various racial and economic inter-sectionalities at play, and their relative privilege in this system. In the end she doesn't. That's one, but there's also the later incident where the speaker is harassed herself: it feels like the moment in the poem when the speaker comes closest to losing her own self-containment. She's targeted outside this restaurant, by a White man gesticulating at her as if he's firing a gun. You recount how she repeatedly appeals for help from the bystanders. It's interesting that in a poem called 'The Passive Voice', the passivity is on the part of the restaurant-goers who say nothing, and the restaurant that does nothing to stop this man just outside their premises. It's a poem that's hugely aware of intersectionalities, of placing the speaker in a net of social relations. Eventually the speaker turns for help to a Black cyclist passing by. Elsewhere the poem explores in some depth the relationship of Asian American and African American communities via the murder of Latasha Harlins, an African American girl shot in 1991 by Soon Ja Du, a Korean American convenience store owner.[4] It's a piece of American history that was unfamiliar to me until I read your poem.

MONICA: The incident outside the restaurant was the part of the book that if I could go back and add to then I would. I think that was one disadvantage of the dailiness of the poem. What I was writing was in the aftermath of the adrenalin rush, and I hadn't taken the time to think it through. What is interesting about that incident is not the harassment by some racist White guy. I mean,

---

4 On the contemporary resonance of Harlins' murder, see for example: https://www.latimes.com/california/story/2021-03-17/latasha-harlins-memorial-playground-black-lives-matter-south-los-angeles

that happens all the time. But what brought it home for me was the fact that this was happening at this restaurant that I used to eat lunch at every day, it was a restaurant outside my workspace at the Center for Fiction. I was constantly there, and that I would be harassed in that way in my own neighbourhood, at a restaurant I thought of as one of my locals, with no one coming to help me was very upsetting. But then what I asked the bystander was not a cry for help, exactly. What I asked him was specifically racialised, which is why I think that that moment was so complicated. My appeal to him was: 'We don't want this racist bullshit in our neighbourhood.' So I was asking him to include me in his 'We.' I was asking him to recognise me as a neighbour and someone with whom he was standing in solidarity, and given the fraught state of Black-Asian relationships in the United States, it was an extraordinary thing to have asked of a stranger in that moment of crisis. I could very easily have said, 'Could you please help me? This guy is bothering me.' And I'm sure he would have done something. I did not appeal to any of the White spectators at the restaurant in that way. I appealed to a Black man not just for help, but for a positive assertion of solidarity, which is tremendously complicated. And he immediately answered that call.

I have been talking quite a bit to a political science professor here at UC Irvine, named Claire Jean Kim, who has a book coming out called *Asian Americans in an Anti-Black World*.[5] Her book is largely about, as the title implies, the situation in America. But her argument is that the way in which ethnic studies and racial dialogue has progressed is that we're used to thinking of anti-Black racism and anti-Asian racism as basically parallel oppressions that are imposed on us by White supremacy, that occasionally come into proximity and that can occasionally intersect. But essentially independent from each other. And what her argument is, is that anti-Blackness is constitutive of Asian American identity in this country. Not to say that all Asian Americans are anti-Black, although a lot more of them are than will admit to it. And that's a conversation we desperately need to have. But also that the reason Asian Americans

---

5   Claire Jean Kim, *Asian Americans in an Anti-Black World* (Cambridge University Press, 2023).

were brought or allowed into this country was largely to undercut Black and Brown people, and to undercut working class White people. And we have been used in that role, and we continue to be used in this role. Right now, in the United States, the Supreme Court is about to rule on a case in which Asian Americans are being used to destroy affirmative action, vastly to the detriment of Black and Brown people and over the vehement protests of the vast majority of the Asian American population who stand firmly in favour of affirmative action. But these White supremacist lawyers originally tried this case with White plaintiffs, and when that didn't go anywhere, they substituted in these Asian American plaintiffs… who I think of honestly as traitors. And every race will have a few of these people who they use as the pawns of White suppression. And this keeps happening—Asian bodies used to beat down Black and Brown bodies. It's been happening since the very first time Asians were brought to this country. And so she says that we cannot talk about or think about Asian American identity without talking about anti-Blackness explicitly and as part of our history.

SARAH: Absolutely, we have a lot to think about on these fronts in the UK too. I learned something else about American history from the way 'The Passive Voice' charts the various waves of immigration in the wake of the various Exclusion Acts; as you say, different Asian peoples brought in to undercut others and undermine other labour forces and other racial groups. A historical consciousness has always been important to your work, not least in the way you work through ideas etymologically—like the idea of Asians as 'buffer' in that poem, another image you circle back to, and slowly unpack.

Going back to my first question about affect, can I ask about the way humour works in these poems? The comic and the grotesque often seem close here. There are several moments that reflect on things that are so horrifying they almost become comically absurd: like the tourists posing for photos inside Sado's rice chest. It's a very witty book, I think, and sometimes it's funny in unexpected places. At the end of the 'Deracinations' sequence I was thinking, 'Oh, she's finally made it! She's finally writing poems and living her authentic life!' Then the speaker has this encounter with her beloved Adrienne

Rich's introduction to that year's *The Best American Poetry*, gifted to her by her boyfriend, only to find there a put-down about anecdotal 'ethnic' poems.[6] That moment of sort of bathos is so beautifully pungent and poignant—the blows just keep on coming!—that it did almost make me laugh.

MONICA: I think quite a lot of that was just played very explicitly for comedy. And I intentionally put those deracination poems in the third person because they are not directly autobiographical. I feel like the person characterised in that last poem was actually—as dorky as she is—actually cooler than I was as an undergraduate. I was basically a tool and was pre-law, not an English major. The Adrienne Rich *The Best American Poetry* was something that I had bought later, but was not given to me by my college boyfriend. I think what he gave me instead was Seamus Heaney's *Seeing Things* in an inscribed edition.[7] And I did have an Asian fetishist frat boy boyfriend, but I had made up the name of the film, just because it was so fun to make up names of porn films as part of an anagram.

I think that a lot of this does have to be comic. You have these moments. They're ridiculous, but they do speak to a sort of community. I feel like the only people who are finding these moments funny in these poems are people who are also Asian, or more broadly, BIPOC people, people who have had similar issues with assimilation, immigrant families, etc. It's really fun reading some of those poems out loud, and to see who feels entitled to laugh and who feels that it's not their right to laugh at these moments. So, I think of the humour as outreach to my community, my community who loves Margaret Cho, and her almost too much on-the-nose skewering of Asian American immigrant families. When I'd watch Margaret Cho with my family, I'd be laughing at more of the jokes than they would.

SARAH: Oh, I love Margaret Cho, too! Can I pick up on the question of audience? Which I suppose was, for me, not really a question at the forefront of my mind when I was writing *Loop of Jade*. Since

---

6   Adrienne Rich (Ed.), *The Best American Poetry: 1996* (Scribner, 1996).

7   Seamus Heaney, *Seeing Things* (Faber, 1991).

that book came out, my musings about what kind of an audience I am or should be writing for almost became so foregrounded in my mind as to be quite debilitating. Crushing even, because it became too self-conscious. I feel like that almost paranoid sense that everyone's listening—which I'm sure is not true—is only just lifting for me now, and I'm beginning to write again. How explicitly were you thinking about audience and readerships as you were writing this book? And was that different to your experience with the previous ones?

MONICA: Yes, I did want to talk about audience in my own work, but I also wanted to talk about audience in your work because I feel like even if you didn't have the word 'audience' written in front of you on a bulletin board or something, it still is very implicit in the movement of the book. Like a poem like 'Crossing to Guangdong,' which brings the reader in, narrativises in a relatively straightforward way, and is accessible to even a Western reader even though it's talking about a private family history. You follow that with one of the most opaque poems in the book, which is 'Start with Weather', which begins with this line, 'whether they will ever return to us is a hard and indeterminate thing.' It doesn't tell us who the 'they' or the 'us' are, that's never specified within the poem. One of the things my graduate students know is that I'm always focusing on pronouns as a way of almost blocking out the potential staging of the work. Do you have your back turned to the audience? Or are you speaking directly to the audience? A pronoun is a box with walls that contains an empty space, and who is in that space and who is outside the walls? So I think that you keep reflexively turning your back at moments to the audience—not in an unfriendly way—but in a way that insists upon privacy for certain of these moments. Or says, 'This is for my family only,' or 'This is for an intimate only.' I don't know if you wanted to speak to that…

SARAH: I haven't thought about the transition between those two poems in a long time…maybe a turn towards privacy, or a sort of scrambling of signal into noise at that point. I feel like there are some poems in the book that consciously start to court nonsense, and that's one of them: whether in a koan sort of way, or an Edward

Lear sort of way, I'm not completely sure. Another poem that works like that is a poem called 'Chinoiserie', which by its title is quite explicitly racialised. And yet, the poem that follows, apart from a few touches, defies its own labelling, and doesn't really do what you would expect it to do. I always had the sense I wanted to play around with transparency and opacity. I imagine I alienated various readerships who were expecting one kind of poem to carry through the whole book: the way more approachable narrative poems give way to these rather confounding, opaque poems, written perhaps just for me. Maybe part of my purpose was to say, look, I'm luxuriating in a free-form, unconscious bilge here: you read into it what you want to read, but I'm just going to please myself.

MONICA: The 'Chinoiserie' poem in particular and that wonderful moment in 'Start with Weather': 'whether guilt's deranged orbit jellies the tar of parking lots / whether the Lord is my coelacanth who shall not weep.' You know, those moments of near nonsense or of sheer, almost self-pleasuring joy. Those are deployed at these moments when the Western reader might be expecting you to act as a tour guide, to be like, 'Hey, here's my culture, come and look at my things—chinoiserie. Here's my souvenir shop.' And once you get inside the door, well, there's a surprise. I was pleasantly surprised. I don't know whether all readers would react to it in that way. But I think that you want to be confounding expectations, and particularly racialised expectations in those poems. You know, there's an American critic called Elaine Castillo, who's Filipina, who writes about the concept of the expected reader—given the demographics of who reads poetry our expected readership is largely going to be White English-speaking, etc.—and how you deal with that.

But an answer to your question—yes, I was thinking quite explicitly about audience. I think most of *From From*, and definitely some of the poems in particular, are addressed with humour to what I think of as an Asian American community. But a lot of them are written in the expectation of a White audience and to say, 'Look, I'm not your tour guide—you may be expecting another exotic, sexualised, taboo, decadent, bizarre story of what I used to call "crazy rich asians," but you're not going to get that here, or if you are, then I want to at least make you look at yourself consuming this, and ask why. Why is it that you keep turning to Asian figures to scratch those particular itches?'

SARAH: Another question comes to mind here: what does it mean for writers of colour, BIPOC writers, to draw on a Western font of myth, as you use Greek myth here? As it happens, you've long written through Greek myth and tragedy. I was fascinated by the way you remake the myths in this book. I remember as an English liter-ature undergraduate studying Greek tragedy and being absolutely compelled by Medea because of the way she's placed as this foreign, Asian woman and wife, who becomes a terrifying, uncontainable force of destruction. In the body of Greek myth, so much is invested in constructing the rational, civilised Greek against the irrational, terrifying 'other', isn't it? You bring that out in these poems, that conflict at the start of Western civilisation, and make it speak to now.

MONICA: Yes, and if you're a little dorky child raised in America, as I was, your introduction to Greek myth is through this pic-ture book called *D'aulaires' Greek Myths* in which all of the gods are pale-skinned and blue-eyed, and many of them are blonde. And you grow up thinking that these figures are universal—a.k.a. White—and you don't realise unless you really start to dig into it that these figures were racialised, that Greek myths, like so many myths, were nationalist and were colonising in their function. And that Asia is a word, a Greek word, that meant 'that area over there where we have colonies'. And that Troy and Medea and her family, which include Pasiphaë, and the royal family of Thebes, all of these figures of taboo and decadence would have been understood by the Greeks as Asian. Dionysus would be understood as Asian and is referred to as the Asian God. And Edward Said writes about this explicitly, but it gets lost in even BIPOC writers' writing about myths. And so I just thought, look, myths are, to a certain extent, a home for me—I grew up loving these stories. If you had asked me in elementary school what I wanted to be when I grew up, I would have said a mythology professor, I just loved this stuff. And it was not until adulthood that I started to understand the cultural and political context of the myths and how they were used and how they were explicitly concerned with this nationalist idea of othering Asians in the project of constructing a specifically Greek identity.

SARAH: Robin Robertson has written some versions of Marsyas well known here, and yet you managed to make him totally new to me as this disembodied, de-skinned, preternaturally calm voice speaking almost from the other side of death, but not quite. He feels, in your version, almost like the victim of a racialised assault.

MONICA: Yes, I've read Robertson's *Marsyas*. But in my take, Marsyas is specifically a racialised figure. He comes from Phrygia, which is understood as Asian. He dares to emulate his White betters, to compete with them, and he is killed in a sickeningly sadistic way—Greek myth is not usually this sadistic—that makes him a public spectacle. I mean, that is pretty much the definition of lynching. All of the hubristic myths around Marsyas and Midas, who was another figure from Phrygia and was the son of Kybele, this Asian goddess who was threatening the Greek pantheon. All of these myths are about punishments for hubris. And that hubris has to be understood as racial emulation. It's mysterious to me why they're not more generally taught that way.

SARAH: I suppose there is also an assertion and a defiance at work in writing about this body of myths, rather than Korean myths, or Chinese myths, or African myths, depending on one's heritage as a BIPOC writer. One of the things that's so interesting about the way you use Sado is the way you point out that he is a historical figure, but has also come to occupy a position in the culture that is somewhat mythic: a figure of horror and an example to be shunned. He's the closest the book comes to a Korean mythic sensibility, alongside the Greek.

MONICA: And I think that's why I was at pains to explain that I had never thought of Korean myth as my home. As in, I am American, I am not Korean, I was not raised in Korea, and I never learned about Korean myths until I researched them in grad school. Which is why I wanted this book to be about deracination as opposed to racial identity, which is why I did not make the book more explicitly

Korean. I'm thinking my next project will be immersed in Korean myth, which is really fun.

From the autobiographical snippets I've been able to get from your articles and from some of the material in your work, it seems as if, for your mother, it was a priority for you to have some grounding in Chinese folklore and traditions.

SARAH: Yes and no, in the sense that, in her completely chaotic childhood—and this is circled around painfully in the poem 'Loop of Jade'—she didn't really have anyone to sing her nursery rhymes, or read her bedtime stories, or tell her the folktales that would pass on that kind of oral inheritance in that way. I think that when she did try to pass on those kinds of traditions to me, she was conscious that there was a break there. I remember she would go round stores in Hong Kong, and later in London's Chinatown, scouring them for English-language books containing myths and stories that would engage me. I think she did want to pass on what she could. But she struggled to do so. She would sometimes say to me she didn't know the songs you would sing to a baby in Cantonese. She didn't know any Chinese lullabies or nursery rhymes, because she never experienced that sort of comforting as a baby, because of the way she was abandoned and then precariously adopted by a mother who was absent a lot of the time. But, I suppose, it was also a choice of hers, on some level, not to speak to me in Cantonese as a child. I think there was this push and pull: that on the one hand, she wanted to pass something on to me, but also ended up effectively excluding me from direct access to that inheritance. I don't know how conscious this was, and if it's something my parents just slipped into. Part of me is still a bit angry and sad about it, but I also wonder if it was a sort of protective gesture, actually: closing me off from native fluency from a culture that hadn't been very kind to her.

MONICA: Is she bilingual herself?

SARAH: She is. She grew up speaking Cantonese. She felt that her adoptive mother, from her accent and various hints she dropped, probably came from Shanghai and was a native Shanghainese speaker. I think my mum didn't start to learn English until she must have been in the later years of her schooling as a teenager. The way she tells it, a kind university student came in, in a sort of volunteering role, and started to teach them English through phonics: my mum must have had a facility for the language, and from that foundation was able to teach herself the language and become completely fluent in it. For some reason she never felt like that route as an autodidact was open to her in Chinese: she's always saying that her own education in Chinese was so poor that she was never even taught how to use a dictionary, so she never understood how to look up the radicals that organise the words in a Chinese-language dictionary. But English was a language she felt she could work out for herself, so she sort of made herself a home in English. It's funny talking about the Greek myths, because my mum absolutely loves Greek myths, too. Like for you, they were almost a bigger feature of my childhood, being immersed in that body of stories and my mum's excitement at them, than the Chinese traditions I was just talking about.

MONICA: That's wonderful. I'm wondering now, in your own role as a mother, what your thoughts are about heritage, tradition, passing things on?

SARAH: I'm still working this out. In some ways, my children are pretty much White, to all intents and purposes, bar our fondness for weekend dim sum. My husband is White, Jewish. Ultimately, I feel like they need to find their own paths in this. I fear that their own connection to the Chinese side of their heritage, via me, is getting ever more tenuous. I guess it will be difficult for them to lay claim to that part of their identity, much as I do pack them off to school in their little Chinese outfits at Chinese New Year. But I mean, how to answer that question... when my daughter was first born, people—including my mother in law—would keep saying to me, 'Oh, she looks so Chinese, her eyes, she looks much more Chinese than her brother.' That was until she grew any hair, which turned out to be improbably blonde. So she's a funny mix. Such markers end up scrambled across generations. I loved your poem about Mendel, by the way.

MONICA: Yes, I think I've had a similar experience with my son. My son is half-Asian and he does read as Asian. I think people looking at him will see him as such. His father, who is White, keeps insisting that our son looks White, which I find bizarre. But luckily, I'm no longer married to him, so it's not a problem. But I did feel, particularly as this anti-Asian hate surge came up, we encountered signs saying 'Stop Asian Hate,' and I explained it to him. But even before that, you know, he had said, 'why don't I get to be White like Daddy, why don't I get to be White like Teddy?' And I had explained to him about Black Lives Matter, about the murder of George Floyd, he goes to a very progressive school, he understands about racial discrimination and the necessity of racial solidarity, but I think he still feels it as a burden. And so I feel like I need to be asserting positive images of Asianness. So he doesn't feel that 'Asian' is the equivalent of 'someone might spit at you on the street, and you need to understand why.' But it's very, very hard to assert that without really knowing this material myself, I've been researching, and I feel like me and the other Asian moms share materials that we find that are appropriate. Very little of it exists in English, especially for Korean materials. Parenthood has really brought out this kind of desperation in me that I need to educate myself so that I can educate my son.

SARAH: I might have to adopt this attitude, and also try to find positive examples of Asianness to show them—I like that idea a lot!

MONICA: Thank you for inviting me to this conversation, and thank you to the editors for creating this space. And gratitude to my student Amaka Nwabunnia for impeccably transcribing this conversation at record speed, which was the only way we were able to complete this interview in time!

***

WHAT WOULD IT BE LIKE
FOR MY PEOPLE?

Romalyn Ante and Louise Leung

Romalyn Ante and Louise Leung discuss the respective colonial legacies of their homelands.

ROMALYN ANTE

Colonisation is a big word for you and for many people. What do you think about our respective encounters with colonial histories and how have these encounters affected us as writers?

LOUISE LEUNG

Colonisation feels like a dysfunctional family. You were born into a nuclear or single-parent family, and then your parent decided to re-marry (whether forced or willingly). Your new parent may do a lot of things 'for your sake' but you are very confused. You're not independent enough to determine if you can truly accept your new family member. And when your new parent goes away, you are free (or become under the care of another step-parent).

But then, do you miss them? Do you love your coloniser because they were trying to better an environment for you? Do you hate your coloniser because they reduced your sense of belonging to your original nation? Do you only realise their worth when they are gone? And when you are detached from their political existence (e.g. an ID card, a passport), are you truly free from such coloniality? They are still here in the photos, in your memories, in our language. There is a part of colonial history inside each of us that we either welcome or are haunted by. And I've tried to capture this sense of double vision chaos in my work, such as 'People on Water' which I wrote while taking a class on postcolonial literature. The sense of dread and hopelessness from the past will meet whatever is ahead of us, be it good or bad. But it is important that while we speculate on our past and future, we should take the present into account as well.

Our reflection and imagination are rooted in the present position.

Imagine a life in a country that has never been historically colonised. What would it be like for you and your people?

ROMALYN

Perhaps I would be writing in our old script (of the people in Katagalugan), Baybayin. When I wrote my poetry collection, *Antiemetic for Homesickness*, one of my poems in it, 'Gunita' or 'Memory', attempted to resurrect Baybayin by incorporating this script.[1] Crafting the poem was my way of recovering and relearning what was lost. That creative process has been a way for me to recover *myself*, as a Filipino migrant in the UK who eventually became its citizen.

Unlike the Baybayin, the concrete and monolithic letters of the Roman alphabet—all its sharp edges—remind me of the architecture of buildings and museums in the UK, my second home. It's very different from my previous world. The characters in Baybayin reflect the movement of nature; just as how native Philippine architecture does. Our roofs are made with nipa leaves, our walls are made with the strongest bamboo. In Baybayin, the ⌒ 'ha' which is the first syllable for 'hangin' or 'wind' undulates like the breeze. The ⌐ 'ta' which is the first syllable for the word 'tangkay' or 'stem' reflects the angle of a twig. Our own script reflects our dwellings, our home.

What would it be like for my people? Perhaps there'd no longer be any of 'my people'; instead, we would still be living in our little chiefdoms. The Philippines, whose name was derived from King Philip of Spain, would have its own chiefdoms, in all its 7,641 islands. Our different languages, folk tales and songs would light up the night and warm the breeze. Perhaps I would have been more proud of my Batangueño accent. Perhaps I wouldn't have tried to change my Filipino accent when I came to the UK, endlessly watching Harry Potter movies to sound more *British*. I would have been prouder in the shade of my own skin, instead of aspiring to

---

1   Romalyn Ante, *Antiemetic for Homesickness* (Chatto & Windus, 2020).

be a *mestiza*. When I was growing up in the Philippines, I wanted to be lighter, scrubbing whitening soap on my skin. Some Filipino women even inject glutathione into their veins.

In our little chiefdoms, there would be different communities singing, appreciating and honouring the warmth of our own campfires.

If there is a positive side to colonialism, what would that be for you?

LOUISE

Better social welfare. Though the British Hong Kong government was trying too hard at the beginning of their rule (e.g. the failure of the Home Affairs Department, the reliance on local business communities and charities), social welfare measures starting from the 1970s were effectively securing people's living quality. We didn't have to endure hardships in contemporary Chinese history because Hong Kong was not considered Chinese land. I know this may sound absurd coming from someone born in the millennium, who didn't have to experience anything I just mentioned and only learned about those matters in textbooks and family tales. But the point is, we owe most of our current social welfare to the development and planning of the former colony.

Thanks to Governor MacLehose, Hong Kong people were provided access to a citywide public housing programme, house ownership scheme, compulsory education, better urban transportation, new towns, improved government structure, elected seats in the legislature... Even nowadays, some government initiatives are a legacy of such colonial measures. Colonialism remains at the root of our present-day politics. I need to thank the British colonisers for my education.

Colonialism often alters a culture in its everydayness, ranging from food to clothes, and more. What are your feelings towards these altered objects or invented products from colonialism?

The way we speak and dress, for centuries, has been a measure of where we came from, and our own cultural divides. I understand that time passes and with it, people and culture change too, but I also find myself asking *at which point do influence and tradition intersect?* From Spanish colonisation (that lasted more than 300 years) to American ruling and Japanese occupation, our culture has altered and shapeshifted. Along with it, the way we look, dress, and speak changed too.

During the American occupation, American teachers in the Philippines encouraged students to abandon their ethnic clothes and adopt American styles of clothing. I grew up wearing more Western clothes such as shirts and jeans; whereas some Filipinos proudly wear printed logos of companies such as Levi's or GAP or high-end fashion apparel like Louis Vuitton or Gucci.

I once had a classmate in my Anatomy class who would spend her bursary on buying expensive clothing. *I might be wiping faeces at the hospital, but outside, I look fab,* she once told me. *Upon meeting, you are judged by your clothes,* said writer Leo Tolstoy. Thinking about this now, not only as a writer but as a nurse in the UK, I can't help but agree with her to some extent. For nursing in particular, we are segregated in ranks by the different shades of blue of our uniform. A registered nurse wears light blue, whether you are newly qualified or have been nursing all your life. This colour reminds me of the Batangas summer sky. The more senior role you take, the darker the blue becomes, until you reach black as a matron. Dark as Wolverhampton sky in winter.

Once, when I was newly qualified, I asked a colleague (who wears a shade darker) to check a bag of blood with me for a patient's transfusion. At that time, in our hospital, blood checks for transfusions were done by two qualified staff to prevent administration mistakes. Even though I was already knowledgeable and qualified, and was the main nurse of that certain patient, my colleague lectured me on the basics of how one should check the correct patient for the bag of blood: last name, first name, date of birth, unique identification number.

Who's that nurse? She's quite condescending to you, my patient whispered to me when I came back to her bedside to obtain her vital observations.

In the staff room, I also observed how our clothes divide us: the grey-wearing healthcare support workers sat in one corner, by the noisy boiler, furthest from the *dark blue* nurses who sat by the window. I often ask myself why the National Health Service chose to present their staff this way. This strange classification leads to segregation in ranks and education. I wonder what if we were to wear only one colour? Would it change the way we look at each other or at ourselves? Or what if our clothes or uniforms paint our true self, our story? The stories of people or patients we cared about? Something that will give us a glimpse of our deeper and abundant personhood, just like how Filipinos' indigenous textiles do. The textiles of the Kalinga people use the art of geometry in weaving, while the T'nalak from Cotabato region or the 'Land of the Dreamweavers' pay tribute in their clothes not only to dreams but to important life events like birth, marriage, or death. There are handloom weavings that attract good health and protection; there are colours, patterns, symbols, used to represent our long history of war and winning, harvest and healing.

How amazing would it be if I could cover my fragile body with a fabric painted with a fragment of my own history or with a talisman woven into textile, passed down to me by the people and patients I meet on this journey.

From our conversation so far, I admire your ability to appreciate both the disadvantages and advantages of colonialism; if you could turn back time and prevent colonialism in Hong Kong, would you or would you not? And why?

LOUISE

I've heard many stories from the elder members of my family of how Hong Kong people were treated poorly by the British colonials at the beginning, such as putting up signboards banning both dogs and Chinese people in certain venues—wow—talk about removing human dignity in colonial subjects. Some of these actually appear in textbooks for primary school general studies and HKDSE's history curriculum. Still, I believe that the benefits simply outweigh the negatives.

To be honest, I think we're just lucky that the British actually cared enough to do something for the people living in the colony instead of simply exploiting our resources and geographical advantages. There are many bad examples of how colonisers ruined beautiful places in history. But, as many see it, Hong Kong history always begins with Hong Kong's humble beginnings as a former British colony

What I'd change though, is how they would initially treat Hong Kong people and the directions they should go with social welfare and the expanded inclusion of local seats in the legislative and administrative councils.

What do you want to say to your ancestors or family members who lived through the first stages of colonisation?

ROMALYN

As you mentioned, there are many instances when colonisation ruined beautiful places in history. And it makes me think of the destruction or altering of cultures, traditions, and values too. I guess if there is anything I would say to my ancestors, I would just want to thank them. Thank them for persevering through the bad side of colonisation but also for preserving what they could pass on to us. I would thank them for passing down their history, their stories, their different views—my extensive family, for example, have views on colonisation both positive and negative—so my generation and the next can absorb these stories and decide for themselves what to do with their inherited history.

***

EVERYDAY LIFE

WRITING OUR DAYS

Victoria Chang and Nina Mingya Powles

Victoria Chang and Nina Mingya Powles share with readers their love for nature and thoughts on how birds inhabit their poetry.

Dear Victoria,

I hope this email finds you well. We haven't met online or in real life before, but I've been a reader of your work for a few years. I'm a poet, zinemaker and librarian from Aotearoa New Zealand, but I've been living in London for the past four years. I grew up in a few different places, with different languages around me: English, Hakka, Cantonese, Mandarin. English is the only one I claim fluency in, though I believe in other kinds of fluency, and I think in some way I'm always writing about the different ways language(s) can inhabit the body, from childhood onwards. I also often write about bodies of water, memory, and archives. I love to swim, and during the pandemic I started learning how to sew.

A week ago I arrived back in London after a few months in Aotearoa and I think my brain and my body are still catching up with the jump in time zones and seasons, from deep autumn to late spring. Yesterday I caught the train across to East London and, walking around Hackney, I stopped by a tiny independent bookshop called Pages. I headed straight for the poetry section as I usually do. I think I move differently in small spaces now, post-pandemic, hyper-conscious of my mask and others' lack of masks, of proximity. I scanned the shelves and the fluorescent red spine of the new UK edition of *OBIT* jumped out at me and next to it, to my surprise, a copy of *The Trees Witness Everything*, which I thought I was going to have to order from America.[1]

There's a lot that I would want to speak to you about, and there's so much that your work makes me think about. But I wondered about

---

1   Victoria Chang, *OBIT* (Copper Canyon Press, 2020; Corsair, 2022) and *The Trees Witness Everything* (Copper Canyon Press, 2022; Corsair, 2022).

starting with birds. Your latest book is full of birds, and I realised that I've been writing about and paying attention to birds a lot lately, mostly because in New Zealand the birds are so loud. The soundscape of birds is so different in London. Back at my parents' house each night I would open the window of my bedroom to hear the owls. The New Zealand native owl is called the ruru (or 'morepork' in English, mirroring its call) and I have never seen one, but every night I heard them. I think of them often now and I think my brain now fills the owl-less silence of the city at night with the soft hooting sounds of owls from memory. The beach where my parents live is also a nesting ground for seabirds such as korora, the little blue penguin. At night they make honking sounds in the distance.

In London I live near a park where there are flocks of bright green parakeets. As summer nears, you can see swallows swooping at dusk. My dad sent me a picture in a WhatsApp message the other day of a pīwakawaka in their garden. The pīwakawaka is a very small, round bird, sort of like a robin, but with a big, beautiful black and white streaked tail in the shape of a fan. Their tails are usually wider than their tiny round bodies. I think it's the same pīwakawaka I noticed a few weeks ago, just a few days before I was due to leave home, cheeping happily in the overgrown jasmine above the path. It's been visiting each day since; it might be building a nest in the jasmine. In Māori folklore, a pīwakawaka is considered an omen of death, but I didn't mention this to my parents. In my family we don't talk about death.

I was just wondering—what birds have you seen or heard recently, near where you live? When did birds start appearing in your writing more often—was it a conscious choice?

Warmly,

Nina

*

Hi Nina,

Nice to meet you here. I love your discussion about birds and they sound really interesting! I am always thinking about birds and other people have noticed that all my books have a lot of birds in them. I'm hardly a birder but I definitely listen, like you do, and try to look at the birds, identify them, and they seem to always end up in my poems and other writing. I have a birder friend I met recently when I was teaching at a conference and I'll now send photos of birds to him and he helps me identify them.

The neighbourhood we live in is called the 'Tree Section' and it's a small forest near the beach. The eucalyptus trees are huge, a hundred feet or more, and they line the streets, alongside other beauties such as the Italian Stone Pines, Melalucas, and more. There are also so many different kinds of eucalyptus trees. What comes with these trees are, of course, birds! There are so many birds here that I walk each night with a pair of binoculars so I can take a closer look at any minute. There are a ton of hummingbirds right now and I've been watching them zip back and forth every day. In particular they like honeysuckles and there's a large bush where I like to stand and watch them. I think they are called the Allen's Hummingbirds or Anna's Hummingbirds. I suspect they are Allen's because they are small. In fact, I am working on a manuscript right now and it's all about a eucalyptus tree, and there are so many birds that appear here already. Two Cooper's Hawks live right near my house and I can hear their sharp and short screeches every day. I regularly watch them hunting in the evenings. They are so easy to spot and are really beautiful killing creatures.

Like your neighbourhood, we also have wild parrots and on any given evening, you can hear them flying around and squawking pretty loudly. Apparently, the area I live in has one of the largest populations of wild parrots in the country. I also regularly spot Dark-eyed Juncos and other sparrows flying around, especially on garbage day when all the garbage cans are pulled out. Lots of squirrels too, crows, of course—they are everywhere. Since I am a ten minute walk to the beach, seagulls are a regular part of the sky highway.

Even though birds and trees and nature in general have appeared in my writing since the very beginning, I'm not sure I always had as close of a relationship to seeing them in the past. I think now, as I get older, I am more focused on looking and seeing. Incidentally, I have your book of poems right here on my desk and, due to travel, haven't been able to dig in yet, but I will. In the meantime, since I was talking about some writing I have been doing over the last two months, I'm curious to know what you are working on? I'm also curious to know how your parents ended up in New Zealand and where they are from originally? My parents both passed away but my father was Taiwanese from Taiwan and my mother was originally from somewhere in Northern China and left during the Civil War. My Mandarin is so-so but I study it when I can and love watching Asian dramas (a lot of K-dramas) but I try and watch Chinese dramas too, so I can learn more Chinese.

—Victoria

*

Dear Victoria,

It's been almost a whole autumn since your email and I'm sorry for creating this enormous delay. The same week in July that you last wrote is exactly when we brought home a puppy—a black fluffy Labrador/Goldendoodle mix named Kaya. She is pure chaos. Ever since then it sort of feels as though my life has been turned upside down. I know it sounds dramatic, but I guess this is my first experience of becoming a parent or guardian. To have a creature wholly dependent on you. So I have been existing almost solely in this exhausting but joyful puppy bubble. The shape of my days has totally shifted, as I knew it would. I get little scraps of work and writing done when I can. It's been really hard to get back into creativity and making again, but I know it will slowly get easier.

There was a heatwave across the city on the day we brought her home. Everything about it felt surreal. It was too hot to step outside for too long. All the leaves on the plants in my garden wilted. The grass in the public forested area near where I live was scorched and dry for weeks. Now, months later, the hydrangeas I planted in a corner of the garden—which I thought had died in the heat—are growing tiny, new, bright green leaves near the roots.

I think it was earlier this year I started following you on Instagram and I'm very charmed by the pictures of your dogs Ketchup and Mustard, especially their Halloween costumes. How long have you had them? Did you grow up with dogs? I had a list of some other food names for our puppy (Pepper, Peanut, Miso) but settled on Kaya. As I write this she's snoring on her blanket near my feet.

To go all the way back to your questions! My mother was born in Sabah, Malaysia, and came to Aotearoa New Zealand for university when she was seventeen. It must have been a slight shock to go from a tropical, semi-rural town to cold, windy, damp Wellington. She was obsessed with languages, but the university didn't have that many options and she didn't want to learn French or Spanish, so she picked Russian. She then went on to join the foreign affairs ministry of the New Zealand government, where she met my father on a posting in Beijing. I was almost born in Beijing. As a result I feel connected to Beijing and northern China even though I've never lived there, only visited. Northern Chinese food is my favourite: baozi, egg and tomato noodles, thick-skinned jiaozi filled with pork and cabbage.

My father was born in Wellington, like me. On his side of the family, I think our ancestors originally came from Wales and England in the mid-1800s, via Tasmania. In my writing and in my life generally I always find I have less to say about my European heritage than my Asian heritage, even though it equally shapes who I am; perhaps more so, because of my white-passing name and face. Maybe I haven't started asking the right questions yet.

I'm excited about your eucalyptus manuscript. Are you writing about a particular tree you know well? What draws you to it? I like what you said about being more focused on looking and seeing as you've gotten older. I think looking and seeing—and just slowing down as much as possible—have become really important to my wellbeing and to my creative practice over the course of the pandemic. Especially now, I think, since my anxiety has been a bit debilitating recently.

I can't say I'm working on anything in particular. I think I want to focus most of all on rest, and on other kinds of making: sewing, cooking, and thinking about how these are connected to my poems. That said, I recently submitted a short manuscript of poems to a poetry prize and they all seem to be about snow and ice.

Are there other kinds of creativity apart from writing that you're drawn to?

Take care,

Nina

*

Hi Nina,

I'm sorry for the delay in getting back to you! It's been such a busy year, and years actually, that my email inbox has become a source of stress for me. I'm sure your puppy is not as chaotic as before, as so much time has passed. I just read a passage in Anne Truitt's memoir that aptly describes parenting: 'They [her daughter and her son-in-law] now have a hostage to fortune. Never again will they lean on a window sill as they did yesterday afternoon watching boats on a sunny river, so wholly at their own command. Their son, yesterday in them, is now beyond them. Born, he cannot be protected, and they will never again be carefree.'[2] So true.

I never grew up with dogs, although my mother took us once to see baby dachshunds but my father wouldn't let us get one. I get very obsessed and fixated on things and always remember that disappointment. So now that I can make my own decisions, we have two dachshunds.

Your background sounds like it's quite diverse. I see some of those

---

2   Anne Truitt, *Daybook: The Journal of an Artist* (Reprint edn., Scribner, 2013).

working out or working through in your book, *Magnolia*.[3] There's a poem, 'Mother tongue' that has a sharp caesura in the middle where you can read the poem multiple ways—horizontally and vertically. If we had more time, we could talk so much more about your book of poems! I was reading it just now and noticed you have a poem in there, 'Happy Holiday' in conversation with Agnes Martin's artwork and I have a whole ekphrastic book on the work of Agnes Martin coming out next year.

Not knowing if you are asking the right questions, it made me think about the poet Paisley Rekdal, who is a friend, who once said something about her books/manuscripts—she thinks that all of her books are asking a central question or corresponding with a central question. I thought that was interesting.

I just turned in my *Tree of Knowledge* manuscript so I ended up completing it in the time that has passed! I am feeling quite prolific lately. It became a conversation with a particular tree that was cut down, and also many other trees, birds, and it became an ekphrastic manuscript too—engaging with various artwork.

I'm so sorry to hear about your anxiety—my eldest daughter struggles with anxiety and on one day, she had four tests (she's a sophomore in high school). Her crying at school reminded me of when I cried in Physics and Chemistry in high school too. I think it is time to go now but it was so nice to correspond with you!

—Victoria

*

Victoria,

I understand about your email inbox becoming a big source of stress. I feel the same most days.

Just to say, I am so excited about your Agnes Martin work. Also, in

---

3   Nina Mingya Powles, *Magnolia* (Nine Arches Press, 2020).

the months since our first emails I've actually been creating work partly in response to *Dear Memory*.[4] (I think this would've happened regardless of whether or not we were corresponding!) It's a sequence of poems, fragments and collages about textiles, sewing, inheritance and memory. I'm drawn to your collage pieces in that book in particular, the way you've used family documents and photographs. Some of the images remind me of Diana Khoi Nguyen's book *Ghost Of*, or some parts of Anne Carson's *Nox*.[5] I think collages made by poets are one of my favourite poetic forms.

Wishing you a peaceful and creative spring,

Nina

***

---

4   Victoria Chang, *Dear Memory: Letters on Writing, Silence, and Grief* (Milkweed Editions, 2021).

5   Diana Khoi Nguyen, *Ghost Of* (Omnidawn Publishing 2018); Anne Carson, *Nox* (New Directions, 2009).

CONFESSIONS

Tim Tim Cheng

In her dialogue with the world, Tim Tim Cheng tells us of a poet's anxiety and of poetry where intuition and institution meet.

I am hungover from my creative writing Masters. I do not know how to transition back to real life, where I need to brand and rebrand myself in CVs, in a new country where I have just spent a year focusing on reading and writing poems. How is that going to help me become a *valuable* asset? Does the UK need another English-as-a-Second-Language teacher, another migrant from Hong Kong? Why did I think it would be worthwhile to give up my five-year career and get a loan, on top of my existing student debts, to become a trained poet?

Before I left the secondary school I was teaching in, one of my students told me that *doing a postgraduate course in writing does not equate to studying literature.* I winked at her and said *I am studying the literature of the future.* I was implying that what I wrote would become literature one day. I was also thinking of how I encountered more diverse texts in the sporadic creative writing classes I had taken, compared with the more traditional English literary studies classes. I was hopeful, sounding more assured than I usually was. But I was leaving my workplace soon, and Hong Kong was going through such drastic changes that even my mother, who once warned that *if I left her, she would break my legs*, allowed me to go abroad to pursue a *happier and less political future.*

By the time I graduated, I achieved my goals: my pamphlet, *Tapping at Glass*, came out in 2023, and my full collection will be published in 2024.[1] I did not tell my mother, who does not read English, that both books explore unhappy and political things that I cannot say in forms other than poetry. Through social media platforms, writing collectives, mentorship schemes, workshops, and festivals, I have met writers who became friends. There are strangers who like what

---

1 Tim Tim Cheng, *Tapping at Glass* (Verve Poetry Press, 2023).

I write, who invite me for collaborations, and who say kind words after my performances. People back home have started to notice me, too. They call me Tim Tim Cheng, instead of 鄭恬恬, in official event releases. Suddenly, the gap between how I live (in Cantonese) and thrive (in English) becomes visible—because I write in English, my name must be known in English, a product of transliteration decided by birth certificate personnel in British Hong Kong, 1993.

Am I not glad that my Chinese name, something that feels unbearably close to my rooted sense of self, is not used?

*

There was a period when I avoided reading Chinese books. I did not want Chinese grammar to interfere with my English. I listened to bands from the UK for at least six hours a day. I consciously changed my Hong Kong accent, wrote Xanga posts in English, talked to myself in English in the shower, and started dreaming in English. I wanted to, as Dior Homme once campaigned, *English my cult*. I was an acne-ridden, alternative, and awkward teenager in a Buddhist girls' school, where English was the medium of teaching, where a teacher escorted me from the basketball court during one recess to remind me that I needed to *catch up on my English*. Being *good* at it meant you were intelligent, which meant you could get into a *good* university and land a *good* job.

I studied there in the early 2000s. Despite their refusal to become a Chinese-medium school due to a change in language policies after the handover, my school had long stopped teaching English literature. Still, they encouraged reading. I devoured Paulo Coelho, Anne Frank, and Patrick Süskind from the library with joy, and cried in the bath as I did not understand *Wuthering Heights*. Discovering new concepts and feelings, I was also proving to myself that my English was *good*. I was so obsessed with learning English through the Internet and the arts that I did not care for other subjects. But you know where being good with words more than subject knowledge could lead you to: I did reasonably well in public examinations—by fluke and paying for last-minute tutorial class notes—for geography, accounting, world history, and economics.

So I got into university to double-major in English and English teaching, where poets like Tammy Lai-Ming Ho introduced me to contemporary poetry. She made everyone in class join a poetry competition (as a course assignment), which I won. The judges wrote a seven-page commentary on my first-ever completed poem. I never knew writing about my first holiday romance in a fragmentary, reverted letter was worthy. I was hooked. I never stopped writing since then but have never won a competition again.

*

Through curricula or reward systems, institutionalising human imagination can be both enabling and crippling. It depends on designs and implementations—could structurally-conveyed values expand the possibilities of communal care, rather than fossilising existing imbalance and exclusiveness? I have met a handful of Hongkongers who stopped caring for English literature after they studied it in school. The few that enjoyed it are now writers. I almost feel fortunate that I lack an early formal foundation in literature that many are forced to endure. That is why I always wanted to learn more.

Poetry, to me, has always been where intuition and institution meet. It is a child's instinct to play with the most mundane of objects time and again, and still find something exciting. Sometimes, experiencing a poem requires no explanation. It is understood through a gasp, a sigh, or a deep breath. Sometimes, contexts add weight to what seems plain and innocent. But once the evaluation of craft takes place, it begs the question of how well-read the poet and the reader are. To say what is good or bad is a socio-economic, thus, political judgement which reflects one's cultural capital. In the ever-expanding library of Englishes and forms, the ladders are moving in all directions. Ours may connect. Can I stay where I am, hovering, and not climb? Will I still meet your eyes?

Once, a poet told me that I sound *refreshing*. He could not locate my influences. It was a well-intentioned compliment. But I wished I could readily name the traditions I came from, the definitive ones that required no further elaboration. Just stating well-known poets and bands among monolingual English-speakers ungrounded me. In retrospect, I should have mentioned Cantopop lyricists like 林夕, 黃偉文, and 阿P without subconsciously thinking that no one would be interested. I should have mentioned my grandmother who expressed herself through horrible Maoist poems (although writing for a student newspaper got her into trouble). It was one of my aunts, whom I avoid now, who introduced me to Chinese Communist Party propaganda ballads (that I, at age six, enjoyed belting out standing at the edge of the bed that I shared with my two cousins and grandmother). And, of course, I should mention my mother who has a mellow voice but sings Cantopop slightly off-key because her Hokkien intonation still rings after living through Cantonese in Hong Kong for twenty-nine years.

*

I was told that being featured in a top-tier magazine is a big break. I was given an honorarium that was a month's worth of groceries for a two-page hybrid poem called 'Field Notes'.[2] I also gained about four hundred followers on my new Twitter account, which I set up to connect with poetry readers. From among the poems I sent, *POETRY* chose the one I was really unsure about. I am aware that 'big' magazines are often gatekeepers, and one could easily find more non-comforming work in 'small' magazines. But the day I received the acceptance email, I strolled for an hour in disbelief and had to lie down when I got home.

I was strategic as to what to share on my social media accounts. On Twitter, I shared a screenshot of 'Field Notes' with *POETRY*'s website header, my name, and the first part which contains the byline 'North East New Territories, Hong Kong'. On Facebook, which I have used since I started secondary school, I uploaded the middle part of my poem without my name and obvious Hong Kong markers. That earned less than thirty likes.

A poet's anxiety: I have been sending my poems to non-university journals since 2018. Yet, I had never actively announced the publi-

---

2   Tim Tim Cheng, 'Field Notes', *POETRY*, July/August 2022, 378–379.

cation of my poems online until a patron lent me the tuition for my masters in 2021. It always felt safer for me that strangers read my poems rather than my friends. I trusted my more sensitive poems with print magazines more than free-access digital ones, too. Out of the internalised capitalistic urge to prove to myself that *I am not a bad investment*, especially after two failed attempts in landing full scholarships for my poetry degree, I started sharing my work and other poems that I love to remind online friends that *hey, I write*. But I still avoid uploading a single image of my own poem in full, which usually attracts the most reactions. It is tricky balancing exposure and feeling exposed.

Coming from a working-class immigrant family, I still ask myself every so often if it is wrong to work on things that are not financially rewarding. One way or another, the citywide grief and anger in 2019 cracked me open. I could not run away from feelings anymore. It was time to overcome my Hong Kong-bred insecurities: *it is not about being good now. It is about striving for something better in the future, even if that is not foreseeable in my lifetime.* Before a version of a version matures into being, I must write. I must. I must. I must.

After a couple of years of incessant journaling and poeming to cope with urgent times, it came to me that *not* writing is an important aspect of transformation, too. I do sometimes wonder if writing poetry is a symptom of my social media overuse and short attention span. A poem is not unlike a status update. Within a word count, one has to create reactions that surface and eventually deposit bottomless timelines. A poem, though, sometimes serves as an anti-status that only emerges much later than the event that seeded it. When the right time for edits comes, I enter into a conversation that leads to an unknown destination. The poem seems to ask: *are you really trying to say this? Is this the furthest you could go?* Feel. Think. Thinking as feeling. You thought that was new. You thought you knew. You thought you were in control. That is not what matters.

Poetry is the one thing that keeps pushing through my presumptions and doubts, and persists with new beginnings.

*

The irony, of course, is that poems demand perfect choices. Give me the best words and the best arrangement. I recall feeling inadequate before classmates who grew up reading more. I mispronounced words during readings. But the embarrassment is fading with practice. If a circle is so sanitised that it has no room for imperfections and accidents, I do not want to be part of it. I am confident enough to stand up for myself now because I am finally *officially trained*. I have paid to have my portfolio workshopped with classmates, teachers, and mentors. Despite being equally lost, I am more proximate to a bigger publishing world than the person I was in Hong Kong, where grants and prizes are scant, if not censored. Does it not say something about my appetite for institutional recognition? How is that going to help with my cause?

I have travelled far to search for ways to set Hong Kong stories in verse, only to find out that Hong Kong has conditioned me into one of its stories.

***

COMMON GROUND

Helen Quah and Antony Huen

Helen Quah and Antony Huen discuss representations of Asia, personal space, and how their own lives led to poetry.

HELEN | 22 June 2022

Hi Antony,

Thank you for sending me your two poems and your Wasafiri Prize-winning essay examining the ekphrastic practices of British poets with Hong Kong heritage.[1] I have lots of questions for you.

Reading your essay, I was really intrigued by your idea of 'seeing and not seeing'. The example you used was taken from Sarah Howe's poetry when talking about Hong Kong. I found that really fascinating and wondered whether you could tell me more? I think your observations of how other Asian poets, in particular second-generation immigrants, are forced to look through a certain lens at their parents' home, holds true. Images and objects become more important as a way to create associations with another place or home. But I wonder whether these associations, created through another person rather than our own sensory experiences, actually makes them more layered in some respects.

Could you tell me about the kind of poetry that you gravitate towards? Who, for you, are the important writers of the Asian diaspora, and do you think there is something that traverses all Asian poetics?

For me I can say that reading Asian writers feels empowering. I feel that about most forms of culture and art: seeing parts of yourself reflected is critical. I grew up in a working class, conservative town

---

1   Antony Huen, 'The "Old Hong Kong" and "A Gold-Sifting Bird": Hong Kong and Chinese Ekphrasis in Contemporary British Poetry', *Wasafiri*, 2022, 13–21.

in England, straddling the border between Essex and East London. My sister and I were the only East Asian students in our primary school. To think of that now is quite shocking. It has since changed over the last decade but that was the reality for us as kids. I think it shaped our self-image considerably—whether good or bad. I naturally gravitate towards the themes of displacement in Asian poetics and the contradiction of heritage. For me, writers like Will Harris and Nina Mingya Powles are incredibly rich and give voice to my own feelings of confusion about my sense of belonging! They are both quite different poets but I feel a kinship with their perspective. Nina uses a lot of pop culture references to make this point actually, that how we consume representations of our culture, particularly those biased by the audience they are intended for, is very significant and probably difficult to quantify. I wondered how you think your physical environment has shaped you as a person and writer? Could you tell me about your life growing up?

Helen

*

ANTONY | 1 July 2022

Hi Helen,

Sorry to keep you waiting and thanks so much again for the thought-provoking questions.

I think what you get from the *Wasafiri* essay has to do with how the second-generation British Chinese can never get the full picture of what it was like to be Chinese in Hong Kong or mainland China. The visual images of postcards and films are both triggers and stimuli for their 'memories'.

I do read more poetry by those who share my Asian or Hong Kong experience but this pool of works is limited so I also look at works by those who come from mixed cultural backgrounds. I try to find works which I can relate to—as a poet I draw on what I've read, which is not surprising.

I don't have an answer to whether there is some kind of Asian poetics. First of all, I haven't read enough. What I try to do as a critic is to recognise the similarities and differences between what I think can be Hong Kong poetics and Chinese poetics. I start with Hong Kong poetics and look at the periphery of it (i.e. how it distinguishes itself from Chinese poetics as well as British poetics). I think of 'Chinese poetics' as a 'pan-Chinese poetics' and 'British poetics' as a similar sort. Of course there are overlaps between all these.

You're absolutely right about how it is important to look at different types of artistic representations of Asia or Asian people and sometimes my access comes from poetry. In Jennifer Wong's poetry I've discovered Zhang Xiaogang's portraits, which are often of family members, but they are eerie and the facial expressions are dull.[2] They remind me of how family portraits are artificial in terms of what they are portraying.

Not long ago I visited M+, a new visual culture museum in Hong Kong and it's the first time I saw Zhang's work. There's only one painting and when I was researching Zhang, I saw many on Google Images. I also realised I really wasn't looking at aesthetics but I was mainly looking at the narrative. In ekphrasis we get *description*, but less of the *painting*, more of what it represents (which is often a narrative embedded in, implied, or provided by the very visual representation).

I've read the work of Will and Nina. I think we've heard of this a lot of the time, which is how we shouldn't expect poets to pigeonhole themselves and to write in a certain way that other writers would expect them to (especially if it's a Eurocentric view). It might be to do with how each of these books by poets with cross-cultural experiences offers something familiar but, antithetically, feels distant. The *uncanny*, perhaps.

So I am the most curious about how or whether we have any common ground in what we write about. What are those common grounds? Should we be known for dramatising those common

---

2   Jennifer Wong, 'Bloodline', 回家 *Letters Home* (Nine Arches Press, 2020), 28.

grounds? Or should we be more recognised by the individuality that we achieve in our work? This also has to do with the private and public distinction. How do we create something out of our 'private' experiences and what do we expect the public to make of them?

You've also asked me about how the physical environment has shaped me as a person and writer. One thing that came into my mind was how I was speaking with a former student and she was talking about the difference between space and place. I think one way of answering your question is how, even though I lived in the UK for four years and the rest of my life I've been living in Hong Kong, it's still the private workspace that shapes my experience (i.e. a room of my own). That was to do with the actual writing space but to broaden the scope it'll be a more difficult question to answer.

First, my poetics is evolving, but back in the UK my experience had a lot to do with cultural differences and how I tried to maintain a connection with home. Ironically, back home in Hong Kong the kind of cultural inputs that I return to are from the West and I'm always caught in this dilemma: how I might always be thinking about somewhere else.

As an individual and writer I try to find certain common ground between who I am and who other people are, but I also create and strive for individualities. Furthermore, being in Hong Kong brings me so much closer to local social and political issues. They often come into my work, sometimes explicitly. Recently I've written a poem about the Jumbo Floating Restaurant, which might have sunk in the middle of nowhere.

To speak more about myself—I grew up in Hong Kong. I got to experience the UK by studying for my MA in Birmingham and some years later after having worked in a Hong Kong university, I returned to the UK for my PhD studies. But there was always some sense of what the UK was like. I had almost 10 years of living in Hong Kong under British colonial rule so there was also my understanding of the shift and transition between what it was like before 1997 and what it is now.

I wonder if you can also say a bit more about yourself: your experience of living in the UK and also how you perhaps negotiate your multicultural heritage. Did you study creative writing? Was it to do with some personal pursuit? I haven't read your poetry yet and it would be great if you could send me some, but I wonder what you think of yourself as a poet writing perhaps about your half Asian half British experience? How do you expect readers in the UK, or Anglophone readers, to receive your work and perceive you as a poet? What do you think are the opportunities and threats faced by poets of colour and poets with mixed heritage now in the UK?

And maybe it's too soon for these questions but what do you think the future is like for young poets in the UK, especially those with Chinese backgrounds? It might be interesting to talk about Chinese as an ethnic group—I am aware of the distinction between Chinese as a nationality and as a cultural group. I think *Chinese* in English is ambiguous, but it isn't in Chinese.

Hope we have enough to keep the dialogue going!

Best,

Antony

*

HELEN | 12 August 2022

Dear Antony,

How are you? I hope you are well in Hong Kong. We are currently experiencing a second heatwave in the UK and are very little equipped to cope! Thank you for your last letter. I've been reading and re-reading your questions for some time and I am not sure I will ever be able to adequately express my answers but I will try.

I agree there is certainly a reimagining that has to happen without that first-hand experience of a place. I think this is also the process by which we experience our parents in general, a kind of half-memory/reimagining which fascinates me. They begin as the most familiar anchors in our small circles of life and as we grow older become stranger to us. I am very much interested in generational gaps in thought which I guess is also influenced by my parents having childhoods in other countries.

Speaking about the uncanny I guess implies a sense of discomfort with this limbo or uncertain state. I think there is an unambiguous difficulty of being mixed and this is very much something I am engaged in; perhaps through voice we express our home nation and through that lens attempt to explore the homes of our parents. Perhaps to a native person this is difficult or unreal. I think Ocean Vuong summarises this uncanny feeling well when he describes how his mother, who he has written for and about extensively, will never be able to read his work. And even if she heard it, it would mean something very different for her. By migrating, there is a cultural as well as generational gap formed and I feel this has always been present for me. I try not to let it frustrate me but grow to enjoy it.

I was thinking about your question of common ground. I think it is curious to try and tie Asian writers' work together with a universal theme or construct. I think, in fact, we are showing the diversity within and between Asian writers' work. I believe that complication is incredibly important. Just like we need complicated characters to read or watch on TV, we need our work to be idiosyncratic and that is how we create depth as a collective. I want to see a community that involves a space for new Asian writers to have role models to aspire to but to not let that model be in any way prescriptive. Merely allow the freedom to expand away from, in any way a writer pleases.

Could you describe your personal space to me? Your room, the things in it? The way you physically sit down to write alongside your teaching?

I love your explanation of moving between the UK and HK and I'd be interested in your experience of that transition in HK. That's so fascinating the idea of always thinking about somewhere else. My partner is a Joyce obsessive and always talks about how Joyce wrote in Italy largely about Dublin. Made me think of that. It's a kind of positioning in order to write or think about place in a way similar to writing about an object or art. You interact with it more critically or less depending on your distance from it. Whilst you're in it perhaps it's even a burden or barrier to writing well around it. I hope next year to travel to Malaysia to stay with my dad's family there for a few months. I am interested in how this will affect my writing. I am conscious of your thoughts about writing about other people's lives without living them and I hope through language (improving my Mandarin) and living with my aunts and uncles I can get a small sense of life in Penang. I am sure I will end up writing extensively about provincial Essex but we shall see…

Ah, I saw that floating restaurant—they've removed it now haven't they? It's an incredible place that must be great material (literally) to write about. I think the Chinese restaurant is symbolic for many things but especially a floating or migrating one. How do you engage with it?

I was very lucky in that I was surrounded by lots of other second-generation immigrants or those from mixed heritages from a young age. My school, despite being in the middle of nowhere in a small village called Ingatestone in Essex, was a great state school specialising in languages that gave places to people from outside the catchment area if they had international links. In that way, I was educated in how people manage contexts. At home you may behave in one way with your family in keeping with their history and cultural background, and at school or around where you live, you may be another person. The kids at my school had this under-standing and were able to create a third-culture environment of sharing some of those cultural reference points warmly with each other. I felt very comfortable in this environment and although I have never met anyone with the same heritage as me, I think as a group of children with the same internal tension, we understood one another. Coming out of that school and that space was very strange, because the rest of the UK is not like that. However I had a good foundation and am so lucky to have close friends who share these core values.

My mother is from Guyana, an ex-British colony that is part of the Caribbean community. She is ethnically Indian/Amerindian and

Chinese. My father is Chinese-Malaysian and speaks Hokkien, but didn't teach me or my sister the language. I am interested in exploring my own parents' experiences of growing up in those countries which, on the face of it, are similarly diverse in terms of religion, culture, and race. Interestingly, my mother's heritage often gets overlooked when I speak to others, who are generally happy with learning that my dad is from Malaysia, as if that is enough to explain my appearance and identity for most people.

I think we are only going to see more people of mixed heritage in writing, because it lends itself to alternate perspectives on the world and expresses a yearning to connect with others with similar experiences. You asked about threats to those groups in writing and I would say the Asian diaspora feeling able to write about anything they want, whether that is related to their race or not, is very important. I am only excited to see what is produced in the next few years from mixed-heritage writers, it can only enrich the perspectives, contexts, and language.

I'd be interested to know your feelings about Chinese groups in the UK and what you experienced when studying here? I really loved your poem 'Self-Portrait as a Steamed Whole Fish', it moves so beautifully and felt very playful.[3] Could you tell me more about it? I wonder how you navigate language in your poems and if you ever write in a language other than English?

All the best,

Helen

*

ANTONY | 23 September 2022

Dear Helen,

Sorry for taking so long to write to you! Hong Kong is still in the

---

3   Antony Huen, 'Self-Portrait as a Steamed Whole Fish', *The Dark Horse*, 2021, 61.

pandemic era and I've heard it many times that the city is 'not' on the world map, which makes me think of how one's 'world' or even 'the world' is all a construct.

To go back to our conversation, I want to first talk a bit about generational gaps. I share your great interest in the childhoods of our parents. In my case, I'm the most intrigued by the childhoods of my maternal grandfather and paternal grandmother. They were the only grandparents I've ever had in my life and both have passed away in the last ten years. I feel that I could have talked to them more about their upbringing.

I'm grateful that you've told me about your mixed-heritage background—I really cannot imagine what it was like to be born with such rich and diverse cultural backgrounds. My parents and I were all born in Hong Kong but, as you know, Hong Kong was a colony of the British Empire and people like me, born before the handover of Hong Kong to the People's Republic of China, could imagine ourselves having a mixed-heritage background (i.e. having had the experience of living in both British Hong Kong and Chinese Hong Kong). But it seems nobody has talked about this in such a way—sometimes, it's not just censorship on a personal level but there's not an ongoing discussion which allows people like me to speak of ourselves as having an imagined dual heritage.

You're right that a cultural or generation gap triggers the imagination. It's really not just about representation but, as you've said, a sense of community. This, however, brings us back to the complex and sometimes generic idea of an Asian community. As you've told me more about your parents, I feel that we belong to the same segment of the Asian community. Maybe it's just *safe* to speak of Asia as a whole, rather than the Chinese community. I think as a bilingual writer, I consciously maintain and increase my awareness of these things. Are you bilingual or multilingual? I can understand simplified Chinese and speak some Mandarin—but I'm sometimes not sure about calling myself multilingual. I can speak Cantonese, Mandarin, English—but does that make me multilingual?

To answer your question about my personal space, I like to really make it *personal*—putting photos everywhere and making sure there are features that reflect my aesthetics. For example, I like things tidy in every sense. I want the desk clean (no mug ring, tea stain or crumpled paper.) I also like having post-its and postcards on the wall, and they need to be arranged in straight lines. I guess this is like my poetics—I'm used to writing in established forms but now like my fragmented, all-over-the-place, accidentally-indented poems a lot.

I absolutely agree with you on how it's difficult to write about the place we are in. Having said that, I've found it easier to write about Hong Kong. Perhaps I was too reliant on the physical distance, when I can actually imagine a sense of emotional or psychological distance. That doesn't make me feel detached from what goes on in Hong Kong but to hopefully see things from an outsider's point of view when I'm actually an insider. As a creative writer in English, I've already been in that position—and I think Nicholas Wong, Tammy Ho, etc., have talked about that before.

You've asked me about writing with someone else's voice and I guess you've seen that in my poem 'Self-Portrait as a Steamed Whole Fish'. The emotions in that are all genuine and I think I had someone in mind when I wrote it, but the narrative, imagery, and setting are all fictional. It's the 'self-portrait' frame as well as the imagination to be a fish served on a plate that allowed me to do that. I'm intrigued by the 'When I Marry a White Man' sequence in your pamphlet[4]—could you tell me more about how you've chosen to create such a temporal context and did the poems begin as a sequence? I've started to like poems that begin with *when* or *if*—the fact that these are conditionals and they don't have to be real or what will actually happen.

My poem about the floating restaurant is less about the floating than its name 'Jumbo Kingdom'.[5] I'm amazed by the fact there are many 'cities' within the city of Hong Kong—there was a 'kingdom' restaurant and the TVB Company calls its studio a *city*. There's also my alma mater, the Chinese University of Hong Kong, often called

---

4   Helen Quah, *Dog Woman* (Out-Spoken Press, 2022).
5   Antony Huen, 'Jumbo Kingdom', *The Oxonian Review*, 15 August 2023.

a mountain city. Jennifer Wong has an epic poem called 'Mountain City' but that sees the entirety of Hong Kong as a city with a mountainous landscape. It's so strange that when the Hong Kong discourse returns to the question of *what is politically correct and what is not*, there's so much in reality that is in fact in the grey area.

Going back to *Dog Woman*, I think it's a small but ambitious volume, speaking of women (mother, sister, cousin etc.), animals, nature, and the connections between them. The poems are often self-assured, as in the 'Marry a White Man' sequence. There seems to me not as much of what we've been discussing, i.e. cultural heritage and differences. Of course you've explored whiteness but I wonder what you think of one's cultural heritage as a theme in your writing. Is *Dog Woman* anticipating what's in your next project?

Could you also tell me more about what you mean when you say that the UK is not like the school you went to? I've learnt from Twitter the contrary opinions on the lavish handling of the Queen's funeral. The Queen has left a lasting impression on the Hong Kong people and I would say that the local news and social media coverage has been quite positive.

Finally, to speak of Chinese groups in the UK, I feel that they tend to be exclusive and diverse. First, my impression was that there was not much interaction between the Chinese groups and the other cultural groups on campus back when I studied in the UK. At York, I saw myself as belonging to an Asian group but I also mingled with the locals. It depends on the discipline though—my science friends would be in a really international community but in my case, there were many local English majors and often 'outsiders' would find it difficult to break into the group. In hindsight, I'd say it's just as difficult for them to 'stand out' from the local group and be close to the non-locals.

I've forgotten to say more about navigating languages. I love including Chinese words in an English poem. Also, 'Cantonese Proverbs'[6] is my attempt at writing a poem that cannot be translated, that is,

---

6   Antony Huen, 'Cantonese Proverbs', *amberflora*, Issue 10, 2021.

the poem would become not a poem but the Cantonese proverbs themselves. It's my translations of them and the sequencing of them that have made the poem—I'd see this as my way of establishing some in-between status. Those who can *fully* understand that poem need to be bilingual. I've tried writing in Chinese but I think my heart is in writing in English. Having said that, I'm practising what may be essentially bilingual (or multilingual) writing.

Best,

Antony

*

HELEN | 8 November 2022

Dear Antony,

I think the feeling you have of dual heritage is absolutely fascinating. Heritage is cultural, political, sociological, and psychological. It makes sense that you feel that way and I think language has a great impact. I was recently watching a short film made up of interviews with Chinese Guyanese people. I am trying to explore the Chinese and Indian migrants that came to the Caribbean as indentured labourers like my ancestors. I am interested in where I fit into the Caribbean community also. They interviewed a woman whose mother was born in China and whose family quite quickly immigrated to Guyana for work. This woman's mother then lived in Guyana all her life. She spoke about the different objects she kept in their home, such as an old silk slipper owned by her grandmother who made it by hand and embroidered it in China. The new generation brought up in Guyana quickly adapted to their new country, spoke English, went to Guyanese schools and that was home for them. Then something bizarre occurred. At around the age of ninety, out of the blue, her mother had woken up and completely lost all of her English. She spoke instead in a Chinese dialect from her childhood. The daughter was shocked and could no longer speak to her mother. They no longer shared a common language even after all that time. I feel this is the metaphor for the generational gaps that are widened when people migrate but also for that black box of understanding we will never have of our parents.

Aha—of course you are multilingual! If you weren't, I'd dread to think what that makes me. I am currently learning Mandarin again as an attempt to speak to some of my relatives in Malaysia and be able to travel more easily around East and Southeast Asia. I think it has always been a goal of mine to be able to communicate fluently in my dad's country, to not feel like a complete outsider although this is nearly impossible. I am also deeply aware of the privilege that comes from speaking the way I do.

'When I Marry A White Man' started as a single poem with many verses of an imagined relationship. It's really talking to the feelings of loss that come with giving part of yourself over in a relationship/ marriage/after having children and deals with witnessing lots of types of distances created in a long marriage, as well as dealing with race. It is both tongue-in-cheek and quite a dark poem, which is how I think of most of that book. It was only while working on the pamphlet that my editor suggested using the sequence as a backbone to the collection of poems that would run throughout. I really enjoyed that in other collections. Rachel Long's short poems throughout her collection, about her face when she sleeps, come to mind.[7] I had written quite a positive backstory for this relationship but decided I would just allude to this by starting at 'part II' and get to the meat of what I wanted to discuss. Happiness is implied by the speaker but not seen. I am really interested in how you feel the pamphlet doesn't appear directly related to the topic of heritage. I think *Dog Woman* doesn't tackle these themes overtly in some respects and more the psychological or internal feelings of displacement or isolation that come from the in-between which I was intrigued by and I feel most intensely. As I said, I am currently looking at the Chinese presence in the Caribbean and hope to think about that part of my heritage more closely—what form it will take, I am not sure yet.

Your piece sounds brilliant. Can you give me some examples of

---

7   Rachel Long, *My Darling from the Lions* (Pan Macmillan, 2020).

Cantonese proverbs you like? Do you feel you have different sensibilities writing in each language?

Are you the same person or are your intentions, feelings even, different?

All the best,

Helen

*

ANTONY | 9 November 2022,

Dear Helen,

What a great idea to end with poems of our own. Before that, I just want to say I'm very moved by that documentary story—it might really be the unspoken, or the inability to speak about things, which marks generational gaps. I'm excited about what will follow *Dog Woman* and your plan is promising! I don't know how writing starts from scratch for you—but I am more driven by feelings or an accumulation or surplus of them. Themes or intentions come later—but my recent poems, or new versions of old poems, are more intentional from the get-go and here is one of them:[5]

---

5 An earlier version of this poem was published in *Mingled Voices 3: International Proverse Poetry Prize Anthology 2018* (Proverse Hong Kong, 2019).

A Bust

The two of us take refuge
        in the artist's head.

A bonsai-like forest: gnarled trunks, dangling
        and swaying roots, two plunging
            cascades, in the dissipating   mist.

In ancient robes, heirlooms, light
                as lace, we play

our Chinese instruments:
        yours, piano-like;
        mine, flute-like;
without dislike or suspicion.

My black hair sticks out
            from under the hat
                with a swallow's tails.

        You face him with your back,
      your head and face shaved,
your eyes evergreen.

The poem is ekphrastic but I have used a bit of ekphrastic licence. I'd prefer it to be first enjoyed without its pictorial referent. It's a landscape painting with two people, by a painter of the Lingnan School.

To respond to your questions, I'm more conscious about how I speak in a different language—I'm more confident and articulate when I speak in English, unless I'm with friends or family. It's also to do with my teaching profession. There are too many Cantonese proverbs that I like and use every day—I'm also picking up English proverbs and idioms every now and then. It seems our inspirations are unsurprisingly from different places: in my case, visual representations, pop lyrics and melodies, etc. I wonder which poem you will share with me. It's been almost half a year since we started this dialogue and I'm very grateful for your insights and time. I hope our paths will cross again in future! Long live our heritage!

Best,

Antony

*

HELEN | 4 December 2022

Dear Antony,

It has been such a pleasure to hear about your writing practice and life, I hope we can meet one day! I will end with a short poem that captures some of the thoughts we discussed over the last six months.

All the very best,

Helen

Ohrwurm

I am Chinese Guyanese I am divorced of all notions
of intimacy until you look at my face and realise
some two people must have got it on in the face of
divorce I am British in the sound that my face makes
a ringing like a glass bottle or eggshell like tinnitus
that goes into the ear and head and doesn't come out

***

ON COMMUNITY, SPACE, HETEROPHOBIA, ANGER, AND OTHER WAYS OF HEALING

Marylyn Tan and Mukahang Limbu

Marylyn Tan and Mukahang Limbu discuss Singapore, Jane Austen and late capitalist queer futures.

MARYLYN

dear muka,

you are a glorious and incandescent poet of a person and i am so excited to write to you.

i've been thinking about space and housing recently. queerness jostles uneasy in a country that demands that the nonproductive and nonreproductive scavenge for what's left of the roofs we are given. if you're poor and brown and gay then pick a struggle because they're all working against you to get a house. sometimes it seems like an unholy test. they don't give you any notice at all before all at once you have to apply for public housing, and you're not quite sure which houses you're eligible for, and you're unsure you'll even get a ballot number at all. because it's illegal for you to be married, so figure that shit out like it's a personal failing.

to be a certain kind of queer in Singapore is to be consistently reminded that you're one fuckup away from everything shattering, that you have to be nice to your idiot landlord because you have housing insecurities, to field inane queries such as 'if you both Singaporean then why have to rent??? [sic]' so this closed-throat feeling, the shortness of breath, the kicking of one's heels uselessly at the kitchen counter while the plastic bag fills and falls with your panicked breaths, you get used to. you get used to the feeling, not of being held, but of being held down against your will.

& now—can i still afford to be curmudgeonly with desire?

is hunger holy? the Catholics will fast if there's something they wish to petition the gods with. in your spiritual arsenal apparently fasting, hand in hand with prayer, is immeasurably powerful.

but i who always seek the surfeit, the abundance, the abandon of decay, forced to live within a margin of austerity—i undergo it but i understand it not.

MUKAHANG

the public housing system in Singapore is a bit cray! i learned a bit about it when i visited SG, and my friend said it's the main reason why SG has a chronic monogamy! Wei Kai said everybody gets married because it's cheaper and it literally opens up doors to more housing opportunities. so when you're poor, gay, and brown, when it's already hard enough being poor, gay, and brown, it does indeed seem unholy, sacreligious, and surely impossible. can't get married, can't go private, finding a sugar daddy in this economy is challenging, it might already be in shattering.

i'm thinking of housing through Austen (forgive me—i'm in deep revision mode right now), as in my girl Ms. Jane Austen, and Singaporean Gurkha wives. the Gurkha wife, as young as Austen's heroines about to 'enter society', who might have only known about their wedding the night before, meeting their husbands on the day of the wedding, tethered for innumerable lifetimes, will have had months to dream of the homes they were meant to make in Singapore. the Gurkha wife, even the most transgressive Lydia of them all, the one who has an eloping loudness, has no qualms sitting at the head of any table, the pick-me Gurkha wife, the non-conforming, well-educated, the one who dared to run away the night before the wedding, even this wife didn't dare to not get married, I 'did it for my mother' she says, or her parents—to make a home in Singapore is a better prospect than staying in Nepal, our dusty, loving, idling Nepal.

and so they arrive, no boxes to tick anywhere, no preferences (how many bedrooms? which floor? furniture?), and are put in the box— the Gurkha Camp flats themselves are quite cubic, and i guess all floor plans are made up of quadrilaterals, and now i'm wondering what the home would look like with triangular, septagonal or decagonal floor plans—i imagine the tick box forming around the young wives. a lot of them weren't expecting anything but i wonder how they might have described these flats: vapid spaces, white tiles, the austerity of tiles, austere because they're both cold and hard. but these cold and hard homes are warmed by footsteps of children who have taken their first steps there, to the older children rushing in and out, as homes with children often seem to have this coming and going, a rush in and out, the doors groaning open close open, the door-curtains whoosh open, close, open.

many days these homes were the wives' only companion. soon after the wife's arrival, the husbands would often have to leave for nine-month fieldwork, and these wives who had popped out babies, some babies themselves, would have to stay in these flats, long periods by themselves, lonely, as you've put it, kicking their heels at the kitchen counter. i imagine my aunt, young, skinny, her eyes cartoonishly round (a family trait, my father's were even more pronounced in anger), so round like a bull's testicle (my mother's poetic description), staring at the wall as she breastfed her first-born. it was the early 2000s, no phones, no internet, foreign tv, and not super well educated to bide the time by reading (all of Austen's heroine's read a lot right—Lizzie reads a lot, well a lot of letters, Fanny reads to experience the world, and Catherine reads too much Gothic stuff, which gives her nightmares and sex dreams). these wives and mothers are in that tick box with all that white space.

i asked my aunt 'but did you have a community with the other aunts' trying to make an afterschool special movie, and she answers 'no not in the beginning, everybody has their own babies; everyone's too busy.'

when i was visiting my aunt and uncle, it felt like a home, not one she had been given but one that was made. as i was washing the mala oil that flew into my cornea with dishwashing liquid, screaming 'help', it felt like i was in a Nepali kitchen; the pans, the vibes. it was also the chicken curry which was like the one in Nepal, growing up in the UK this one felt closer to Nepal, and it was what i needed. they have had almost two decades in these spaces, and then without any choice they are forced to leave.

after many decades of service, after making their cubes into a home, after hanging up their typical Nepali white lace curtains, after raising their children there, who are in the midst of their A levels, who barely speak any Nepali, who are well versed in rapid Singlish that i find tricky to understand, after learning which hawker centre sells the better char kway teow, after overcoming their depressions, after the friends they've lost and the friends they will lose, their names will one day become just a familiar sound, after accepting all the rules and regulations of SG, rules implemented on their bodies, their beings, rules that tell them they can't get a Singaporean nationality even if they were born there, rules that don't let the wives work, nor their children, rules that drive the teenage boys to take on cash-in-hand summer jobs, laborious jobs, dangerous jobs like building stage sets or slicing metals, after having and breaking up with Malaysian, Singaporean boyfriends and girlfriends, after feeling dare-they-say Singaporean, they have to leave. with the surety of a full-stop when the Gurkha dad's employment is over so is their time in Singapore. they must leave, pack all their belongings. they must attend a hundred farewell dinners hosted by other Gurkha families who themselves will be in the same position in a few years. as hard as they might try they will put on some weight. they will complain about all the weight they've put on. the wives will nag at the husbands for drinking too much beer. the husbands will keep drinking too much beer, beer bellies and flushed smiles.

then they move back to Nepal. there is no argument, no petitions, no resistance. this is the way things have been. and so, they leave with their memories, with all their unfinishedness and with their washing machines.

(also housing with Jane Austen—my girl had to live in so many different places. when i was living in Berlin, and i was lonely, unanchored, aimless and bored, i read *Persuasion* and watched this long documentary about Austen's housing situations. she moved constantly from her family home then to various places including Bath, to look for marriage, then Lyme, the seaside place they visited in *Persuasion* and there's that mad accident where Louisa falls down the stairs—this was when Austen was at her poorest. shifting from family members to family members, brothers who wouldn't look after her— the poor girl she deserved better. partially, Austen's complete uprooting was relatable, and she realised a great fear of being a poor creative—*got any tips for this?*—and her story isn't unique or singular but she was in constant anxiety over her housing; she's not our brown, queer, poor—scratch the last two, there are theories she was queer, and she became poor—template. but she allows me to re-think notions of space, think through that shortness of breath, of being caught in a gale so straight you can't push your breath past your chest, that anxiety in your chest, in the words of one Katy Perry 'like a plastic bag/drifting through the wind.')

the anxiety of housing is maybe a plastic bag i guess—all flimsy and easy to tear.

haha not sure if you wanted all this, infected by my finals but i miss Singapore! looking forward to your response.

MARYLYN

i appreciate what you say about space—as in the confines of the physical space, being located geographically/geometrically within the boundaries of a room or a residence—as well as finding community and making space for a community—which sometimes isn't even possible because 'they all have their own babies', that is, when the petty vagaries of life demand too much for you to reach out to some-one else. i've been thinking a lot about running on fumes and crisis mode. i've been thinking about being stuck between abusive home environments and late-capitalist queer futures and the endless crush towards legal monogamy in Singapore, and how it makes me a more heterophobic person, because in Singapore being married (marriage between a man and a woman, the only real kind, not the fake kind that gay people pay a photographer and a willing solemniser to do overseas in taiwan or new zealand to commemorate) is another way the state realises you as being human with civil rights—what little we can glean of them, of course. and i am thinking about taking up space with stories as well—how the Infocomm Media

Development Authority (IMDA) will play these sexy little mind games with artists, mindfucks really, where if it's a queer-centred show or performance they sometimes (read: often) won't issue you the show licence until the day before, or the day of, so you have to put in all of your time and effort into a show you don't even know is going to be happening. i was organising a queer conference that happened over last weekend and one of the panellists on a talk on party organising noted that as lesbians running women's parties for over a decade, it's a historical fact that they would expect to get raided and shut down by the police every single night for a while. even as recently as 2019 was their biggest party issued only a partial licence, with a day's notice, such that beachgoers who expected a beach party had to cram into an indoor space. the point i think i'm making is that these things may seem trivial to the state or the sexual majority when we complain about them but i think that when it comes to alienation and isolation every little bit helps. every little push towards choosing the 'right' life, meaning the easy life, meaning easy to categorise and slot into the social institutions that serve a dominant superstructure, meaning live life in a way that is convenient to govern. i don't mean to sound angry, it's just that i am, and i think tiredness is a way to deaden our connection to pleasure to peace and to notions of home, which are only ever expanding.

to me notions of home and moving a lot are also close to my heart, because often the people who move a lot happen to be either extremely well-connected or have to by virtue of circumstance, which means it's either romanticised or just an endless torment of housing insecurity. i have lived with my partner for four years now and have helped her move four times in the span of two years. when you move to new, usually more expensive lodgings, there is often a feeling of upgrading, as well as the unshakeable fear that you won't be able to maintain this new lifestyle, and this new expenditure, in the long term. does this also count as housing insecurity? because the rental market in Singapore is so unforgiving, and landlords are so unabashedly racist and classist, i think it also forces questions of worth, of self-categorising, of trying to show landlords that we are good tenants, we will *not* fuck up your house, we are *full-time employed*, we are *educated*, we are *clean*, and always get the chinese person (if you are lucky enough to have a chinese person) to talk to the agent, because it makes the chances of even getting a text back so much higher. sure, it's shocking that some rental ads flat out say 'no [race]', but it's even more insidious and pervasive that almost all of the others say 'all races welcome', because it's a thing you very much have to specify. if i feel traumatised by having to hunt for leased rooms in very-much-illegally-partitioned apartments it is an infinitesimal fraction of what space means to the disenfranchised, especially the migrant worker.

when you speak of Gurkha wives and displacement i often think of the migrant worker populations in this country and how the drive towards community and the crush of dehumanisation characterises almost all we hear of them. the pandemic resulted in their being locked in the dorms for months on end. i think of mental wellness and the way we discuss migrant workers' rights to rest as a debatable point. it wasn't until very recently that we implemented the notion of a 'rest day' formally, as in legally, as in:

> *From the Ministry of Manpower's website:*
>
> *Rest days*
>
> *Your MDW is entitled to one rest day per week. You and your MDW must mutually agree on which day of the week she should take the rest day.*
>
> *From 1 January 2023, all employers must ensure their MDWs have at least one rest day each month that cannot be compensated away.*
>
> *If your MDW agrees to work on the remaining rest days in the month, you must compensate her with one of the following:*
>
> *At least 1 day's salary. Note: This is an additional payment and is not counted into the MDW's basic salary.*
>
> *A replacement rest day taken within the same month.*

all of this is just to say that i think the importance of making art, both for the 'poor creative', and for the marginalised body, is in being able to imagine. Brian Gothong Tan, a theatre practitioner and artist, on a panel i was moderating recently about queer art and the future, said that you either had to be 'very brave or very stupid' when you make a decision to create queer art in Singapore, and part of me suspects that is also because it is healing, it makes us take pleasure in an activity that does not prioritise consumption, and it breaks and re-coagulates structures in the imagination. i often think of Audre Lorde's assertion that women are psychically milked and maintained at a distance of inferiority to men, so as to be utilised for their immense powers of eroticism, rather than have men examine this depth of feeling in themselves, and i think the same is true of all hegemonic social groups—all others in service to, but that which is too authentic, too mired in something uncontrollably real—is dangerous. and therein i think is the absolute clusterfuck pleasure that i think must undergird all of our organising, all of our writing, all our advocating for better things for each of us.

xxx

marylyn

MUKAHANG

i might myself be a heterophobe; in fear of being cancelled as a hate monger of 'heterosexuals' i can only say that i'm much too full with resentment at how much easier it is for the heterosexuals in the world, case in point in SG. i've seen instagram reels of the gay couples who celebrate their love through the classic wedding photoshoot, but there isn't an actual civil licence that recognises their existence. and i think it's sad. i hate how hard it is, so like you i'm done, i'm angry. i'm angry that gay couples have to find some loophole, some roundabout way to confirm their union, that they're denied spaces so easily accessible to heterosexuals, that all the structures around the templates that we have been melted to are het-structures, and so habitating, accommodating, and even loving is just so damn hard—the queer future, as much as the queer past, is unable to escape loneliness. sorry this is a tired tale. but i've been thinking of loneliness. queer loneliness—are we lonelier? can it be quantified? should it be even a competition?

i'm sorry that you have to prepare for a tornado even after you receive the 'ok'. and, even more, that the tornado is a certainty. this does make me love the UK a little more, or living here, even with its greyness, the dampness, the greyness of our pavements made grey by all the grey rain (i'm glad spring is coming, although we get sun for three months—the only three months where i think *i love living here*). we're lucky that queer spaces are not preparing for a police raid, or events have to be given the 'A okay', that we had *Queer As Folk*, *Emmerdale*, Graham Norton, Alan Carr, and *This Is Going to Hurt*, to buffer the homophobia, and that as a nation, and just people, they're indignantly against being governed. that's why the lockdown was such chaos here—even the most tory or upper class people i know were against the government trying to put a holster on their life. but i'm thinking about how policing events is an act of reducing and redacting space, and so i understand your anger. it is reasonable. it is the only thing that seems to make sense. confinement, you watching your island being eroded around you can only instigate anger. this is a feeling i've written about recently:

I don't know what happens when the curtain of rage is drawn in; from where I'm standing, I see her porcelain skin, her cheeks flush, her freckles like soil, crease, knowing that it's something not unlike lava, like a tsunami, or maybe an earthquake of heat. She'd asked that afternoon why Bollywood celebrities live in high-rise apartments when there were so many earthquakes in India. Isn't it dangerous? And apparently there are earthquakes every day in Japan but why don't the tall buildings fall? I told her something from YouTube; I mumbled something about engineers having discovered a way to make buildings flexible, so they wobble from the shock, but they don't crumble. And I saw her, this almost five-foot skyscraper, gaping at me in woollen leopard print pjs, both wobbling and crumbling. Her tall shadow looming over my horizon. She'd also asked why we get earthquakes in Nepal.

I wonder what she sees, in her mind, when she's this angry, like canines teething around the bars of a cage. I'm thinking about Rilke's Panther endlessly circling its cage looking out at the poet to make him feel things; the poet immerses himself in the Panther's gaze, trying to penetrate its mind, to see through the Panther's dark brown eyes, its cyclical emotion, watching daily how the sun rises from one side to set on the other; this poet is to be so moved he makes the lines of stanza material, each quatrain like the cage's walls. For the Panther doesn't know the world outside this cage, and it doesn't know the world outside this form, the world outside of the poem, like how my mother in this moment refuses to see anything outside of her rage. My mum doesn't know Rilke, and I don't know how to translate panther. But she's seen a cougar, the expensive one my grandfather brought home to keep in our zoo; the one that escaped into the jungle. And so, I'm thinking her anger is like this cougar escaping—visions of a future where I'm crying on the phone, visions of me not living at home, visions that are darker, too scary for me Reader to even write, or think about yet she has already imagined and lived in her mind, slips through those bars like a wild cat. It escapes out into the wilderness and becomes the jungle itself. It engulfs this jungle, the trees, the shadows of wild mushrooms, and all its unnavigated fear, running, cutting in all directions.

so this is a little prose essay written in the hour after my mum and i had an argument (well she was angry and i accepted her anger) regarding where i applied for masters. but i was just angry at how angry she was, and i think a lot of it is a product of love, her worries, her fears, but a lot of anger is instigated by her confinement. like Gurkha wives, my mother lives in the army barracks with my two young step-brothers. she can't really leave the barracks because she can't drive, and has to look after the kids. she can't go clubbing like she did when she initially split from her abusive husband, my father, and she's not out in the world meeting up or catching up with her friends. she had a rich social life, independence, and stability. but she does love my step-dad, he's a patient man and he does a lot for her, but still she doesn't have much of her own space. it's the kids and step-dad, which is an equilibrium of smothering confinement in both directions. it's this displeasure that makes her so angry. she asks me 'why do you ask why i get so angry? do you not see my life?' and i'm still like 'why are you so angry?'

i am so sorry that you and your partner have so much trouble with housing, and that constant relocation, and the constant need to advertise yourself, and make yourself palatable for classist, racist, homophobic, hegemonic agents must be really tough. housing insecurity is the worst; it is a trauma, and manifests, behaves and prowls like a trauma.

i think of all the houses i've moved from—sorry going to do a little count—Nepal, Tyne Road, council estate after my dad retired in Littlemore where my mum couldn't sleep because the walls and the carpet smelled like cigarettes and people were shouting on the streets all night, then relatives house in Rose Hill, Lenthall Road, my teacher's shed—cus when i went to uni we couldn't afford our house, my mum wanted to move to a small room to save money—Church Cowley Road, then Queen's College, Queen's College Annexe, Berlin for my year abroad: three different apartments in Berlin, back to Queen's College, and now Portsmouth where my mother is based—but next month my step-dad is going to have to move again cus of the army. hmm, to constantly shift, to be constantly relocating is definitely shattering—this is why my mum wants a house, so i gots to get a job ahaha. unfortunately as you say the migrant workers were not given the opportunity to stretch their bodies or their minds. being locked up, abandoning you with yourself, is a punishing experience, i feel i can vouch for that. *#healing*—my best friend is on a healing journey and just inspired by what i still have to get done—i like the idea of 'rest day' though, it's the very least.

Brian Gothong Tan, oohhh i'll check his work out. let's be 'very stupid' and 'very brave'; i hope this can lead to buying a house someday. that is such an interesting quote from Lorde—where is it from? i'm still wrapping my head around it; but there is a voyeur. recently, my teacher said to me, cus there was this very strange and weird review of my work—remind me and i'll send you the link— that queer asian men are treated how women writers have often been treated. hahah let's just say he used the words 'domestic', 'tender', 'exotic' etc… but i'm moving towards that reconciliation of how this old white man is reckoning with my work and forming it in a canvas to present it to the world, in a very 'tricksy' and abject way of saying 'i understand this work, it's good and not good' and 'i'm going to go read it by the beach' because 'it's that kind of book'. i guess being a creative or as you wisely put it 'dangerous' (fuck yeah why not!), comes with this kind of thing as well. but thoughts?

stay dangerous! the cold winds of spring are cray here—missing you and Singapore!

much love

Xx

MARYLYN

dear muka—

i think it's very interesting that you frame it as '[your mother] was angry and [you] accepted her anger'. i think it's a very good way to think about anger without yourself getting displaced by the frustration and uncomprehending that can sometimes manifest when witnessing someone else's eruption. i'm sure that in its own way it's a healing exercise as well—allowing the anger to seethe and then pass through us leaving our physical husks unharmed. it *is* a tired tale, like queer anger is tired, and some days i seem to pass from fatigue to rage to fatigue, and these are my two moods, but i think it's in the state's best interest to make sure you are worn out and too weary to find community and organise, so i try not to let the energy deplete.

it's so hard because you're a wage slave, you're 'born to squirt but forced to work', as a shirt i saw recently from Malaysian designer ghostboy says, and if you say you're anti-labour, especially in Singapore, people find that difficult to compute. in a place that prides itself so strongly on the myth of meritocracy, where things such as the right to live, to housing, to water and electricity, are earned and not freely given, i don't really believe it's possible to not work, in any case.

the closest i came to witnessing a life that might be anti-work was when i was staying with punks in Berlin in a squat, and they were talking about collecting bottles at a festival to be recycled for money later on. that was the job, and other times they just made art and went to parties, to clubs, to exhibitions. i'm not saying that's the ideal life (although it may come close in certain aspects). i just think being able to have enough to live on should be easier to come by. and it shouldn't sound like such a radical idea, but to me the idea triggers an immediate fear and anxiety response, like what i'm proposing is the collapse of society, but what it really is is the proposed downfall of forced labour and making capitalism angry. i don't know how to change that. universal basic income, expecting less, consuming less, perhaps, mutual aid, spending time building community and social networks instead of monetary accrual, but really, what do i know about money? what do i know about holding space? it's like you said—*are we lonelier? can it be quantified? should it even be a competition?*

i don't know that i am good at competitions, or trying to quantify pain. i just think that oppression is too-often a zero sum game, and maybe that is also a trite sentiment. i don't know if there is anything new i can say about suffering. i think it's easy for us to say, let the suffering of the past connect us to the suffering of the present, and in that we might organise across generations and time, when what so frequently happens is a collective amnesia, a breaking of history, a new generation every five years (queer people regenerate more quickly than others) trying to reinvent newness, queerness, thinking, ideas. i love that image of the panther-proxy stalking in your post-argument prose essay. it is so easy to say 'become ungovernable' and then live wholly domestic. i feel defanged by my own tiredness. i feel inspired by others' passions but it goes away quickly.

i've said before that art-making is my one throughline to community, that i find it difficult to connect with people otherwise, and i think it's a kind of magic to be able to create and have it have legs, where people are having conversations about the work independently, and they can see what it's about, it has a voice and an ethos and aesthetics—to me, i understand that, rather than organising. sometimes i feel i can only come towards the future from the dream-sphere, from imagining the far end of fucked up, and then by saying the ugly thing, or imagining the horrific or subterranean or visceral thing, we open up space to imagine in which potential ways we could connect to each other. it's why horror is so important to me as a genre, it's why i always say i trade in disrespectability politics; it's the greatest treasure to me to be able to act faggy and weird and off-putting, to subvert the push towards milquetoast/banal/inoffensive representation. i think that for me that's what healing looks like—unlearning what is attractive and pleasing to the status quo and maybe sometimes actively rejecting or subverting it. what about you? what does a healing journey look like to you?

yes, please, show me the strange/weird/tokenising review of your work! the Lorde quote about the aphids is from her essay 'uses of the erotic: the erotic as power', and i refer back to it frequently whenever we talk about how women and sexual minorities are distanced from their own erotic power as a means of commodifying them or making them a consumers' market. mmm, 'exotic' is a definite red flag, 'tender' less so, but then there's the whole 'tenderqueer' (derogatory) rhetoric that goes on—historically, cishet white men's ways of receiving my work have been, i want to say, a little repellent. there was this guy who asked 'who wrote that' in an incredulous voice after i'd performed at an open mic, and this other guy who dismissed my work but asked for my bibliography/recommendations lmao. that was so odd. so you'll read it as long as it comes from a western source? but you won't take it from my mouth? it's very funny to me because i think there's a sort of backlash happening where these men perhaps feel like, 'oh they're only playing the minority card and that's why they're receiving adulation'. i'm not sure. that being said, anyone who feels that way is likely not my audience, and one must fantasise an audience, right? that's what Divya Victor told me when we were embarking on the first draft of *GAZE BACK*, and i envisioned an audience that was very queer and very female and

Singaporean, and i think there is home in that specificity, just like appealing to everyone is the enemy of focus.[1]

stay dangerous, but stay safe! you will have sunlight soon! we tend to take it for granted here but i actually, deeply, enjoy the sun, and not having to wear clothes, because i am a tropical girl and get cold for no reason.

xxx

be well, Singapore waits for you,

marylyn

***

---

1 Marylyn Tan, *GAZE BACK* (Ethos Books, 2018; University of Georgia Press, 2022).

A LETTER TO TAO QIAN

Arthur Sze

I wish to tell you but lose the words—
    more than a millennium later,
on another continent, in another language,
    I know adversity strengthened you.

Today we possess antibiotics,
    cars, cell phones; scientists
use infrared scanners, check a wildfire
    that has charred 341,735 acres.

When you picked chrysanthemums
    by the bamboo fence to the east,
then gazed at mountains to the south,
    at birds homing at sunset,

you turned in three directions,
    centring yourself; though you omitted north,
I posit *mortality* as you sipped wine.
    Today we have no spell

that lessens loss; a neighbour's backhoe
    beeps as it excavates a slope.
Sifting your words, I dig at this site
    where pines scent after rain;

a black swallowtail lands
    on Russian sage, bending the stalk;
as it imbibes nectar and sways, I sway;
    light slants all that we do.

WRITING

WORK IN PROGRESS

Li-Young Lee, Jennifer Wong and Eddie Tay

Li-Young Lee, Jennifer Wong and Eddie Tay exchange thoughts on the poems they are currently working on and talk about the pandemic, spirituality, and love.

EDDIE TAY: Li-Young and Jenny, it was great being able to share my poems with you, to communicate through email and also to meet through Zoom. Writing is such a lonely affair. Yes, there is a difference between loneliness and solitude but sometimes it's hard to tell which is which. When we write, we are physically alone, aren't we? And we spend so much of our time writing. Li-Young, I am sharing an extract of your poem here:

> I meant to send you a message
> this morning via wings, but
> all the mourning dove knows
> is the logic of what's missing.
> And the redwing only ever speaks
> to reminds us to look far off,
> there are no answers on earth.
> And forget the crow with its,
> Error! Error! Error!

It is sometimes hard to communicate, isn't it? I think we are all caught up in our solitudes which ultimately is a kind of loneliness, and language is that special magical connection, a path we cut through the jungle of everyday life. All we can do is reach out. But everyday language is often not pure enough. We say one thing or a few things but there are always lots more left unsaid simply because the jungle is too big and we can't cut enough paths through it. Or to use another metaphor and to play on a cliché, language provides a window into our souls but the window is most of the time tinted or muddy. Here's a third metaphor (sorry): I think as poets we are aware that language is a knot we are all trying to unravel in our own ways.

LI-YOUNG: Fascinating, Eddie. I love that image of language as a knot. Maybe it's one of the primary knots. Maybe another knot is the body. Maybe time and space is The Knot of Knots, the Knot that gives rise to all other knots. Or maybe consciousness is The Knot of Knots, since consciousness gave rise even to time and space.

JENNY: Eddie, I love the way you see language as a tinted or muddy window. I remember talking to Eleanor Goodman in Beijing, who said that language for the Chinese poets is impure or unclean, and we must find a way to navigate that.

Throughout the pandemic, I struggled with language in a way as I struggled with silences from loved ones and friends, including two years of silence between me and my mother. It was painful back then and still painful to articulate now. I tried to find my way out through poetry, through metaphors. It led to a poem, 'The truth is when you stopped talking to me for a year' published in *Poetry London*, my first in that magazine. Later, I wrote another poem, 'Kinder to self'; I looked for a way to fuse together the sense of lived time, self-care, and the longing to be understood, to be forgiven, from one generation to another:[1]

> I mean to send you
> a gold-embossed paper crane with
> cherry blossom wings,
> [...]
> I would have wished instead
> to have sent a postcard
> of a picturesque childhood:
> a doting mother's heart
> brimmed with pride

---

1   Jennifer Wong, 'The truth is when you stopped talking to me for a year', *Poetry London*, Issue 102.

but my memory
is a clock with eager hands
pointing forever towards
Forgive, forgiveness [...]

EDDIE: That's a wonderful piece! It starts with wanting to communicate, which is the job of poetry. I would love to receive a gold-embossed paper crane. It speaks of such care and hand-crafted labour and thoughtfulness in the age of convenient and disposable online communication. Isn't that what poetry is, a gold-embossed paper crane or a postcard? Even a literal postcard is not good enough, because how would you convey a picturesque childhood given the limited space? That is where poetry comes in, to communicate thoughts and feelings as much as possible in a compressed form.

And here's an extract of a poem I offer as a response to yours:

I am afraid I can only give you a stone.

Yesterday, a student read me her diary
of wilting flowers.

There is no nectar in my heart.

Yesterday, in the news,
there was a young couple who fell.

I can't recall a paper crane
in memory's pages.

I am afraid I can only give you a stone.

The news in the past years has been depressing. There is an epidemic of mental health issues in Hong Kong (and everywhere else, I suppose) in relation to the pandemic. In addition to physical health issues, there are economic hardships which then lead to anxiety and related mental health issues. Yes, it seems that we are emerging from it all now, some of us being more battle-scarred than others. But scars aren't always visible.

LI-YOUNG: I'm lit up inside like an old opera house in Shanghai! I'm so excited and grateful to be in this exchange with both of you. I'm deeply moved by your poetry. I see that we three fit Thomas Mann's description of the writer as someone who, contrary to what others think, has the most trouble with language. I think when our tongues are checked by awe (in awe of beauty, in awe of horror), when our mouths are stoppered by shock or trauma, when our speech is seized by an experience beyond our understanding, when we can't speak because of a wound between us and another, or a wound so deep and early we can't find it, though the pain it causes radiates throughout our being to inform our every breath, when even the impulse to speak is arrested because of an experience of solitude or isolation so deep that we feel no words can bridge it, then poetry emerges.

Theodor Adorno said something like after the Holocaust, poetry is not possible. I'm convinced the opposite is true: After the Holocaust, only poetry is possible. Where our philosophies fail us, poetry begins. Where our theologies can't reach, poetry begins. Where our discursive theories dry up and blow away, poetry begins. The experiences of 'O, my God!' or 'O, my Love!' or 'Holy, holy, holy!' all experiences of speechlessness, demand poetry. For me, all lyric poems are informed by 'O!' The 'O' which is an exclamation of both speechlessness and a need to speak at all costs. The 'O' which demands of us the most potent speech. The 'O' which forbids us to speak. For me, this 'O' of speechlessness is the mother of poetry.

And I see the three of us coming to terms with this in the poetry we've exchanged. How good it is, Jenny and Eddie, that we're all three in the right place. How sad it is, Sweethearts, that we find ourselves bereft of philosophy, bereft of any inherited meanings of the world. How terrifying. How lucky, dear ones, if we find our poetry. We are 'free in the tearing wind', as Roethke, the other Theodore, has said of us.

But let me say one more thing about the void and the silence of our speechlessness. It's my conviction that a psychoanalysis of that silence and that void might reveal the Mind of God, that wonder of wonders and the beginning of awe. Isn't that why we read poetry, for the wonder?

JENNY: I agree, because poetry goes beyond words to give shape to our longings, disentangle complexities of the world, despite the ambiguous or even contradictory beliefs that surround us from day to day. And I am moved to think that though we live in different continents and societies, have experienced different kinds of conflicts or cultures, were brought up by different family values, as writers we can find a home in poetry, in that poetry is trusting and forgiving, capable of holding multiple truths.

Eddie, there's so much in that line in the elegy—'I can only give you a stone'—I feel that pain, as someone whose heart is with Hong Kong even though I wasn't there. And why the young would deserve a bleak landscape of wilted flowers. There's so much contained in that stone: trauma, guilt, hidden sorrows of the living. Guilt in the things that are not. Eddie, I also sensed that this is a new voice you're experimenting with, this more authentic and distilled voice to blend the personal with the political.

EDDIE: Yes—for me, the personal is the political is the professional is the aesthetic. It's all blended for me. I'm intrigued by your personal memories. Jenny, you wrote about your grandmother, not in the way she lived but what you'd like her to see.

> In my mind I'd carry you, because you have such tiny feet. I'd carry you to try my handmade dumplings even if you complain about the thickness of the dumplings skin, and share soup-spilling memories. I'd carry you to see Big Ben, turn the clock hands like Mary Poppins surely can, all the time your frail body regaining its strength, as we take a ride on an ombre-pink, sheepskin-soft rickshaw to cross the Thames, feeling triply young, singing Jasmine Flower in the river breeze.

It's a comfort, isn't it, to be able to return to an imaginative treasure-house. Home is where your lived and imagined geographies are.

Perhaps this is how you find home. Is that right? Though you're from Hong Kong, you're living in England now.

JENNY: I was thinking about places marked by people's presences and how our family follows us everywhere like a shadow. I often think of the contrast between my body and por por's body. Por por's bound feet meant that she found it difficult to make long trips. She could not run. She never took a plane. My womanhood is so different from hers.

LI-YOUNG: Your relationship to your por por's body is deeply important. I wonder if being yourself a woman allows you easier access to your subject matter. I wonder if it's less fraught with fascination, awe, and wonder on the one hand, and fear and confusion on the other hand, than for a man. Or is it just as mysterious and uncharted?

JENNY: You're right. I have always been intrigued by the relationship between women's bodies and their minds, having read books by feminist thinkers like Simone de Beauvoir at university, who prompted us to rethink the woman's body as a site of conflicting desires, knowledge as well as anxiety, and the challenge of women to claim their bodies as their own. In writing this poem, I wanted to reimagine por por's possibility as a woman, despite being filial, despite her bound feet and fate. I also try to understand my mother through reimagining how my por por brought up my mother.

What about your thinking of The Mother? It seems that notions of the female or the feminine have been present in your writing too, often on symbolic terms.

LI-YOUNG: I've always suspected that I've been trying to create something like my mother's body with every poem I write. I've always been worried that there's something regressive that drives me to write poems, as though I'm trying to enter or return to a primordial one-ness I've never felt since the womb.

My own relationship with The Feminine has always been potent and a little confounding. When I was around three years old, I was initiated into knowledge of the feminine body by a babysitter and her friends, and it lasted until I was about five. It was mostly a gradual and gentle initiation, although there were terrifying moments, especially when there were so many bodies, all of them towering over me.

I also recall one day heedlessly walking into my parents' bedroom to find my mother and two of her sisters and two of their cousins all trying on different things they'd bought that day at a women's clothing store. I just remember seeing a group of beautiful grown women in various states of undress standing in a room littered with colourful fabrics, dresses, underthings, hats, and scarves. They all burst out laughing when I walked in, and my aunt, bare-chested, lifted me and carried me out of the room.

I think every boy's first love affair is with his mother. I was definitely in love with my mother. Several years later, caring for my mother, bathing her, changing her, feeding her, I was greatly privileged to witness the mysteries of death and her naked body in a state of complete vulnerability and fragility. I wonder, Jenny, when thinking about your por por's body, are you thinking with your head? Your heart? The soles of your feet? Your hips?

For me, most of my thinking about my mother's body begins in the soles of my feet and reaches to about my heart, and never quite makes it to my head. I can feel my mother and my grandmother in my hips and in my ribs. What's it like for you, Jenny? Do you remember being in love with your mother, Eddie? Were you in love with your father, Jenny? You know, I really believe that the grail we're all in quest of is not the poem, but that thing which the writing of a poem enacts: A Psyche Well-Informed of its Own Parts. That is, a consciousness aware of its unconscious contents. That consciousness, that psyche may be the most serious and important human artefact.

I'm grateful on so many levels, but I'm the most grateful for the pressure-cooker feeling which this project instilled in me, for it was that pressure that elicited the writing of 'Telling Secrets in the Garden':

109

Telling Secrets in the Garden

1.

O, Hummingbird,
why is the universe
searching for you?

Here you are, the jewel
of jewels
in the universe's belly button.

Here you are
bearing the universe
on the top of your head, one feather
of your iridescent crown.

O, Hummingbird,
why is the milky way
searching for you?

Here you are,
the stillest eye
at the heart of the milky way.

And here is the milky way,
the tear in your eye
when you remember home.

O, Hummingbird,
why is all of Space expanding
to find you?

Here you are,
the tear-shaped pendant all of Space
keeps between its breasts.

All tears are made in your image.

And here you are, Master of Space,
entering where there are no doors,
exiting where all the doors are locked.

O, Hummingbird,
why is Time seeking you?

Here you are
at Time's crest,
in Time's trough,
Time's plaything,

and Time won't find anything but your last disguise,
a little haste in living colour,
a bit of hurry in someone's telling of a story.

And here you are, Master
of stillness and motion, Time's mother,
Time your initiate.
O, Hummingbird, you

are the mother of all fletched things.
You are the bell and you are the peal,
the prompt, ignition, and initial.

O, Hummingbird,
why is Eternity
looking for you?

Here you are,
the green earring
dangling between
Eternity's lips.

2.

O, Hummingbird,
the universe
is in love with you.

You, the quick
itself, you,

the darting pupil
of whose eye?
Only death

loves you as much
as the universe loves you.

That's why your heart races.

O, Hummingbird,
the milky way longs
for you.

The milky way lies awake
every night thinking about you.

O, shining-headed one,
O, feathered sacrum,
scaley, tufted engine
revving and insane for sugar,

only death yearns for you as constantly
as the milky way yearns for you.

That's why
your heart burns itself alive.

Only death
knows you by as many names,
O, sweet per cent,
O, ratio of ratios.

That's why
you make your body a pyre,
your hunger a cauldron,
and you cook your heart.

O, Hummingbird,
the Earth adores you.
See how morning gazes at you,
see how evening lingers for a look at you,

you bright knell struck from rock,
you vaulting note, you note
leaping out of the mouth
of the volcano.

From the moment it was born,
the Earth has done nothing but call your name.

The Earth was made in your image, O, Hummingbird,
and you are the Earth's destiny.

And my beloved and I are your secret audience.

You are the small of her back,
and you are her wrist
turning over the cards
to show me my future.

And only death loves us
as much as the Earth loves us.

That's why our hearts burn unquenched.

Only death finds us as precious.

That's why I can hear your heart from here.

3.
There you are, O,
Hummingbird,
don't go.

O, green
glimpse, blue clasp
to the hour's locket,
blurred hem of the invisible,
I waited for you.

In your stillness, hovering
in perfect place,
you are the bird most like a flower,

and your stem-like beak seems to spout
from the narrow throat
of the open blossom you plunder.

In your quickness and flurry,
you are the moment missed, the lost hour, O,

pulse, spark, syllable, token
of the sun, fetish, charm, flint
to my mind's dull edge, key

to this morning's secret doorway. Is it true
what some say about you?

Is it true
you were a soldier once
in the war for dominion
between the winged and the unwinged?

Is it true
you gave up offices, titles, and thrones,
to follow a path of nectar?

Is it true
when you heard the immense sadness of the stars
as they departed faster every year,
you mistook it for music,

so you copied it down,
played it for God,
and now that's all God wants to hear?

Once, I called the ocean my mother and father,
but the ocean told me,
'I am not your mother and father.
The Hummingbird is your mother and father,
as The Hummingbird is my mother and father.'

Once, I called the mountains my mother and father,
but the mountains told me,
'We are not your mother and father.
The Hummingbird is your mother and father,
as The Hummingbird is our mother and father.'

Once, I called the stars my mother and father,
but the stars told me,
'We are not your mother and father.
The Hummingbird is your mother and father,
as The Hummingbird is our mother and father.'

Is it true
you are the hub of all worlds,
the rock of ages,
mother and father of everything?

Is it true that you discovered the prime numbers,
that you taught humans the uses of fire,
and that yours was the first tribe?

Is it true
you witnessed the creation
of the world and barely survived
to tell about it?

Is it true
you travel back and forth
between the living and the dead,
and that you collect the nectar of both worlds, O,

Master of The Veils, is it true
you saw through The One, The Three, and The Many,
and now you do nothing
but feed on God's best parts?

Pollen smudged
between your eyes and on your chin,
you bear The Lord's seal
upon your dark brow and bright breast,

the way to the nectar inscribed upon your heart.

O, Quintessence, my gem, fled
tenant of my heart's perch,
feathered inkling, don't go.

I've heard you've been to The Promised Land.
Show me the way there
over the seven mountains
and through the seven valleys.

Quite simply, I sat down to write something that might cheer up
Eddie, who seemed appropriately hurt and deeply disturbed by the
tyrannies of principalities and powers in the world. I tried three
times. Those three attempts are the three sections of the poem. And
while my poem in all likelihood failed to bring relief to anyone, it
allowed me access to something I've been obsessed with my entire
life: finding a governing symbol for me to contemplate 'The Dao'
and The Christ Principle as different names for the one governing
logic undergirding all of manifested existence, material or otherwise.
My hope was that by relativising the domain of principalities and
powers to the logic of a deeper domain, the seraphic domain, one
might gain some peace of mind.

JENNY: There's so much tenderness, especially 'In your quickness
and flurry, / you are the moment missed, the lost hour [...]'. To me
the poem has to do with the pilgrimage of being a poet, the search
for life's nectar.

Having read a few of each other's poems, I wonder if we can share
with each other about recollections of what prompts you to be a
poet, and the way poetry has changed your life?

Quite a lot of the poems we just shared have to do with courage,
with being understood, and with healing. How does poetry bring
about courage and healing? Can you think of any specific example
or occasion when poetry brings such?

Also, thinking of our own journeys as poets, do you feel at home being where and who you are now?

EDDIE: What prompts me to be a poet...I suppose it's an unromantic way to say this, but I enjoy writing poetry the way some people enjoy playing tennis. Once you start writing, there's an imaginative space of one's own, a language bubble of one's own. Imagine playing tennis and then suddenly deciding you'd like to change the rules so you can aim for some fanciful shots. I think that's partly what poetry is. Has it changed my life? Well, for me poetic thinking (thinking with language and through language as an aesthetic form) is part and parcel of my day job, which is literary scholarship and teaching. So it has allowed me to embark on a life and professional trajectory suited to my temperament and interests.

Courage and healing—I'm not sure about courage but I do know writing (and the arts in general) can be very therapeutic. With funding support from my university, I've worked with a creative writer and creative arts therapist for the past few years, to conduct online creative writing and creative arts wellness workshops for secondary school students. Judging from the feedback received from teachers and the students themselves, the workshops have helped them through the school closures during the Covid-19 pandemic.

I do feel at home where I am, in both Singapore and Hong Kong. My Cantonese is not very good so I don't fit in so easily sometimes in Hong Kong, but that's fine as I'm ok with being an insider and outsider at the same time. You need a bit of discomfort to grow as a writer, much like the muscle aches one feels after a hard workout.

I think it's the same when Li-Young spoke of the 'pressure-cooker feeling' which helped him create the poem above. Thank you, Li-Young, for the poem! So yes, poetry does heal because it allows us to communicate with one another in a special language. This is why we speak of forming a community unravelling the knot of language together. (Every anthology is the formation of a community, is it not?) 'The Hummingbird' is that focal point, the 'still point of the turning world'. There is always a spiritual aspect to your writing,

Li-Young, that I find fascinating. Would it be fair to say your poems seek to attain a form of spirituality without religion?

LI-YOUNG: Yes, Eddie, I do experience the practice of poetry as a spiritual practice. I notice, for instance, when I'm writing, I move from feeling that I'm doing the writing to a feeling that something else is doing the writing, from 'my doing' to 'not-my-doing'. I also move from 'my logic' to 'another logic'. If that shift from my rationale to a deeper and bigger rationale doesn't happen, I've failed. That's exactly what I'm trying to attain in my life, surrender to a deeper, more comprehensive logic, call it 'The Dao'.

You raise an interesting subject regarding community. I know community is important, and I know we are trying to bridge the chasm surrounding our solitudes, but there is a part of me that feels that my pursuit of poetry is taking me into greater and greater solitude and inwardness. In fact, the voice I'm most interested in is the voice of one who is 'alone with the alone', as the Sufis say, or alone with God, or alone with the Beloved. But that might be an essential role of the lyric poet, to introduce each member of the community to the inner riches of his or her own interior.

I have to admit that I never got the knack of feeling at home anywhere. I think that must be a talent some of us are born with. I so very much want to feel at home, but I never have. Maybe it's part of my family's culture. Until the day she died a year ago, my mother maintained and often reminded us that no country is or ever will be truly safe for us or anyone who isn't in power. Maybe she was right, I don't know. And while it shames me a little, I have to say that my siblings and I all agree that we never truly assimilated to life in the USA. We've learned to speak with almost no accents, and we are all functioning taxpayers, but there's something strange about us, and we're uncomfortably aware of that.

Friends have actually referred to us as 'The Chinese Addams Family' (from a TV show that aired in the mid-60s in the USA). We've talked about it with each other, but none of us can put a finger on it. We've met fellow immigrants who arrived here relatively recently compared to when we arrived, and they seem much better assimilated and more comfortable than any of us are. Even they say that about us.

By the way, my living situation is four siblings and our families living together in one building and caring for our mother (until she died a year ago), and at one point there were 17 of us all dining together every night. A dear friend of mine once started calling us, with much love, his favourite family of charming Chinese vampires. He noted that we seldom ever left the house, that we were unusually close knit, that we never slept (almost all of us were insomniacs), and a few of us were so nervous around people, we'd scatter and hide when someone knocked at the door. It sounds comical when I describe it, but I'm not sure it was healthy for our children.

As for courage, I wasn't born with that gift either. I've been a coward my entire life, terrified of death, terrified that I don't know why I was born, terrified that I might die and never learn to love another person fully, unselfishly. Personally, I've broken every promise I've ever made in my life, and I've left no painful words unsaid, no bitterness unspoken, no cruelty resisted, no heart given to me in good faith unhurt, so there's no hope for me.

It takes so much courage to love. I failed and continue to fail because of fear. Maybe this is a good place to address Jenny's question regarding the writing of 'The City in Which I Love You'. In a nutshell, that title poem, as well as other poems in the book, were informed by my horror at the realisation that without Love informing our relationships, all we're left with is Power informing those relationships, and given the fact that power dynamics are so unconscious and natural and easy and convenient, while Love is a heart-practice that is so conscious and unnatural and difficult and often inconvenient, I came to the conclusion that we're all headed for hell on earth, the triumph of power over love.

Also, we were living in one of the worst parts of Chicago. Also, I was madly in love, and I still am, when I wrote that poem. Maybe a quick word about love. I was born in-love. My third grade teacher and the school principal paid my parents a visit at our house one day to explain to them that I had to stop kissing each and every one

121

of my fellow students every morning as we were getting seated. I remember the feeling of being in love with them. Each and every one of them looked so adorable and beautiful to me, I couldn't resist holding their faces in my hands and kissing them. I don't know what was wrong with me. Maybe, because I couldn't speak English, I was trying another way to communicate.

But here is the problem of problems, and we're back to knots: might a psychoanalysis of silence render the Mind of God?

***

COMING TO POETRY

Mary Jean Chan and Yanyi

Mary Jean Chan and Yanyi reflect on their personal beginnings as writers and the importance of trusting one's writing.

MARY JEAN CHAN (MJC): Can I ask what your corporate job was?

YANYI: I was a software engineer.

MJC: Interesting! And you wrote poems during that time as well?

YANYI: Yeah, I wrote *The Year of Blue Water* during that time.[1]

MJC: That's awesome. I basically kept studying, then decided to go straight into academia. Did you keep those two worlds separate—i.e. your tech job versus your creative work?

YANYI: It was like having a double mind. Like going to work and then pottery class. For me, it was a writing class.

A lot of things are not possible when you work a corporate job. It's very difficult to do a residency because you'd use all your vacation or wouldn't have enough. There was a lot of me figuring out how to write in the crevices. It became kind of untenable. After my first book came out, I wanted to try not working, even though it was a really important stability for me.

MJC: I can imagine that, in a way, it might make the poetry you were writing even more sacred, almost like that creative space seems more valuable. At the same time, you're exhausted. It's doing two jobs, essentially.

YANYI: How did you start as a writer?

---

1   Yanyi, *The Year of Blue Water* (Yale University Press, 2019).

MJC: I started off in business school in Hong Kong. So I was in Hong Kong for nineteen years, until I went to university. After my first year at the Chinese University of Hong Kong (CUHK), I transferred to study Political Science and English Literature in the US.

I was going to be a lawyer initially, as I'd gotten into law school at the University of Hong Kong, but then I ended up as a Global Business student at CUHK.

YANYI: I was going to do Economics.

MJC: How interesting that we both started off studying Economics/ Business. In my first year at CUHK, I was quite depressed. I kept going to the poetry section of the main university library when I was supposed to be studying statistics or something. I was staying up till 5am to finish my Accounting problem sets. It was so hard. I was trying to keep my grades up. I didn't want to be getting Bs or Cs; it was just devastating. Thankfully, I took an elective class called 'Meanings of Life in Cultural Anthropology' with Professor Gordon Mathews. The course was asking these big questions: culturally speaking, what are the 'meanings of life' for different groups of people? I kept going to Prof. Mathews' office hours. He finally asked me, why are you here? I said, I'm really miserable. I miss the humanities and social sciences. He then asked, have you ever heard of liberal arts colleges in the US? They're really good, you should apply. Long story short, I ended up transferring to Swarthmore College for my sophomore year. In hindsight, it was the best decision I'd ever made.

YANYI: I also tried a bunch of things. By my third year, my mother was like, you are not allowed to major in anything but these. So I picked Computer Science. I did actually enjoy it.

MJC: Sounds like you were really good at it.

YANYI: I still am. [*laughs*] So you went on to do a PhD?

MJC: Yeah. In the UK, PhDs last a minimum of three years, three to four years is what they normally are. I got a partial scholarship for the MA in Creative Writing at Royal Holloway, University of London, but for the PhD, I was classed as an international student and they had no scholarships for that year for internationals. They just cut it that year; normally they have like at least one or two. My parents are very Chinese; they were like, don't stop now, you should continue your studies. I'm fortunate that they were happy to fund my PhD. But I was like, I don't want to pay this much, as international students pay so much more than local PhD candidates.

Two years of international fees for my PhD was roughly the same as three years' worth of local fees. So what I ended up doing, which was crazy for my mental health, is that I did my PhD in two years. After submission, there's a period before the viva. I knew that even if I got revisions, I didn't have to pay more. So I knew I'd have to go into the viva knowing there would be revisions, but I was going to submit my PhD within two years. Had I gone one day over the two year mark, they would have charged me the full fee for my third year. So I was working seven days a week non-stop, trying to get the PhD done in time.

YANYI: So you submitted a manuscript and an analytical dissertation.

MJC: It was my poetry manuscript for the book that is now *Flèche*, plus 40,000 words of criticism.[2]

YANYI: You got it in the crevice.

MJC: I suppose. I think literally the day of the submission, my now ex-partner was like, we have 10 minutes before the post office shuts, you need to hurry. I was still finishing my bibliography. It was stressful. Apart from the poems, I ended up with two chapters on the work of Kei Miller and Sarah Howe. I initially had a third chapter, but I just didn't have time to do it justice. I titled the analytical

---

2   Mary Jean Chan, *Flèche* (Faber, 2019).

chapters a 'postcolonial poetics of relation', inspired by Édouard Glissant's *Poetics of Relation*.[3]

YANYI: Wow. And then you just revised it and submitted it?

MJC: Yeah, I had my viva, and my examiners gave me some really useful comments. I always felt like I needed to prove that I could be just as good at criticism as any scholar of English literature. It felt like I had two things to prove, the creative and critical, because sometimes there's a presumption that creative writers can't do criticism. Anyway, that's me. Tell me more about you. How did you get from Computer Science to poetry? How did you start writing?

YANYI: The Common Core at Columbia University includes a literature class that I loved. I loved literature but the prospect of majoring in it would have been unthinkable to my parents, who were footing my undergraduate bills. The graduate instructor of that class encouraged me to write. I applied for this intermediate poetry workshop, because I had been writing poetry all throughout high school, but I was also studying economics. In the end, I took three workshops. After my Introduction to Economics class, when they told us that all people are rational, I thought, Oh, my God, this entire field is fake.

MJC: Yeah. I had that moment as well in business school. It was also during Intro to Econ.

YANYI: Yeah. So I left Econ. I was so uninterested. I was leaning toward Anthropology and History, then that episode with my mother happened. In retrospect, that helped me. I did the Computer Science degree in two years, including a summer class to get all of my requirements, thanks to my parents footing the bill. Their support made a huge difference. I worked in music, event-planning, social media management, and design. After graduation, I became a software engineer and did that for six years, slowly moving up the ranks. The MFA came after that.

---

3   Édouard Glissant, *Poetics of Relation* (University of Michigan Press, 1997).

Financial independence changed my life. I could pay for my own therapy; I could survive the blowback from coming out to my parents. Self-sustainability meant I could take writing classes whenever I wanted. In New York, you can take a poetry workshop and meet other artists very easily. The city was a formative part of my artistic development. I went through some writer's block too. After some success in school, I started to believe I had to write in a particular way to be published, and that I couldn't experiment or explore. So I stopped writing for a little while and did this other life, this other career, that not only occupied but also stabilised my time. Towards the end of it, I started working on what would become my first book, *The Year of Blue Water*.

MJC: That's so cool. Was the MFA helpful for you to write your second book? I presume that was when you wrote it?

YANYI: Somewhat. By the fall of my second year, I had already drafted my second book. That year was cut short by COVID. There are some poems from that time that ended up in *Dream of the Divided Field*, but most of it came from before then.[4]

MJC: Did you do the MFA thinking it would be useful for applying to future academic jobs, or was it that you wanted an environment that would help you grow as a poet? Or both?

YANYI: Both. I thought to myself: I want to be a writer, I must be a professor. To be a professor, I must get an MFA. But also, nothing helps me grow more than access to top-rate research libraries.

I'm in the valley of my third book right now. That time when you think you'll never write another book again and that you're a terrible writer.

MJC: I feel like I did go through that when I experienced eight or nine months of not writing during the pandemic in 2020. Writing my second book felt—now that I've written it—like a calmer process.

---

4 Yanyi, *Dream of the Divided Field* (One World, 2022).

It's interesting that even with two books, for you, it hasn't eased that feeling of 'I'll never write another one again.'

YANYI: Some things do happen with the second book. The first book, I agree with you, is always like, well, what if this was just a fluke? What if this just happened to be the marriage of fate and ability? The second book, whether or not your first book was received well, contains that doubt of whether I can write another book. And then there's also the issue of whether I can maintain my artistic integrity in terms of growing and changing, even if that means moving in another direction? There's that niggling question: since people liked what I did last time, shouldn't I just do what's safe?

The second book is the first time I really had to consciously make the decision to write whatever it is that is coming. It was really hard. I probably will go through that every time. I work on a book, I have a sense of direction, I try to plan it, and I just can't. My ability isn't there yet. There's something outside of me that I have to learn. I have to go looking for it and be open to finding it, though I'm impatient. I think to myself, I have all this time! I should just be able to do it! And that's not true.

Was that your experience? Or did you have something different happen for you?

MJC: *Flèche* came out in July 2019. By early 2020, I thought, I really haven't written anything for a while, maybe I'd written one poem or something like that. I was starting to get anxious about not writing. The struggle was that I simply didn't feel like I had anything to say. I was feeling a lot of stuff, but I wasn't able to express those feelings in language yet, it was all caught up in emotions or images. I was kind of okay with that for a while. But ten to eleven months in, I did start to feel like I wanted to say something, but I didn't know how to say it. So I was reading a lot instead, and on the good days, I would just read a novel and be like, that's fine. But on other days, I'd be like, this inability to write is proof of my failure to actualise something.

Obviously, you've written your second book. Was there a breakthrough moment?

YANYI: It's not so much that there's one breakthrough moment as there are multiple. Each one is the new poem you wanted to write that you didn't know how to write. One day you're doing it. It only comes one piece at a time, piecemeal.

Whenever I write a book, there do seem to be seed poems that are clearly important for the book and my development as a writer. They show that I've moved something.

There were a couple of poems that did that for me in my second book. 'Translation' was a strange and important poem for me, though I don't know how many people understand it. [*Laughs*]

There's seeds for the third book, too. Where am I going next? In *Dream*, 'Ambulance! Ambulance!', a really long poem written in an older voice, comes to mind. I have different styles of writing that are best for getting at different values. The voice that I was writing in for 'Ambulance! Ambulance!' holds joy and hope. It's exuberant, a this-or-that kind of voice that I developed when I was younger. The voice didn't die away but took more of a backseat as I've moved toward, say, the tender tone of my first book or the more metaphysical or mystic voice of some of the poems of my second.

Do you have different styles that go for different kinds of things in your writing?

MJC: That's such an interesting way of thinking about voice. I think I have a pretty consistent voice. In the first book, it's tender, and quite sincere. I don't really go for irony. There are some poems that made people laugh when I read them aloud. I don't think of myself as a funny person, but apparently there is some humour in my work.

With the second book, *Bright Fear*, there is a movement in some poems towards, in general, a more confident voice, since there are certain things I'm calling out.[5] Where I'm saying: this is what happened.

I sort of have that in one poem in the first book called 'Written in a Historically White Space'. It's a bilingual poem, with the Chinese characters left unglossed. It addresses the reader; towards the end, I say something like, 'can you tell me what it is that I should do next?' That's the only poem that's maybe slightly snarky, or quite confrontational.

I have more of that tone in the second book. More poems where I'm just going say what it is that I want to say in a completely unapologetic way that's not meant to be tender, or meant to shield the reader from the impact of it. It's more forthright. That's maybe the slight shift. The tender voice is still there, but my newer poems are more able to access a kind of anger.

YANYI: Anger is the boundaries of the self—your little tripwire.

What did you learn from your first book that was useful in crafting your second? I don't know how far along you are in the second collection, but also then the same question for the second collection—what do you think you will take from that?

MJC: Having gone through the process of having a debut collection, not so much in the writing of it as the reception of it, I feel like sometimes there are people who will read whatever they want into the poems, or they will choose to receive it in a way that makes sense to them. So it makes me feel even bolder in saying what I want to say. A friend said something like, 'Oh, these new poems feel sharper to me.'

I suppose I tread similar ground in my second book, but it has a looser structure compared to that of my first book. It didn't start out that way at all! The tight structure was foisted onto *Flèche*, in the sense that I found the structure once the book had been written, rather than the other way around. I'm going to let the poems breathe

---

5   Mary Jean Chan, *Bright Fear* (Faber, 2023).

a bit more in *Bright Fear*. It makes me slightly insecure, because the three sections aren't as intricately interwoven, and there isn't as clear a narrative arc.

Tell me about how writing your first two books has affected your third book.

YANYI: I've learned so much since *The Year of Blue Water*. It's hard to talk about the book without talking about my life. Since that book, I've been making all these measured decisions to focus my life on writing.

The thing I learned from the first book was the confidence to have a radical intimacy with myself and to share that voice, those thoughts, and those emotions with others. At the time, I was writing the book I wanted to read. I was comforting myself in a time of intense emotional and mental isolation. I wanted a balm to that. It was a blueprint to keep connections with people, with the world.

In tough times, you spend most of your time in the void. You're hopping from island to island of *That was something good. That happened.* So I wrote and presented a book about those islands. I needed it to live.

This is what I generally think about first books: they're the big introduction. The first time you're on stage in the world. Once I established my 'I', I was able to, in the second book, go in the directions that I wanted to with that. I proved to myself that I could write a book. I proved to myself that I could write one that got to the heart of things. And I wanted to explore other things.

The second book came together in a surprising way. I'm going through a very similar process now. I spent many months not writing. A big struggle for me was becoming interested in writing again. Because with every book, I'm learning, I have to transform and find a new voice that I want to be in. I've got to catch up to the different person I've become in the interim. Even the poems in my second book now feel like an older voice for me. It's weird to embody an old self often two years after the fact. I'll say to myself, I like this book. It's a good book. And I'm not this person anymore.

MJC: I like the idea of accepting that you're no longer the same person who wrote your previous book. That's an important realisation.

On a slightly different note, do you enjoy being edited? How does that work for you?

YANYI: Oh, I never enjoy being edited. I can be very set in my ways when I make decisions. So I've had to learn how to circumvent myself. I'm much more open to editorial comments earlier in the process of working on a manuscript. So I have been trying to figure out that sweet spot between 'I'm not quite done yet and I'm open to comments' and when I feel very done.

MJC: I have a slightly different relationship to being edited. Maybe it's a confidence thing. With my first book, I saw the editorial process as a sieve. A sieve that would catch anything that wasn't working. I had a sense of being a 'good' poet, but maybe I wasn't as confident about my internal editor. I got asked how much feedback I wanted by my editor, and I said the more the merrier. I received very detailed notes. Each poem had line edits, image edits, punctuation edits. It was very detailed, and it wasn't that I had to take all of it on board. But I felt quite reassured by that editorial document that 'nothing can go wrong now'. I think it's a bit like a buoy, right? I needed that.

YANYI: Being edited ultimately is a very good thing. It is about someone asking you, Well, why did you make this decision? And as a writer, if you don't have a good answer for every single thing you have done, then what? That is when I'm open to a different decision. I'm such a perfectionist that I just send in my work really, really late in the game. It's more vulnerable to send the earlier drafts that I'm not as sure about.

MJC: You're right, because it is letting people you trust see the way in which some poems fall apart. I'm particularly open to small edits; I feel like I'm being edited without it feeling too vulnerable. I often let friends read the earlier drafts. I'll say, this is a draft, so please don't expect anything, and please tell me whatever you feel needs to be rethought. That somehow feels easier than being edited more formally. Do you feel the same?

YANYI: I have a couple of first readers. They understand my work already and what I'm trying to do. So that is helpful. But if you change your voice from book to book, who knows? There's still a little bit of vulnerability.

MJC: It's interesting, because what you're saying reminded me of friends saying certain things like, I gave your book to my best friend, who gifted it to her partner for her birthday. On one level, it says nothing about the poetry, but the fact that my book has now become something that is a gift that meant something to a queer person, or, I remember someone at a literary festival saying, I'm going to buy your collection because my daughter is queer, and I want her to read it. That almost transcends the poetry itself, because if I wrote something that meant something to someone, or that might provide some kind of comfort or solace, that's the ultimate dream for any writer. In a way, I really value these comments, maybe because I never had that growing up (in terms of having queer role models in literature or the arts). In contrast, a book review feels quite different. It's like, someone is taking my poetry seriously. That a critic has close-read a poem of mine and has understood my poetics feels valuable to me. It makes me happy in a different way.

YANYI: I totally know what you mean. The book being a physical object makes such a difference in how it can be part of a gift economy. It becomes imbued with the love from one person to the next. Or even, you know, the fact that the book was requested at a library is always really meaningful to me.

MJC: I like that. Poetry is increasingly commodified, but it can also be freely given and shared. In a way, people can now access poetry however they want. I do like the fact that people can take photos of a poem. Of course, they can Instagram a paragraph of a novel, but you can't quite do the same thing, right? But you can just take a photo of a 14-line sonnet and post it online. It feels too commodifiable because you can just share poems, but then actually it's also great, because it reaches people and they get to experience that poem in its entirety. Whereas you can't really do that with long form prose.

YANYI: I feel like it's a creative act to share stuff like that. It takes time and energy to do it. I've definitely received artwork that has included my words and that's cool. It's a different form of artistic homage that's not quite the same as getting a review. Artistic rather than intellectual, I think.

MJC: Yeah. People quoting a line from my work feels really beautiful to me. I'm just like, you used this as a generative source for your own poetry? It feels miraculous when that happens to me. Not only does my poem exist, but it's enabled someone else's words to exist. I mean, that's sometimes how I write as well. Often, I read someone else's work, only to discover the language I needed to write my own.

***

ON REVISION AND HAUNTING

Jay Gao and Jenny Xie

Jay Gao and Jenny Xie discuss the creative process of working on a manuscript.

JAY

Recently, I have been thinking about what revision means. I sent the final proofs of *Imperium* to my publisher not so long ago; up to the final minute I was revising a word here, a punctuation mark there.[1] Yesterday, I was rereading my manuscript and, again, the question of revision floated back to me. There were entire lines and poems I wanted to revise, some quite radically. I almost wanted the entire book to melt down into a puddle of words before coalescing into a new form or shape. It does not escape me that revision has the word vision nested inside of it. For me the question of revision is a problem about seeing and being seen: it is a type of work that implicates light. I am curious, Jenny, is there a line or a moment from *Eye Level* that you have thought you might want to revise?[2]

JENNY

Jay, I completely understand your impulse to revise down to the wire and, oftentimes, even after a work has emerged in print. I'm an inveterate tinkerer, through and through—someone who revises texts and emails, even bits of stray conversation I replay in my mind. Given this disposition, it should come as little surprise that a great deal of my creative process, even the generative stretches, revolves around rereading and revising language, lineation, pacing, the calibration of tone, formal containers, and so on.

What is behind this restless revising, if restlessness is the right way to characterise it? For me, part of it must be tied to some deep-seated perfectionist tendency: an inability to be satisfied by what came

---

1   Jay Gao, *Imperium* (Carcanet, 2022).
2   Jenny Xie, *Eye Level* (Graywolf Press, 2018).

before, because one's ambitions always exceed the mark one can hit at the precise moment. On the other hand, the impulse to tinker might not spring from just harbouring rigid, exacting standards, but rather from the other end of the spectrum: not taking one's work too seriously. The work is malleable, ongoing; it's to be played with. Even though it's been read by others, or met with praise, or accepted for publication, one can still engage it as a live thing and continue to shape it according to one's present vision and preoccupations.

I've revised nearly every poem in *Eye Level* that has previously appeared in publication in journals and even in chapbook form, prior to the publication of the full-length book. Looking back on the book, four years after its publication, there are doubtlessly things I would revise on each page, if not re-write altogether. It makes sense to me—I'm a wholly different person than I was when *Eye Level* was submitted for publication, and I now look at the poems equipped with radically different eyes, ears, internal rhythms, interests in new poetics, and bodies of knowledge and feeling. So, to re-see the poems means revising them from new vantage points.

Pivoting back to you: I'm deeply excited for *Imperium*, and the journeys your book will go on once it's been released. At the same time, I'm curious how you feel around having your work circulate through publication, to be encountered by new readerships. Most writers I know crave readers and engagement; some secretly, or not so unabashedly, seek out the flood lights. Still, though, publication— which you are no stranger to, of course—shifts one's relationship with one's work. How do you feel about inviting in so many eyes onto the page, which at one point was yours alone? My mind goes to Maggie Nelson, who describes the 'mourning' involved in both writing and publication. In one interview, she says, 'I miss the blue I loved before I wrote *Bluets*; blue now is not the same as it was then, when blue was my secret.' Are you preemptively mourning anything prior to publication?

JAY

Talking about restlessness and revision, I am reminded of something the poet Erica Hunt practises. For her, writing poems is a type of

136

rehearsal: a rehearsal in order to live freely. And Fred Moten, too, uses the analogy of rehearsal and *study* in order to think about intellectual restlessness. Revision as a restless dress rehearsal. The fifteen minutes or so before one reads at a poetry event. Or the seconds right after you submit a poem to a journal or a grant application. An itchiness. Sweat under the collar. A rehearsal for what? What's laid out on that stage?

A lot of my writing carries a restless undercurrent, an anxious heart, the awkward laugh—I find it odd to realise how content my poems are in becoming unsettled things themselves, in their willingness to play and to be playthings. I love what you wrote about 'not taking one's work too seriously.' To go back to the idea of revision, there's also that informal British usage of the word as in 'to study', for example, to revise for a test. Now, when I am revising a poem, I see that I too am studying it—studying myself, my place in the world—not for any particularly serious major or minor test, but to ludically 'engage it as a live thing' as you wrote.

To answer your question, Jenny, with *Imperium*'s publication date rapidly approaching, I find I am continuously revising my relationship to the book, to the book-as-object. I feel as if my book and I have displaced each other; we have moved out of phase now that it has moved beyond the confines of my poiesis. Publication has been an invaluable lesson. I realised I actually do not love all the publication and post-publication *noise* (or silence) as much as I thought I would. It's stressful! I am trying to go back into a state where I can just be left to write the thing that needs to be written. But I admit circulation does seem crucial for poetry. There's a sociality to the genre that, I believe, sets it apart from other modes of writing. The book of poetry becomes especially defined by the conversations surrounding it.

I do want to move on. The next book. The next project. A newer, fresher poetics or direction. Publication, so often for me, is like being granted a special license to move on, to try something drastically different, oriented towards the otherwise. I am always on the lookout for those opportunities that allow for radical departure. My relationship to my published work is a cooling one. Like putting hot metal into cold water. I hope this does not come across as overly cynical but I already feel wearied by the thought that for the next few years, or so, I will have to drag *Imperium* around with me, around my neck, hawk its wares, perform it, that I will be compelled to explain its intentions, to reduce it to a select few buzzwords and themes—turning poetry into rhetoric—in order to ask people to connect with it. And I do want people to connect with it, more than anything, but I am figuring out the ways in which I can convey my work authentically, poetically. It is no surprise that this anxiety comes in part from my experiences of being a queer poet of colour in a country that, so often, tokenises minoritarian poets.

Reading the poems from *Imperium* is like an excavation of sorts. Like coming across intimate bodies begging to be buried. Ultimately, all these ugly feelings are a symptom of not quite yet coming to terms with the theatre of the book being put out there, of putting oneself out there. There is something to be mourned but will I have the time to mourn it? And uncannily, just as I was typing out my response, my author copies of *Imperium* arrived. I opened the package and, when they slid out, I thought to myself immediately that they were like pristine tombstones or funerary stele.

Perhaps I can weld two questions together for you, Jenny. What has shifted for you in terms of publishing your second book? Earlier, you mentioned your interest in new poetics—what are these new poetics, and are they present in *The Rupture Tense*?[3]

JENNY

Jay, I admire the candour of response here, and the real reckoning behind your ambivalence with regards to publication. This is a tonic during an age when it seems, oftentimes, that only certain emotional tonalities are permitted when announcing that one's work has made the passage into print form. We're allowed gratitude, glee, pride, cheer, joy—all tempered, or marbled, by some degree of modesty. What gets discussed far less, at least in public, is the private discomfort and alienation. The strange postpartum deflation.

---

3   Jenny Xie, *The Rupture Tense* (Graywolf Press, 2022).

Perhaps at the root of all this is some sense of being distanced from the thing that one lived privately with—work that hadn't yet 'cooled' or congealed into its final form. I'm sincerely happy to hear of your author copies of *Imperium* arriving, but I admit I'm also amused and enlivened by your comparing the copies to funerary stele—hah!

I can see the linkages here between the ambivalence of seeing something in 'finished' form and the invigoration of revision. You draw marvellous connections between revision and study, revision and rehearsal. In both study and rehearsal, there is a striving for or toward: a desire to learn or to test out. The act of revising has desire in it: desire for the unknown, something that hasn't yet been articulated, hasn't yet been stitched into form. My mind goes to Anne Carson and her writings on eros: 'When the mind reaches out to know, the space of desire opens.'[4] That is to say, revision injects kinesis into the creative practice. Something is not yet done and, therefore, there is still the unknown and the possible.

Publication, on the other hand, can signal an ending of that kinesis, perhaps. You employ metaphors that the work has cooled, or passed on. Likewise, I sometimes fear that the promotion around the book as a marketed object creates fixity and muffles what was unruly, possible, wild. The work that was once thrillingly inchoate is jeopardised by the book copy, the Q&As, the two-sentence summary of what the collection is 'about'.

To respond to your questions: with my second book, I tried to prolong the private relationship I had with my work for as long as possible. Unlike the poems in *Eye Level*, my first collection, which emerged from poetry workshops and other exchanges, *The Rupture Tense* was written without any input. While I submitted individual poems to journals, I only ever showed a draft to my partner and my editor, at a late stage. I was protective of an experimentative space I had with the unfolding work.

As for new poetics: I think the second book is much more interested in long sequences—some thirty pages long—and in the poetics of

---

4   Anne Carson, *Eros the Bittersweet* (Princeton University Press, 1986).

fracture, indeterminacy, dissonance. In the first book, I see poems that are satisfied with being clicked shut. In this second, I wanted more unruliness, restlessness—more of what resists narrative closure.

Going back to your analogy of older work that feels like 'bodies begging to be buried', I'm curious what feels alive to you in this moment, in past projects, present or future. And what kinds of burial do we owe our older work, if any? What kinds of hauntings do you invite?

JAY

I love the questions you are asking, Jenny, and I wish I had the ability and space to meet them fully. *What kinds of hauntings do I invite?* Often, I find myself haunted by the legacy of others, the afterlives of texts. Theresa Hak Kyung Cha writes about hauntings and afterlives in her great book *Dictée*: a book that, I am sure, has been so influential for our work and for Asian diasporic poetry writ large. It is a book I often find myself returning to; am I haunting it just as much as I feel haunted by it? Cha writes about *phantomnations* and *ghostwords*, and I love how much of *Dictée* is preoccupied by different types of haunting and hauntologies.[5] To be haunted is to embrace a suspension of time, to pause the past, the present, the future. And I think poetry can suspend time too. To bring those temporalities together is something I want to keep inviting whenever I write a poem.

I think we are both invested in these questions of time, memory, and how we bury or unbury it. We both are drawn to that 'desire for the unknown, [for] something that hasn't yet been articulated.' And perhaps that is why we both write in long sequences, as a way to expend that which cannot be said. Is form an unburied manifestation of memory? I think our hauntings materialise through poetic form. What is haunting but friction, the rubbing through of boundaries, borders, spaces; it reminds me of that ghostly mark, smudge-like, in *The Rupture Tense*. An inarticulable presence. Haunted matter.

5 Theresa Hak Kyung Cha, *Dictée* (University of California Press, 2009).

Formless yet constantly reaching out towards shape. Haunting resists closure. It rejects it.

But I think this conversation around haunting and burial, as you are alluding to, should not be taken pessimistically. The aliveness of language, its capacity to resurrect itself from all that is rendered mundane and inert, the afterliving of poetry—*that* feels endlessly sustaining. And I strongly believe experimental writing can really cultivate a space for that, a space for renewal, for the renewing of poetic energies from the afterlives of past work. Burial and decay give way for fertilisation and regrowth. You bury the seed believing it will grow into a poem rich with vitality, matter, and enchantment.

I have been thinking a lot about trees recently. The ways that trees shape the poetic imagination. The ways we have shaped trees and the spaces where we find them. My next book will be one that focuses on the arboreal, on this idea of a poetics of grafting, on how we can come to a confluence of thought and sap. And I can see, quite clearly, where my interest in trees has come from: the ecological moments in *Imperium*. It is as if I had to write the entirety of that book just to discover the few seeds, picked out from that massive bank of words, that will become the foundation for the next project. I really feel invigorated by the dizzying and myriad ways in which I, and others, have approached trees.

In the act of renewing that writing space, renewing it towards experimentation, I undergo all those processes we have talked about: study, rehearsal, revision, desire, kinesis, fracture, restlessness, dissonance, afterliving. To be at this fertile stage of writing, to feel the work unfolding out, in a way that resists control and completion, and all the baggage that comes with the distant thought of publication, is one way I can renew the inchoate energy that lingers in my older work. This becomes my way of paying my respects. The poem might end with the line but the poetry manages to continue way past it, burying itself into the future.

***

READING

READING OTHERS TO KNOW OURSELVES

Kit Fan and Ethan Yu

Kit Fan and Ethan Yu discuss Simone Weil, Li-Young Lee, Susan Sontag, Kierkegaard, Wallace Stevens, Plato, and Emily Dickinson.

5 August 2022 | Scattering showers | York

Dear Ethan,

Since you'd mentioned Simone Weil in your last letter, I rediscovered my copy of *Letter to a Priest*, a lovely re-edition published by Routledge in 2002.[1] I found the sentences and paragraphs I'd underlined ten years earlier. What should I do with them now? Weil wrote in her rice-grain-like handwriting back in autumn 1942 in New York while waiting to join the Free French Movement in London. A turbulent time. It was unclear if Fr. Édouard Couturier ever responded. If I were Édouard, I wouldn't have a clue how to write back to Simone. Re-reading her letter, I'm still astonished by her bullet-train-like inquisitiveness. She was so certain about uncertainties. I find her affinity with pre-Christian antiquity very seductive. It tickles my blood pressure every time I think of Jesus as Dionysus and 'I am the Way' as a Taoist derivative.

You asked if the bookshelves are in my house. Instead of ordinary bookshelves, ours is a poetry wall in alphabetical order. The beautiful shelves were made by Geoffrey, Hugh's history teacher from school, and I proudly gave Geoffrey a hand with the wood-glue. I'm glad you like books. I gather you're from Hong Kong. I was brought up in a local library in Hong Kong from the age of six to twelve. When I say 'brought up', I mean my mother left me there after school and during summer holidays. She was a cleaner. I read like locusts, finishing one shelf then moving on to the next, bingeing on words and stories I mostly failed to understand. Why was there a gingerbread house in the middle of a forest? Who would believe

---

1   Simone Weil, *Letter to a Priest* (Routledge, 2002).

a tortoise can outrun a hare?

Recently, someone asked if I could provide a bookless background for my author photo. I didn't know what to say. After googling I noticed that books now rarely enter an author's backdrop. Backgrounds have become mostly monochrome, soft-focused, abstract. I was told ideally no background at all, as if phenomenologically and humanly possible. I'll have to find myself a void.

I hope August is a good host to you.

Kit

*

6 August 2022 | Writing from midnight | Sacramento

Dear Kit,

I'm so glad Jenny and Eddie have connected us. Thank you for your letter. One last comment on your bookcase before I begin: But it's so big and tall! I love that it is handmade from wood with such love. I hope I have a big enough house to store all my books when I become a professor!

As I've gotten the chance to ruminate on your poems from your second collection, *As Slow As Possible*, since the last time we talked, I am more and more convinced that, like young Kappus with Rilke, I have found a friend who I can trust with my rough-draft words and my pre-formed thoughts without harsh judgement.[2] I wouldn't be surprised if Simone Weil didn't know what to do with her words as much as Fr. Couturier did, or you or I for that matter. I just read a short biography on her by Francine du Plessix Gray today and I am both terrified and astounded by how strong her heart is to act equally with both body and soul, on issues both spiritual and political.

My favourite poet, Li-Young Lee, when he's asked about how he relates to his Asian American identity or contemporary culture

---

2   Kit Fan, *As Slow As Possible* (Arc Publications, 2018).

and politics, usually answers that poetry exists in a locus between a horizontal plane of temporal, cultural existence and a vertical plane of transcendental, metaphysical existence. Every poem is supposed to unfold the layers of our selves, from the one we wear most outside to the one deepest within us, to the one of which we are not even aware. Of course, I think you can tell what kind of poetry he prefers. 'A poem is that one [temporal power] which must play host to something beyond the human.'[3]

Yet I struggle with this. There are days when my Dad is telling me over our morning coffee, the ones I make sure I wake up an hour earlier for before he leaves to work at the last Chinese restaurant my family owns, about the latest anti-Asian hate crime in San Francisco or the most recent threat China has made against Taiwan or the US, and all I want to do is close my eyes and my ears and dive, without returning, into the thick, black pool of pure philosophy. But I know the day my heart grows numb to the world's suffering is the day I am no longer human.

Kit, do you have any thoughts and advice for me struggling on this matter? What you said in your previous letter about your mother and in your poem, 'My Mother In a Velazquez', moved me very much. What must art redeem? What is there to be saved?

Thank you,

Ethan Yu

*

3 September 2022 | Excited birds after a storm | York

Dear Ethan,

August was not a good host. I was sick nearly all month— coronavirus then norovirus. Quite similar spellings but completely different symptoms. These days, it's hard to feel fully recovered from anything. Illnesses focus the mind through the battered body. On

---

3   Li-Young Lee, 'Red, White, & Blue', *Poetry Society of America* (2012).

those bed-bound days I kept wanting to re-read Susan Sontag's beautiful book *Illness as Metaphor* and trying to summon a quote for solace. Instead, my head was a void and I binged *Stranger Things* alongside *Uncoupled* on Netflix. When watched together they seemed the perfect medicinal cocktail.

Auden, however, did enter my hollow brain during the dark hours: 'About suffering they were never wrong, / The Old Masters: how well they understood / Its human position'.[4] I'm pleased you read Francine du Plessix Gray's gem-like biography. In many ways, Simone is a master of suffering. You're right, she puts her words and thoughts into direct actions, a straight line without detour or shortcut. In the Brueghel painting Auden referred to, Icarus is falling from the sky. We only see one leg and a small splash.

I hugely admire Li-Young Lee's work, but if anyone tells us poetry (or any disciplines in the humanities, sciences or social sciences) can be explained in two dimensional terms, we need to take it with a pinch of salt. If we have to use metaphors, I'd prefer it to be about hiddenness, the unsaid. Just like Brueghel's Icarus, the less we see, the better. We learn to draw the eye away from the centre of attention, or in Simone's words, 'to see a landscape as if I am not there.' That said, Lee's explanation does tap into something real. A poem should take us somewhere outside ourselves. It should time-travel beyond the parochial into the unknown.

I'm moved by what your father told you over the morning coffee and your wise intransigence. Both worlds exist with intense poignancy. Many racist languages came my way during the height of the pandemic, with strangers calling me all sorts. On the other hand, our beloved Hong Kong has changed beyond recognition, while my ambivalence with the political might in China is as extensive as the Great Wall. Internal escape is an understandable survival instinct. But can philosophy really be 'pure'?

Like you, I too share the strange territory called intergenerational

---

4   W H Auden, 'Musée des Beaux Arts' in *W H Auden, Selected Poems*, ed. Edward Mendelson (Vintage Books, 1979).

pain. It runs so deep. I think it's the mystery of time. We see those closest to us age, diminish and, one day, disappear. There will be a time when your morning coffee with your father becomes a memory. We know it by heart, the passing of time, the erasure of human traces, and yet the thought of it still burns our flesh. Nevertheless, we should let it char us. See how our ancestors use burned pigments to leave handprints in the caves?

Let's open our doors to autumn,

Kit

*

10 September 2022 | Full moon | Sacramento

Dear Kit,

I'm sorry that August did not turn out to be a good host for you. I've never heard of norovirus before, but reading the symptoms online, I do not envy you in the slightest. While I too love Sontag (she was also close friends with Susan Taubes, that other great modern mystic who plunged the depths of her soul in search of meaning, in the face of the Death of God), some TV sounds good when you're sick hahaha.

I think it is both our greatness and terrible human, all-too-human, penchant to seek meaning where it is not meant to be understood. I was reading Kierkegaard's diaries this morning and I was so struck by how we will continue to be able to feel the contours of this radically unique, individual, isolated soul, so long as books continue to exist and there are people to read them. I don't think he ever settled accounts with the angels he was wrestling before he passed away. But I do think he has done us a great service, by displaying his soul for posterity on the torture-rack, so that perhaps we can better understand suffering's 'human position', if it is true that suffering itself cannot be understood, as Job had to learn the hard way. To become masters of our own suffering, and if that phrase is an oxymoron, we must try. Right?

149

I think you're right about how poetry isn't a simple duality between transcendence or immanence, as Li-Young Lee would have us think. Hiddenness seems closer to the essence of poetry. But that seems so hard to capture, or rather, I'm sure that's the point. After all, no one said writing poetry is easy. I tried looking back at some of the poems I've written since I started this journey two years ago, to see if anything fits what you were saying. This was the only poem I found that I thought came close to what you mean. I hope you like it.

How did I forget?

How did I forget
how cold a winter
in Sacramento
can be?

How did I forget
how long it's been
since I've returned
back home?

I don't remember
my mother in spring
planting the four cypress trees
in our front yard.

I don't remember
my mother bringing
me and my brother to press our hands
on the cold and wet concrete.

I don't know
where they are now.
At the feet of the cypress trees,
my mother's roses have grown.

Could you elaborate more on what you mean about the hiddenness of poetry? How do you try to capture it in your poetry? I combat deeply between the philosophical urge for the precision of concepts and the poetic awe at the power of words. Or rather, the cataphatic with the apophatic. I guess what I'm asking is: how do you find your void?

Thank you,

Ethan Yu

P.S. While I didn't respond to the last two paragraphs of your letter, please know that they were the ones that touched me the most and I thought about them the most this week. Thank you. I took your words to heart and seared a few memories in my head today at my family's Mid-Autumn Festival celebration. My grandpa, drunkenly, raised his hands to the sky, and praised the full moon.

*

7 October 2022 | Torrential rain
York physically, Greece mentally

Dear Ethan,

Wallace Stevens says, 'Death is the mother of beauty', though for me Death seems more of an entrepreneur, a monopolist. It must be so boring to always be the winner.

I'm speaking of Death casually because last month I travelled to the Mani in the Peloponnese, driving all the way down to Cape Matapan and spending some time in the so-called the Gate of Hades. It is where Odysseus enters the Underworld and meets his mother, only to see her dissolve again. Despite its potential corniness, I found myself rather moved by the Death Oracle. People have turned it into a shrine, leaving ordinary items there as a way to remember and summon the dead—a pair of Nike shoes, a bag of dried figs, photos of the disappeared faces…I wonder if Kierkegaard would have visited this place where the souls spent many dark nights behind the stone walls, divulging the hidden meanings of the afterlife to the living.

I don't believe in posterity. It's a fantasy. All things deserve to end and disappear, even the words of our most memorable philosophers or poets. Many galaxies had exploded into dust before our Sun was born, so why should human endeavour be the exception? The sense of an ending helps me breathe lighter and remember more.

On the surface, Death collaborates with the past, as the dead are left behind to mind their own business. And yet, simultaneously, Death is the future, as we, the living, look ahead to the Gate. That's why I think the Dark Lord is entrepreneurial: he has taught us to invest in Time, to laugh and eat while we can, to mourn and grieve while we must. For us, it's both a win-win and a lose-lose situation, as Time, after all, is our only dividend.

Thank you for sharing your poem. Can I take the liberty of offering a suggestion? The interrogative mood is moving but I think the poem wants to be freed up from the explicit formula of 'forget' and 'remember'. Hide these two words and cut the materials to the bare minimum, to the bones. Then, you will hear what the cypresses are trying to tell you.

You asked if I could share with you a poem-in-progress. This is it: one day, I'll turn this letter into a poem. You also asked what hiddenness means. A poem is hiding here in plain sight. So here, you have it.

Let's toast to the moon, our shared, most beautiful void,

Kit

*

Dear Kit,

I did not expect to be writing my last letter to you for now on my phone in the lobby of the Chicago O'Hare International Airport, but it will have to do.

A lot has happened to me since your last letter. I got a job at my local community college library, I went to Chicago to visit my mother's side of my family and attend a conference at the University of Chicago on theology, and, if all things go well, I might spend my spring in New York to be with some old friends, and perhaps make new ones. But Kit, pardon this digression, I am just as lost as you. I suppose we had better learn how to enjoy ourselves if we intend to live for as long as possible.

When I first read your letter, I have to admit, I was a bit overwhelmed. I think Wittgenstein once said something along the lines that his entire philosophy has been a struggle to refuse facts he knew to be true. Maybe you are right that posterity is a concept that is overused: in trying to immortalise ourselves, we never get to live our own lives, because we ourselves carry on hopes and dreams that those who are now dead were not able to achieve. But is there another way of viewing our human endeavour, just as you and I are doing together right now, in face of the oblivion of the stars and night sky?

Can joy ever be something in excess? One can want not to be too sad, but no one ever says they're too happy. Happiness as an emotion must constitutively be incapable of being completely filled. Perhaps that is our deepest void. Kit, I have still yet to learn the breath as light as air that you talk about, because living in a world of finitude, I still choose to will the eternal. Yes, Death is the operator of the threefold ecstasies of Time. It leaves the dead to bury the dead, the present living to play that bittersweet wager that you so perfectly described, where we only win as much as we are willing to lose, for all love never comes without the price of incurable melancholy, and death promises us to take the callouses away around our hearts, like memories neither remembered nor forgotten, as in, *un-made*.

Thank you for the suggestion, I'll see what I can try to do to take your advice to heart, but, like you, I'm horrible at revisiting the past. I really look forward to seeing what hiddenness you reveal when you turn your letter into a poem, and I hope you can answer my question in some way by the end, or help me find a bit more peace.

It has been truly a pleasure getting to know you through the black scribbles of these white pages. Maybe we are like Simone Weil's two prisoners on opposite sides of the wall, us tapping our fingers onto the keyboard or screen, with the Internet separating us so far apart and keeping us so close together. You've made me feel so much less alone on my journey, and I've actually been able to write a lot of poetry again these past few months, all thanks to you. Whether or not they actually become any good is up to me.

I leave it to you to find for our reader our final words. Thank you. For everything.

Sincerely,

Ethan Yu

*

1 December 2022 | York
Mist as dense as the opening of Throne of Blood

Dear Ethan,

I adore Plato's idea of *metaxu* which Weil beautifully resuscitated in her image of the two prisoners. The mist outside my window looks like a wall. What's this urge to connect? Curiosity? Solidarity? We've never been so connected in human history, but look at how disconnected we are with our planet and other species. COP27 in Sharm-el-Sheikh didn't help my state of mind, plus the ongoing

Ukraine war and cost of living crisis around the globe. November was lampblack.

Your optimism for the future is invigorating and cheered me up briefly. '"Hope" is the thing with feathers', Dickinson writes. But I always think that Emily is canny and embraces ambiguity, even in the case of 'Hope'. Note the quotation marks. Also, anything with feathers eventually flies away. The last two lines are the most perplexing: 'Yet - never - in Extremity, / It asked a crumb - of me.' Is the 'it' 'Hope'? If so, what does 'Hope' do for us in extremity if it asks us for nothing? Is it because we ask 'Hope' for too much?

Extremity is a cutting word, especially in 2022 and perhaps the remaining decade, or beyond. The word must be a sibling of *un-make*, as it's hard not to think that we spent the last two centuries creating and sustaining the myth of growth and now we're in the Age of Disappearance, of Unmaking. This year, we lost the Pinta giant tortoise, the Yangtze River dolphin, the Ivory-billed woodpecker... George Monbiot writes urgently and eloquently about our age. Reading him gives me solace as, like Weil, his words are actions.

I often ask myself why I spend time making poetry, fiction, and other forms of art when what I should do is to act, to reduce my traces on this planet. The more I create, the more there is to unmake. A friend told me that art is most vibrant in times of chaos. I do feel very selfish to dwell too much on poetry, music, and art. Almost like the survivor's guilt. Perhaps because I know there's a real possibility that the crisis ahead may not be survivable, certainly not for everyone. But why should I assume that I would be in the position to survive it?

Pardon the gloom. I blame winter, the fast-disappearing daylight. I left the page unattended for hours and now as I return it's ink-dark outside and the central heating has just come on. Ink looms large in my mind as I've been editing the poems in my forthcoming collection *The Ink Cloud Reader*.[5] There is an assumption that a poet progresses over time; their understanding of poetry—the art

---

5   Kit Fan, *The Ink Cloud Reader* (Carcanet, 2023).

and craft—deepens as they publish more books. With this third collection, on the one hand I feel I've a stronger grip on the lexicon, breath and music. On the other hand, poetry is no fun without taking risks.

I don't want this letter to end because I like writing to you, Ethan. It's astonishing that we were strangers in September, and now friends. Letter-writing, by its nature, is elegiac, especially in this day and age. I read a soul-shaking elegy yesterday, 'Elegy for Leo', by Andrew David King, a poet based in the San Francisco Bay Area. Nearly every line is pitch-perfect, but these are better than perfect: 'he preferred his poems be stumps of jade, / snail-tracks on rice paper, / glass thorns in the headless forehead of the world.' I was struck by lightning when I read them. I'll hold onto these three precious lines and objects as the year draws to a close. I hope they chime with you.

I've always wanted to visit Chicago. Two of my favourite TV dramas, *ER* and *The Good Wife*, are set there. I'm sending you a million congratulations on being a librarian, a truly romantic job. Smell the books for me, my friend. Against pessimism, I've an inkling that this is not an ending. It's ink that flows through us, between us. Let's speak next month when nobody can eavesdrop.

Salute to the arrival of the two-headed Janus,

Kit

***

VOICE NOTES ON READING AND WRITING

R. A. Villanueva and Eric Yip

R. A. Villanueva and Eric Yip discuss how poetry moves from the personal to the ethical.

ERIC YIP

Hey Ron, thanks a lot for the voice note. It's really great to be able to hear you again. I have thought some more about the conversation we had at the bar and have been trying to write some thoughts related to our conversation.

R.A. VILLANUEVA (R.A.V.)

I'm such a sucker for voice notes. I think it's an easy way to talk, especially when I'm driving back and forth from Brooklyn up into the Bronx. The morning commute from home to various teaching commitments takes a long while and it's been a joy to keep our exchanges alive across distances.

It's lovely to hear your voice, too. It really has been a great gift. If I didn't describe it before: there's a tunnel on my route that goes under the East River and there's no reception; my radio, my Spotify, my connection to the network cuts off for some time and I reserve that for you—and for us.

A project like this is a testament to how we have to make space to make poetry—and by poetry I mean, in part, our kinship with other people who also care about poems. We have to weave it into our day to day, right? Like the extraordinary stuff of creative energy has to be woven into the gorgeous minutiae of juggling responsibilities to our families, communities, and the pressures of workaday existence.

And we're not alone in this. There was a series called 'Correspondences' published in *TriQuarterly* between two poets I really admire, George

Abraham and Bradley Trumpfheller where they were engaged in an incisive, caring, prismatic conversation about Claire Schwartz's debut collection, *Civil Service*.[1] I love their letters so much. Over the course of weeks, they share passages from across her poems, thinking through things. What we're doing feels linked to that precedent.

ERIC

Hi Ron, it's so great to be able to hear from you again and very excited to know that your new manuscript will be mostly sonnets. I really love sonnets. They feel like such an intuitive form to both read and write. It has amazing longevity as a form and it's so fun to see other people play with the form, to subvert it, and break it apart.

Recently I've been thinking a lot about the personal in poetry. When I started writing poetry, it was this private thing, and it became a reflex to write autobiographically, or at least from a semi-autobiographical perspective. But now that I realise that people might read my poems, it makes me feel a bit vulnerable. It's really interesting to me especially how people from 'marginalised communities' are expected to write more autobiographically, and there is a certain invisible expectation, or even a subconscious trend, that people feel compelled to follow. That's why I'm always looking out for ways to subvert this, and I think when you mention Richard Scott's *Soho*, one of the reasons why it's so great, at least for me, is how it pierces that game of expectation.[2] I remember there are several poems in the collection that directly address this relationship between the reader, the poet, and the reader's perception of the poet through the poem itself. It's not that often you see this topic being brought up in a poem so I just thought that was interesting.

I remember there's this Adrienne Rich line in a poem that says: when

1   George Abraham and Bradley Trumpfheller, Correspondences: On Claire Schwartz's Civil Service (letters 1-3), *TriQuarterly* (2022). Available at: https://www.triquarterly.org/craft-essays/correspondences-claire-schwartz%E2%80%99s-civil-service-letters-1-3

2   Richard Scott, *Soho* (Faber, 2018).

I write about you, 'am I simply using you, like a river or a war?'[3] I'm simply saying that I hadn't considered the effects of using, let's say, other people's personal lives or events that are traumatic to an entire community and putting that in a poem. And even if it's handled with care, is there some responsibility that has to be dealt with? The biggest takeaway from these two points is that I'm realising that I'm becoming more afraid to write about either personal things or even stuff about my family, because it makes me feel like I'm intruding upon someone or something by taking material. Even if I alter it, I'm still taking material from other people's lives. And then it becomes a poem that belongs to me and then it's published. And that feels both very vulnerable and bizarre to me. And I don't know if I've just constructed this mental hurdle in my head, but that's the problem that I've been thinking about. I'd really, really love to know your thoughts.

R.A.V.

As I was listening to you, my synapses were firing with the names of texts and quotes that I wanted to share. I've set aside reminders to send you links to an interview with Muriel Leung where she addresses dimensions of what you're wrestling with: 'I don't believe I have the authority to say how people should write or not write, but I hope that there is an awareness of what we unconsciously covet or desire in poetry about violence and identity…I hope we read for our sustainability as much as our devastation—let it be known that as much as it hurts, we intend upon thriving.'[4]

And that, in turn, takes me to a podcast with Teju Cole, who discusses this core question in his work: 'How do we enjoy, benefit from, and remain awake to the world at large without cannibalising the world of others?' And that feels in tension with a poem from

---

3   Adrienne Rich, *The Dream of a Common Language: Poems 1974-1977* (W. W. Norton, 2013).

4   Lauren Eggert-Crowe, 'Behind the Editor's Desk: Muriel Leung', *Women Who Submit* (2018). Available at: https://womenwhosubmitlit.wordpress.com/2018/01/24/behind-the-editors-desk-muriel-leung/

Franny Choi's *Soft Science*: 'If they used it against you / it is yours / to make sing.'[5]

Each of those, I think, offers a different approach to consider and to complicate. What if there's no easy or untroubled, unbiased or un-haunted way to do our work?

Of course it's a question of ethics. What inspires one's first attempts to make a poem anyway? How often do we encounter or talk with writers who take-on writing a persona poem because they say they're giving voice to those who don't have a voice yet?—as if somehow writing from another point of view will automatically validate and or amplify that point of view. That, to me, is a deeply egocentric approach. Like: no matter what you say about why you hope to be in service to someone else, that effort is inevitably filtered through the prism of your own desires to feel like some kind of saviour.

That's why it feels deeply important to reckon with the motivation for writing the poem—the impulse. And I would say your fear and your awareness and your conscience is not necessarily something to be lamented.

Those tensions may alter the pace with which you create those poems. The dilemmas may alter those initial images or (if the poem has already come to life) perhaps that self-consciousness is the very thing that guides your revisions. Ultimately, if the poem needs to be written by you, it will be written by you. If the poem needs to live and its issues, problems, worries, concerns, falterings, self-doubts, triumphs—when all that needs to get made, you make it.

In fact, why the compulsion to publish everything you dare to draft? What if an element of the process is: you keep that mess in the cistern of your journals; you don't show anybody else except that

---

5   Between the Covers Teju Cole Interview, *Tin House* (2021). Available at: https://tinhouse.com/transcript/between-the-covers-teju-cole-interview/ See also Franny Choi, 'Turing Test_Love' in *Soft Science* (Alice James Books, 2019).

one caretaker, you—a you who goes down there and is free to just sort of check on things.

Trust that there is a difference between writing and publishing. And there is a difference between being 'a writer' and being 'an author.'

And every day, I grapple with those nuances in a fuller way. And/ or whenever I ramble on about these kinds of things—as I talk to a friend or a colleague or a peer or a hero or whatever—I start to realise that I'm talking to them and *through* them back to me.

But it seems important to recognise, where are you bringing this work? Are you bringing it out into the world because it needs to be said? Are you bringing it into the world because it needs to be said and then it may find some family in a manuscript or in a literary magazine? What's the initial impulse? If you could trace it back to that, perhaps it's a way to, on your own terms, come to grips with some of those ethical dilemmas.

Have you read Paul Tran's *All the Flowers Kneeling*?[6] It's Paul's first full length. I highly recommend it for its formal grace, its willingness to be vulnerable. Near the middle-ending of the book, Paul shares a long poem that's an invented form called 'The Hydra.' And maybe if I have a second today, I'll send you a PDF of the poem and the note. I haven't been able to stop thinking about it since I read it this summer. I first heard Paul read from their debut at Sarah Lawrence College (where I teach) as part of the annual Poetry Festival in the spring. After Paul's lecture and performance, I read through their poems obsessively, coming back, trying to metabolise something about their ideas. Truth be told, I'm intimidated by 'The Hydra' because it's virtuoso work, astonishing in its obstructions and rulesets—*and* also how it feels sort of bizarrely inviting, too. It's somehow both intimidating *and* hospitable. And I don't know if that makes sense. Maybe I'll send you the poem along with their imaginative constraints and maybe my challenge to you will be: don't read Paul's clarifying note until you finish reading the poem and just get a sense of how it's made. What if we try a collaborative one?

---

6   Paul Tran, *All the Flowers Kneeling* (Penguin, 2022).

Hi Ron, hope you're having a great day. Thank you so much for the generous guidance regarding my questions about the ethics of writing about other people's stories, or the impact that other people's lives have on you. It's interesting to be introspective and really try to consciously think about the initial impulse—often we don't really think about that as it's something that's so natural. It's almost like a reflex because we write poetry. When people go fishing, they don't really think about why they go fishing. You have to actually ask them, *what do you enjoy about fishing?* And someone will tell you, *oh, it's the calm waiting*. It's the *skill* or just the *joy* or the *feel* of fishing, but you never really think about it while you're doing it or when you're not prompted to.

So I do believe it is important to take stock and really think about what makes me or any of us want to write poetry, especially if that poem in particular is addressing something difficult. I guess there is a very human impulse in looking for meaning in past events or events that feel important to us. There is that impulse of, I don't know if I should call it rationalisation, but definitely some sort of questing, some sort of ritual that we try to perform to make the past, to make memories, make sense in our heads. And some events, I suppose, are so muddled, so confusing and so complicated that they can only make sense within the malleable world of poetry—it's difficult, I imagine, for a lot of people to write directly, very plainly, about things that concern them, but it's easier in poetry because there's so much space in poetry.

I remember reading a study somewhere about the effects of meta-phor on brain activity. I don't remember the name of it, so I might be like completely making this up in my head, but basically they had people come in and read a text with visual metaphors in it, and what they found was when people were reading these visual metaphors or these images, the language actually led to brain activity in the visual part of the brain. It was stimulating the brain as if it were seeing. And that has always stuck with me because a lot of people see text as something that's very passive, something not as engaging as other forms of media like watching a movie. But to me, text remains the elemental form of meaning-making because it gives the reader so much imaginative space. And I don't think there's other forms of expression that can hold that much meaning on a granular level and at the same time allow for so much freedom in navigating those meanings.

Poetry is a generous way of seeing the world because it confers equal importance to everything. You can make anything interesting in a poem if you have the skill and courage. And I think that is what's most liberating about poetry: it can be so varied in its ambition. You can write a long sequence, or it could just be a tiny poem about an apricot. Part of the reason I fell in love with poetry was each time I read a new poet, I'm amazed at the things that they do. It's almost weird for me to say this, but sometimes I think I enjoy reading poetry more than writing it. It's always good to read other people's work and be reminded of the possibilities that a poem can take.

R.A.V.

I'm very intrigued by the difference that you're feeling between visual media and language as relayed through text. I guess it's like how with movies or television there's a kind of 'tyranny of the image' at play, right? Which is to say, when you're a viewer watching a screen, what the creators imagine is dictated to you—and you are under their influence in a very complete way. The totality of sound and sight, it kind of overtakes your ability as a viewer to do anything. You really have no choice but to follow what the director or the cinematographer gives you. What other choice do you have? Whereas with a poem or something textual, it's a *conjuring* as you said. I think that's a really fascinating distinction.

ERIC

Hi, Ron. Today was my sister's wedding, and I'm flying back from Hong Kong in less than 12 hours. It's been a really surreal week because I remember in my last voice notes, I mentioned I was curious about how my way of observing my surroundings would change when I return to Hong Kong. And I remember the very first day, five or six days ago when I was walking through the streets, there were these small details, like the way the pedestrian light beeped, the rhythm and the frequency of beeping, it just reactivated a certain memory that I didn't even know that I had stowed away somewhere in my brain.

I think being in the UK for a while has changed the way that I look at certain parts of the city. Things that I previously would have found very mundane or not noteworthy at all, suddenly became quite interesting and unique in relative position to the infrastructure and the architecture of the UK. But it was a really bizarre reorientation thing that was happening in the first few days.

And extending that train of thought led me to think about how something being defamiliarised can actually help us form more interesting ideas and observations. If we don't pause to think about an object, then the object loses its properties. It becomes something that's purely functional, and we don't really think about the features or special things about this object that we can potentially extract and use as the sapling of a poem. When I first came back to Hong Kong and walked through the streets, I went to many different districts to reconnect myself to places that I haven't been to for one or two years. It gave me this new appreciation for streets, which I had previously thought to be purely transitory, as in they're a site of transit and I didn't really pay attention to what was happening in those streets when I was younger. But, now that I'm back, it's a very ephemeral feeling of knowing that I'll be leaving in a few days. So it's pushed me to try to capture little details in my mind.

R.A.V.

Hey, good morning from the road. About your reorientation as you said going back to Hong Kong and seeing things; it really struck a chord with me because that's how I felt coming back to the States after living in London for a while. We were there in 2014, which is when my wife and I first moved. Then, we came back to the States because *Reliquaria* was set to launch and I spent a month travelling a bit, talking and performing with the collection.[7] When

---

7   R.A. Villanueva, *Reliquaria* (University of Nebraska Press, 2014).

we headed back across the Atlantic, I remember realising how different everything looked and felt. I was struck by the spectrum of light in New York City and how it played against the architecture, its materials. Even the shadows along the shades of asphalt were distinctly New York when compared to London.

There was something about the feeling of warmth from that light. I mean that in terms of both the colour temperature as well as the literal temperature of that light diffused through the air.

It's such a privilege, this defamiliarisation that you talked about. It's such a privilege because it allows you—or *forces you*—to reconfigure and recalibrate yourself. Against certain kinds of reality, the multiple realities and the rival truths that are all around us. It's palpable and necessary. I think nothing radicalised me more than facing differences while living abroad. Like: the NHS is far from perfect, of course, but in profound ways it felt more humane than what we have here in the States.

Having a child in the UK as opposed to having a child here, it draws those dissimilarities into such painful focus. I think that many of the poems that I wrote while I was in London are relentlessly aware of the sudden strangeness of the familiar becoming unfamiliar (and vice versa). I was being oxygenated by contrast all the time. It seemed to be a necessary condition—or at least a fundamental condition—of writing or creating, that experience of tension, that experience of the unlikely and the surprising.

ERIC

It's so interesting to hear your perspective on defamiliarisation. I love the way you describe the light being different, the tone of it, the way it reflects and refracts. It is a privilege to be able to travel to other places, to stay in other places, or relocate—when I was 18 years old I hadn't ever been to the UK, or Europe in general, and coming here to study was actually the first time I'd ever been in the UK.

Yesterday it snowed here in Cambridge and the pavements were white to the brim. Before coming to the UK, I'd never seen snow in my life, because it never snows in Hong Kong and I didn't travel anywhere during winter that has snowy weather, so snow in my mind became an exotic symbol of a world that I'd never been to. Obviously there are a lot of places where every year it snows and snow is just something that's completely expected, but it's interesting how for some people such weather can carry a certain connotation or meaning simply because they were never exposed to it. When I was young, the only times I ever 'saw' snow were through pictures and videos, so yesterday when it was snowing at night, I walked out of my dormitory to feel the snow landing on my clothes and on my lips and realising that this is a thing that *exists*.

Speaking of snow, I just remembered this great Anne Carson poem called 'Merry Christmas from Hegel', which I read in a bookstore back in Hong Kong. I'll send you a picture of the poem in case you haven't read it.[8]

***

---

8   Anne Carson, 'Merry Christmas From Hegel' in *The Penguin Book Of The Prose Poem*, Ed. Jeremy Noel-Tod (Penguin, 2019.)

INSPIRATIONS, SPARKS, AFFINITIES

Lora Supandi and Chen Chen

Lora Supandi and Chen Chen share their thoughts on language, word order and serendipity.

July 19, 2022

Dear Chen Chen,

I came across your poem, 'Summer', while browsing through the Poetry Foundation's LGBTQ+ page. It was the beginning of June, and it stayed with me. I'm excited to start this correspondence with you. Right now, I'm based at CalArts in Valencia, California (teaching film and creative writing workshops for a summer arts program). Where are you this summer?

I am an avid sender of handwritten letters, but if the digital world suits you more, I'm open to all formats and forms. What are some ideas, topics, and reflections on your mind? Are there any stories/songs/artworks that you find yourself returning to?

I think, in this era of my life, I've been fixated on the concept of a placeless place, distorted memories, diasporic nostalgia, queer kinships, and forms of grief. The red, blinking lights on cranes currently exist as a motif in my life. Other snippets of inspiration and art: *Katatsumori* (dir. Naomi Kawase), 'Limerence' by Yves Tumor, and this poem by Ada Limón:[1]

> was how horses simply give birth to other
> horses.
> …
> A horse gives way
> to another horse and then suddenly there are
> two horses, just like that.

---

1   Ada Limón, 'What I Didn't Know Before', *The Carrying* (Milkweed Editions, 2018).

Finally, a sonnet I wrote about Wisconsin, where I lived last summer (a place I miss):

> in our quiet explosion, we wrote
> our way through the backcountry
> greeting the cryptid offsprings of
> MustangMan and CrowBoy as they
> gallop through the codeine cornfields.
> the coyote-limbed teenagers set off illegal
> fireworks by the Culver's drive-thru, shining
> billboards for an elixir + ButterBurger combo.
> we tasted the hemlock horrors of Winnebago
> County, where beautiful Miss. G hid your
> black walnut regalia in the meshes of Fox River.
> we hiked in unremarkable heath, facing the wicked
> malfunctions of life: too kind for the everglades,
> too cruel for the pacific, too alive for a ghost tale.

I'm excited to connect with you, to experience a glimpse of your world.

Best,

Lora Supandi

Dear Lora,

Happy spring. I'm glad to finally—finally!—have a moment to respond to your initial message properly. As it happens, life has been so very full of living, which gets in the way of sitting down and writing—but we need to live if our writing is to be worth reading.

First, thank you for sharing your passions and inspirations. I'm sure you have all sorts of new ones since last summer, but let me go ahead and respond to what you've shared and asked, and we can continue from there.

I, too, enjoy handwritten letters, though these days I have not had much time for that beautiful practice. Maybe I need to make the time! A return to the handwritten would help me slow down, which I keep realising is something I deeply crave and need. After all, the way I process experiences tends to be slow. And I prefer writing (a primary form of how I process) slowly. Carefully. Though I'm also very active on Twitter, *the* speedy genre. I don't know what to make of these contradictions at the moment. But, I'm noticing how slowing down does allow me to admit that: my contradictory impulses, tendencies, ways.

Last summer I was in the Boston area. This summer followed my final semester teaching creative writing (mainly poetry) at Brandeis as the Jacob Ziskind Poet-in-Residence. My partner and I moved at the end of August to Rochester, New York, a smaller, more affordable city that is more my pace. I've been making attempts to slow down in my life overall, though it still feels like I've taken on too much and things are moving too fast. A big part of that has to do with the fact that I had a new book come out in the fall and also a new chapbook that's just been published in January. So, while I've been teaching much less, I've been on tour, I've been in promotional mode and travelling a great deal. Right now I'm again reflecting and reassessing what I should give my energy and care to—and what would most give me what I need in return.

I so appreciate what you've named as inspirations, sparks, affinities—
we have some overlaps when it comes to 'diasporic nostalgia, queer
kinships, and forms of grief'. I would love to read more about what
these mean to you, perhaps how they've evolved for you since last
summer. For me, I keep thinking about how I used to romanticise
solitude as *the* way to live a writer's life. I still cherish alone time,
quiet time, but increasingly I see how crucial conversation and
collaboration are for my writing. I've been working on a very weird
poem with the (literally) quotidian title, 'A Day in the Life' that
contains these lines:

> to art even a second requires being
> a part of life, which means trying to say the simplest things
>
> to the unsimplest others

I'm thinking about how the making of art that is fully alive (and not
merely an aesthetic exercise) demands a living among and with other
people (and trees and squirrels and lakes and algae…). At least, that
has proven to be the case for me and my art. Conversations lead to
poems and a lot of (borrowed or completely imagined) talking often
happens in them. What role does conversation, broadly defined, play
in your thinking and making?

At the same time, I'm considering how students I work with, usually
novice writers, have this misconception of poetry as experiences or
memories dressed up in fancy language. As in, one takes something
simple and makes it sound complicated. When I find, in the poems
I'm drawn to, it's the opposite: something deeply complicated conveyed in the simplest way the poet can manage. But that 'simplest
way' occurs as the strangest utterance.

Like that Ada Limón poem you've shared, 'What I Didn't Know
Before'. The horses! The turn that comes with the sentence 'That's
how I loved you.' Which sounds so direct and simple. But it refers
to the horses giving birth. How strange. How wild yet clear. It's a
love poem, ultimately. One that gives us the experience of falling/
being in love via this wacky metaphor—dizzying yet with its own
rightness, its own 'logic'.

And thank you for sharing your own poem, the sonnet. So much gorgeous imagery and I'm a big fan of how this poem describes Wisconsin in such a mix of natural and cultural details—for instance, 'the coyote-limbed teenagers set off illegal / fireworks by the Culver's drive-thru'. It feels more truthful to have all these details side by side, rather than paint a purely idyllic nature-filled picture or a purely cynical one about people.

How have you moved through the seasons since your first message? How have the seasons moved through you and your mind, your art, and your living?

Sending a handful of snowmelt from Rochester—

Chen

March 24, 2023

Dear Chen Chen,

I'm writing this letter beneath soft sunlight, just days after the equinox. The warmth feels like a recovery. We are emerging from California's atmospheric river storms, those nights—unrelenting, dark, on the brink of endlessness.

Funny, here we are now. It is spring and, maybe, things will be okay. The seasons remind me that the great cycle will go on and on, even without us. Yet, I am still here, pushing onwards, yearning to embrace fluidity and surprise: in my relationships, friendships, day-to-day observations, how we move within our kinships, how we dive deep into our human experiences. I ache thinking about the ways we love and care for people even when it's sometimes unbearable to do so: the soul-intensity of orbiting one another. Even in solitude, we inhabit space alongside critters and ephemeral bits of nature. Grief, decay, and birth exist all around us. It is always evident. I guess it just stings much more during the cold and rainy months.

This winter was a difficult one. There was grief, loneliness, and the inexplicable pains of existence. My writing practice served as a silver lining. This quarter, I completed a Levinthal Tutorial with a Stegner Fellow at Stanford. My tutor, Jalen, brought new perspectives to the power of revisions. For the first time, this practice became a meditative act. Each draft unveiled something new about my consciousness and how I interact with the world. Instead of striving towards perfection, I learned to examine rewriting as a mode of metamorphosis/a tool for adaptation, fluidity, and transformation.

I've also been thinking about Ross Gay's response when asked about his decision to omit a period: 'What does a sentence do? How does it contain? How does it capture? Is it a grammatical replication of structures of violence?' This winter, I've been recontextualising societal transgressions and diasporic joy. In a world where punishments result in a sentencing, could poetry serve as a tool to construct new realities beyond these harms? I do not know, but I want to believe in this power.

This then brings me to your question. The times when conversations spark that 'a-ha' moment are rare yet special, but to be frank, adult conversations (especially in academia) drain my creativity. Children, on the other hand, move through the world with the most surprising bits of wisdom. It is their tender curiosity. These conversations pierce the heart. My nine-year-old cousin was digging a hole in backyard soil when he asked, 'Why do people make up stories? Is it to feel what these worms feel?' …I don't know, it was so off-hand and it stuck with me.

I then thought about how my cousin appears to the rest of the world, and I was pained by the social labels and preconceived narratives that are often fixed onto him: undocumented immigrant, Southeast Asian, feminine boy in a hypermasculine community… One day, when he discovers how stifling this world can be, I would only hope that he still converses with the Earth, that he crafts his own story and slowly feels the pain, joy, and hope of reclaiming his own narrative.

Well—in my personal life, one thing remains certain: life is surprising.

In the fall, I fell in love.

At the end of winter, I finished college (not gonna lie, hanging by a thread).

This spring, I'll be working a part-time job in art and diversity programming. I'm also letting myself relax as I slowly discover my next steps in life. These uncharted spaces—it is all so scary, so perplexing, so oddly beautiful.

My heart is preparing for many looming goodbyes.

What are you yearning for this spring? Have you experienced any new realisations/formed any new fixations? I hope you are well, that you find time to bask in the sun's playful warmth.

Wishing you joy and little green sprouts,

Lora

Dear Lora,

Thank you for your beautiful, thoughtful and thought-provoking letter. I really appreciate how you're considering the seasons and I'm moved to learn about what's changed for you, your interests, the external and internal landscapes you occupy, your grieving and your living.

I started this year with the loss of a friendship and, while I agree with those who say not enough is written about this genre of breakup, I'm not sure if I will write much about this particular event in my life. I've certainly talked about it plenty with friends! Or maybe I just don't know yet how to find the written language to describe it properly, fully. Or I'll write about it but I won't publish it. I'm thinking about how important writing is for me in processing life, especially the upheavals and the general unpredictability—and how little that has to do with publishing or with making the work publishable. Writing has many roles, including deeply private ones.

Letter-writing can be that kind of writing, though in our case, we share an understanding that this correspondence will be made public in the form of an anthology—so, there's an additional layer here that's sort of funny. Of course, we're not sharing all the life details that we might have if we were close friends who regularly talk. Nonetheless, I'm glad for the opportunity to share in some vulnerable thinking and feeling here. I'm struck by how corresponding with someone new and in a different format can open up the mind in unexpected ways.

I love that Ross Gay quote about grammar and the ways that violence might be embedded in the very structures of our saying. Ilya Kaminsky has suggested something similar when he's talked about the English sentence being so reliant on word order—how it has to 'march' forward like an obedient soldier. And I recall Ocean Vuong talking about grammar in a similar spirit—the importance of paying attention to how easily we can slip into language that implies war or any type of violent conflict, rather than taking the time to imagine a different relationship. What comes to mind is all the rhetoric around the pandemic, phrases like 'the war against this virus', or the way people often refer to cancer patients as 'battling illness' and eventually 'losing', as though it were a matter of sheer willpower. When we don't care enough about words, we become less caring toward one another.

As a so-called professional writer, I fail at this, too. In fact, I sometimes feel that the academic and publishing worlds prefer it this way: that I should care very much about words when the professional systems can benefit from my participation... but outside of those systems, why bother? When in fact, it's in my day-to-day interactions and off the page moments when my words likely have the greatest effect. I should care about my language all the time, in every context, with each person. And if I find that I can't in some instances, I need to take a step back and ask: What is keeping me from showing the depth of care that I should? Have I spent every last ounce of my energy, of my caring, elsewhere? Am I prioritising the wrong places for where I give my care? Why am I not resting enough, not taking care of myself enough such that I am this depleted and incapable of taking my time?

I'm yearning to take my time. More. And more.

Thank you for sharing that wonderful, truly *wonder-filled* moment with your cousin. It makes me think of one of my younger brothers, who loves hearing the story of his own birth (I ended up writing a poem about this!). A cynical perspective might view this eagerness as something self-centred, when I've always experienced his asking for and enjoyment of the story as a great reminder of how stunning it is, the fact that any of us are here at all. These lines by my former (but forever!) teacher, Aracelis Girmay, are flying into my head:

> Beloveds, making your ways
>
> to & away from us, always, across the centuries,
> inside the vastness of the galaxy, how improbable it is
> that this iteration
>
> of you or you or me might come to be at all

You probably already know, but for anyone else reading this correspondence, that's from a sequence of poems called 'The Black Maria' (from the book with that same title).[2] By the way, I've been considering for a good while about getting a tattoo of this poem's last line: '& so to tenderness I add my action.' Maybe this year will be the year. I'm also planning on (finally) getting my ears pierced!

I'm writing this while sipping some black tea and looking forward to lunch. I'm always so excited for lunch. It's usually a time when I let myself be less busy and frantic. It's fitting that you used the word 'bask' toward the end of your letter. My partner just said to me yesterday, 'You don't bask enough!' Now that there's more sun, I really should. Bask and remember that my core state is one of care—towards language, towards living, which includes loss. A core state akin to that of 'tender curiosity', as you put it. I hope your cousin holds onto that, yes. He's lucky to have you in his life, someone who sees him and, it seems, helps him hold onto himself.

And I hope that the 'oddly beautiful' is giving you some ways through the 'looming goodbyes'. What helps you hold onto your own tenderness and hope?

Sending leafy light and slow stretches of simply being here,

Chen

---

2   Aracelis Girmay, 'The Black Maria', *the black maria* (BOA Editions, 2016).

Dear Chen Chen,

When I reflect on friendships, as well as platonic breakups (which, for me, are sometimes more painful than romantic ones), I remember that platonic joy is a core element of life. Of course, the heartbreak of such losses will be immense. Human bonds allow us to endure: we are fuelled by that capital-L 'LOVE' that defies the boxes and labels tied to the spectacle of relationships. Quite silly, but have you seen *Ponyo*? When I think of love, I think of Ponyo, Sosuke, and a child's approach to friendship and intimacy.

When grieving a human connection, leaning into the ache is so important to me. We are letting go of something that was once beautiful. Thus, there is a human madness to this loss. There is also immense joy to be 'all in' or else what is living for?

On the note of feeling deeply, I have been turning to Lucille Clifton for guidance. Her poem, 'water sign woman', moves me like no other. I am in love with the first stanza:[3]

> the woman who feels everything
> sits in her new house
> waiting for someone to come
> who knows how to carry water
> without spilling, who knows
> why the desert is sprinkled
> with salt, why tomorrow
> is such a long and ominous word.

Clifton's water sign woman emerges in my life, time and time again (perhaps, I am simply a cancer). I too find myself in the ominous lingering of tomorrow, and I find myself feeling everything even when it hurts me. Unrelated, but I think I will take a visit to the

---

3   Lucille Clifton, 'water sign woman', *How to Carry Water: Selected Poems of Lucille Clifton*. Edited by Aracelis Girmay (BOA Editions, 2020).

ocean or a small creek tomorrow. Water, its fluidity, brings ease. And as the weather warms up, I have been in awe of the crisp, spring-green quality of forest streams: blazing, like liquid opal.

In holding onto tenderness and hope, I am also yearning to take my time. When confronted with looming goodbyes, I fixate on time's finite eclipse—its anxious ticking. I'm reminding myself that we all have a lifetime to explore tenderness with one another. There is no rush. Nonetheless, I will continue carving out moments of sweetness: chopping basil and cilantro with my housemates, taking long drives into the Redwoods, sitting in silence with those I love.

Yesterday, two beloved friends and I discovered a makeshift forest bungalow. We huddled in its shadows, below a green canopy. We are twenty-three, but it felt as if we were brand new to this world. I found myself thinking that it will all be okay. I can always return to this childlike state.

The tending of language: I find myself failing at this, too. I care so deeply about words and sentences, but I let myself down when the language I release in my mind inflicts flashes of gloom and cruelty. It is often a reflection of the societal harms inflicted on us. I want to unlearn this; I want to be kinder with my words and beliefs... and through this intention, I hope to create a personal world of tenderness ('& so to tenderness I add my action.' Wow, what a closing line. Girmay, her cosmic power, that human honesty. It leaves me speechless.)

As I conclude this final email to you, I am thinking about the word *serendipity*.

On the rare occasions that I find myself going out, I am most comfortable when I connect with a stranger who also lingers and observes from afar. Through our shared nature, this person usually becomes my 'best friend for the night', and although a societal expectation is to exchange numbers when we depart, the magic exists when we refrain from doing so. Serendipity springs up in my life when I find out, weeks or even months later, that this stranger and I are connected by a mutual friend, or a family member, or a particular summer camp… sometimes, the same childhood neighbourhood.

Our email exchanges are different, certainly. Still, the closure of our correspondence evokes this emotion for me. There is a diaristic element to what I share with you in the way I might share with a stranger whom I may never see again. Nonetheless, the window of possibilities remains open. Perhaps, serendipity will come in an unexpected way. I'll keep an eye out.

I wish you surprise and warmth.

with softness, with tenderness,

Lora

April 28, 2023

Dear Lora,

Thank you for taking the time, making the time, to engage so fully and attentively and tenderly in this correspondence. This last letter of yours—I'm holding it close. I may print out this entire set of emails we've sent each other so that I can literally, physically hold them. Now. Though I know they'll be in a physical anthology, I need to experience them as something I can hold with my hands much sooner.

It's so wonderful (serendipitous!) that you reference *Ponyo*. It's one of my favourite Miyazaki films—also because of how it looks at friendship and intimacy. And, just the other day I was in a bookstore in Brooklyn (shoutout to Community Bookstore in Park Slope!) and I came across a *Ponyo*-themed notebook with some behind-the-scenes artwork. I wasn't sure I had room in my luggage for this item, but I kept walking around the store, browsing, while I couldn't stop thinking about it. Eventually I added the notebook to my stack of books. I couldn't help but get some poetry books (by Monica Youn, Shelley Wong, and Jenny Xie) as well as a new nonfiction book I've been meaning to read (Jenny Odell's *Saving Time*)—all of which made one of my bags much heavier... but much happier.

Another happiness: your phrase 'leaning into the ache'. Why is it that running away from ache just leads to more right around the corner? Ache knows how to find us. Maybe because ache is life, too, alongside non-ache. They are neighbours. I say that reading your phrase, 'leaning into the ache' is a happiness because it articulates so clearly something I've been mulling over but didn't have the words for... or rather, my words for my own experience weren't as clear nor succinct. This reminds me of high school, when I was obsessed with Aimee Mann's songwriting for how it could articulate exactly what I was feeling when I didn't even know what those feelings were. I mean, I'm still obsessed with Mann's lyrics, though in some ways they're less close to my interiority now; I continue to admire her craft. Anyway, I'm thinking about how I've avoided leaning into the ache at particular moments this year... and how I've avoided leaning into the joy, sometimes, because I became overly focused on the ache.

I'm thinking about something an artist friend (shoutout to Vincent Chong!) said to me recently when I mentioned my need for rest. I'd been defining rest mainly as a pause in activity and Vincent pointed out that rest can also mean a greater variety in activity. He reminded me that too much of the same of anything can lead to stagnation and the need for a break.

But that break can look like many different things. And maybe it's the 'many different' part that's important. There's rest that involves literally lying down and shutting your eyes, your conscious mind. Then there's rest that involves reading a book that opens up deep reflection. There's rest that involves company, good company with lots of good food and loud laughter. There's rest that takes the form of a long walk in a favourite park. There's rest that takes the form of a totally new experience, one that allows you to lean into joy without pretending all the ache is gone. There's rest that takes the form of rewatching *Ponyo*. There's rest that takes the form of journaling or, say, letter-writing.

Your sharing of that first stanza from Lucille Clifton's 'water sign woman'—another form of rest for me. By the way, you probably know this already but in case you didn't, Aracelis Girmay recently edited a selected volume of Clifton's poems and she chose the phrase 'how to carry water' for its title! What a beautiful title. And what a gift, to read that phrase again within its full sentence. Oh and I'm also a water sign! Pisces! I feel like I'm a truly classic, stereotypical Pisces: romantic head and idealistic heart always dreaming, dreaming. Though I don't love being in water, I do enjoy being near it, observing it, watching ocean waves or a pond's ripples carry life, ferry loss, tug themselves through—

These Clifton lines from 'blessing the boats' come to mind:[4]

---

4   Lucille Clifton, 'blessing the boats', *ibid.*

may the tide

…

carry you out

beyond the face of fear

And these lines by Girmay from her poem, 'I Am Not Ready to Die Yet':[5]

I want to love you longer

& sing that song

again. & get pummeled by the sea

& come up breathing & hot sun

And Girmay's poem is after a poem by Joy Harjo with the same title—here is a stanza from Harjo:[6]

And when it happens, as it certainly will, the lights

Will go on in the city and the city will go on shining

At the edge of the water—it is endless—this earthy mind—

Wishing you water and light, wonder and song, and more questions that are good company—

Chen

***

5   Aracelis Girmay, 'I Am Not Ready to Die Yet', *Kingdom Animalia* (BOA Editions, 2011).

6   Joy Harjo, *Conflict Resolution for Holy Beings* (W.W. Norton, 2015).

TRANSLATIONS FROM LANGUAGES I NEVER LEARNED TO SPEAK

Natalie Linh Bolderston

1.

Four years after a day referred to as Ngày Giải Phóng or Ngày
mất nước — depending.

My mother steps off a plane to find she is only worth what she
can interpret. Police bring in two boys and call on her to translate
their crimes. Jagged nouns held by their edges: Đột nhập. *Break-
in*. Kiếng. *Glass*. Dây đồng. *Copper wire*. Máu. *Blood*.

2.

Mid-nineties. A hospital
with rose-dotted walls. My birth
as a frothing at a newly drawn equator.

She chooses an English name
derived from an old word for Christmas
and a Vietnamese name that means *soul*
      (a midwinter offering)
      (a hybrid that can live through snow)

3.

She speaks to me as if sounds are inscribed in blood
and can be inflated when the right valve is opened.

Listen, two ways to say love —
>   yêu

>   (a woman lying underwater,
>   chest bubbling light)

>   thương

>   (the sun reaching for her wrists)

>   yêu

>   (the last seed in a bird's dying throat)

>   thương

>   (the hibiscus that bursts
>   through its ribs)

>   yêu

>   (the sky darkening with God's shadow)

>   thương

>   (the peaches that keep him immortal)

4.

Our names written on a funeral service sheet
in a language Ông Ngoại never passed on:

>   玲 [líng]
>   *tinkling of jade pieces*

>   真 [zhēn]
>   *loyal; faithful*
>   *chaste; virgin; virtuous*
>   *to practise divination*

5.

The millennium. A VHS tape of Paris By Night 53.
A song called Cô Tấm Ngày Nay: *Modern Girl.*

Four singers wearing swirl-patterned áo dài,
dancing in front of two stacks of moons.

My mother's favourite: the girl in blue.
As beautiful as liễu rủ màn che.
> (a willow concealed behind a bolt of pure silk)
> (the mother goddess of a red-cloud realm
> cradling two halves of a jade cup)

6.

After Ông Ngoại died, Bà Ngoại played the same chant every
morning:

Nam Mô A Di Đà Phật
> (a way of obeying the light
> or inviting it to come back)

7.

The remains of my great-grandmother's house in Xiamen.
An outdoor shrine beneath a tin roof; damp smoke in our hair.
A surrounding rubbish tip. An old woman living in a hut nearby.

My mother wants to say something
but doesn't have the language for it.

A stone column; a dedication chiselled in a script she can't read —

It was like my mouth was broken.

Later, we use our phones to find what we need:

悲哀 [Bēi'āi]
sorrowful

强忍悲哀 [Qiáng rěn bēi'āi]
to suppress one's grief

8.

A platter of crab served at a place with pale green walls
near my mother's birthplace.

A woman pouring yellow lotus tea —
Where are you from?

My mother describes a gold-lit shop
and a rooftop fruit garden that no longer exists.

A nod, a hand hovering over the teapot.
Việt Kiều?
(one wrist tethered to the sea)
(back teeth unrooting at a sealed border)
(a body half-hidden inside a pink shell)
(a body divided by a line of coarse salt)

***

(First published in *The Rialto*, 2021)

LANGUAGE

YOU UP MUD SPRING:
ON KONGISH AND SINGLISH

Joshua Ip and Felix Chow

In this correspondence, Joshua Ip (from Singapore) asks Felix Chow (from Hong Kong) what Kongish is, and Felix asks Joshua what Singlish is.

KONGISH

JOSHUA: *What is Kongish?*

FELIX: The short answer would be the way English is commonly spoken in Hong Kong, a mix of accented English mixed with Cantonese expressions. It's characterised by its playfulness and its use of purposeful 'language errors' to create new meanings. One example would be:

> Try my best (English)
>
> 搓 my breast (Kongish, literally 'rub my breast')

Another example can be seen in this poem from Louise Leung Fung Yee:

> Mom's blue sky is brew sky,
>
> a borscht brewed blood red:
>
> The distance between daughter and mother

For reference, this is how the term was defined in an academic paper:[1]

'Kongish is a blend of English and Cantonese that is characterised by the use of Cantonese words and expressions in romanised form, especially verb phrases such as hai (係, 'is'), ng hai (唔係, 'is not') and ng wui (唔會, 'cannot'); there is a high degree of sys-

---

1 A. Sewell and J. Chan, 'Hong Kong English, but not as we know it: Kongish and language in late modernity', *International Journal of Applied Linguistics*, 27 (3), 2017, pp. 596-607.

tematicity in these patterns.English usually predominates, but the Cantonese-ness of Kongish is asserted in multiple ways, including literal translations and unconventional spellings. The latter draw attention to Cantonese influenced pronunciations of English words (e.g. 'actually' as actcholly). The words with infixes (sor(9)ly and exac7ly, also written as sor9(r)y and exact7ly) represent so called 'bad language', and demonstrate how the availability of keyboard characters is exploited to create the forms of Kongish. These forms also creatively exploit the fact that some number terms such as gau (九, 'nine') have multiple meanings. There is abundant language play, for which Cantonese provides rich resources with its colourful idioms and ever-changing slang. In short, Kongish demonstrates various kinds of 'bilingual language play and local creativity'.[2]

JOSHUA: *Why Kongish and not Honglish or HongKonglish or Kongnese or Ganglish / Gonglish?*

FELIX: I don't think there was ever one universal name for the language before, but the term Kongish was popularised by a hit Facebook page called 'Kongish Daily'. The page, created in 2015, posts regular news commentary in Kongish.

JOSHUA: *Do you have challenges with Kongish not being taken seriously or being used solely for entertainment?*

FELIX: Yes. Perhaps this a relic of the colonial EMI (English as a Medium of Instruction) education system used by top schools in the city, which instilled in students the idea that standard English was the only acceptable form of English. Studies after the Hong Kong protests in 2014 and 2019 showed that speaking Kongish correlated with a stronger sense of having a 'Hong Kong identity.' However, while there has been an increased acceptance of Kongish after these protests, it is still seen as an improper and unofficial version of standard English, which in turn is something that most of the population accept as 'good' English and the degree of acceptance

---

2   Jasmine Luk, 'Bilingual language play and local creativity in Hong Kong', *International Journal of Multilingualism* 10.3(2013), 236–250.

of Kongish shown in these studies was still lower than 50% even amongst university students.

JOSHUA: *Does Kongish intersect with other Cantonese diaspora internationally? Are there different flavours of it? Or is it exclusive only to Hong Kong?*

FELIX: As far as I know, Kongish is not exclusive to Hong Kong. Cantonese is seen as a strong marker of the Hongkonger identity, and speaking Kongish is a way through which recent first and second generation immigrants can coalesce. There are a few diasporic comic and meme pages on Instagram (e.g. @ricelumpy) that use Kongish in their works. However, I am not sure what the differences are between HK Kongish and diasporic Kongish.

JOSHUA: *What is the relationship of Kongish with class?*

FELIX: Interestingly, the usage of Kongish seems to be correlated more with age than with class. People of an older generation (50+) rarely speak Kongish, either preferring to speak entirely in standard English or in Cantonese. Perhaps this is because in the colonial era they grew up in, speaking standardised English was seen as a sign of civility and intelligence. The younger generation tends to speak more Kongish, across educational and socioeconomic levels. Not only do university students type and communicate in Kongish, local rappers such as Takeem, Tomfatki and Akiko also use frequent Cantonese-English codeswitching in their songs.

JOSHUA: *Are there loan-words from other languages included in Kongish besides Cantonese and English? Does Mandarin feature in Kongish? Or other Chinese dialects?*

FELIX: Mandarin and written Chinese are also included in Kongish. While Hong Kong is made up of a hodgepodge of different Chinese subgroups (e.g. Hakka, Hokkien, Shanghainese), the dominant group is Cantonese. Due to the need to achieve communicative efficiency, words from minority languages or dialects are rarely included in Kongish.

JOSHUA: *At what point was 'Kongish' created as a term and when did it start to enter the public consciousness as a distinct entity?*

FELIX: The origin of Kongish can be traced to the so-called 'martian language' used on Internet platforms and forums such as Golden Forum and ICQ in the early 2000s. Before the emergence of user-friendly Chinese input software, many Hong Kong users tended to just type out romanized Cantonese words or used literal Chinese-to-English translation to communicate. For example, instead of semantically translating 你噏乜春 (what the heck are you saying), the phrase is translated phonetically or directly as 'You up mud spring'.

The new language gained popularity due to the emergence of these forums. While it was initially seen as a 'low language' or as evidence of the declining English standards of Hongkongers, Kongish further entered the public consciousness as a marker of a distinct Hong Kong identity. Kongish was used frequently during the 2014 and 2019 social movements as a way to differentiate protesting Hongkongers from their mainland counterparts.

JOSHUA: *Are there literary works written entirely in Kongish or known for featuring Kongish?*

FELIX: The most groundbreaking Kongish poem would be Nicholas Wong's 'Golden', which won Third Prize in the 2020 Hawker Prize for Southeast Asian Poetry.[3] The poem, named after the Internet forum HK Golden Forum, is an exploration of the poetics created through Kongish use on local internet forums. Quite a few of Wong's works make use of Kongish, including 'Advice from a Pro-Beijing Lobbyist' and 'No/No'.

Other users of Kongish in poetry include Tim Tim Cheng ('Rudimentary Cantonese', 'Salt and Rice'), Antony Huen ('Brain

---

3   The Hawker Prize, *Sing Lit Station*, http://www.singlitstation. com/2020interviews. See also http://ofzoos.com/8.1=NicholasWong.html

Sea') and Louise Leung Fung Yee ('First One Fifteen', 'Red Soup', 'Level').[4]

JOSHUA: *Are there popular media / popular culture phenomena that celebrate Kongish?*

FELIX: I can't think of any examples from the mainstream media that celebrate Kongish. The closest to that would be the usage of Kongish in the songs of Serrini, an independent singer who is now one of Cantopop's leading artists, and the bands My Little Airport and GDJYB (雞蛋蒸肉餅), whose songs predominantly feature Kongish. In fact, the lyrics of GDJYB's songs are written entirely in Kongish!

JOSHUA: *How is Kongish viewed by the government and by the education system?*

FELIX: While there hasn't been anything like the 'Speak Good English' movement in Singapore, there has never been any implicit endorsement of Kongish by the government or education system. Moreover, markers' reports from the Hong Kong Examination and Assessment Authority provide guidelines on how teachers can help address Kongish issues in students' compositions. It can be said that the government sees Kongish as a problem instead of a cultural marker.

SINGLISH

FELIX: *How is Singlish seen in the broader Singaporean community? Is it seen as something to be proud of, or perhaps even a symbol of national identity?*

---

4   Tim Tim Cheng, 'Rudimentary Cantonese', *Cantocutie* Vol 3 (2021) and 'Salt and Rice', *Rabbit Poetry Journal* Vol 33 (2021); Antony Huen, 'Brain Sea', *Poetry Wales* (2021); and Louise Leung, 'First One Fifteen' in 'Auditory Cortex', *Asian Cha* (April 2022) https://www.asiancha.com/wp/category/auditory-cortex-2021/ and 'Red Soup', *Ricepaper Magazine* (May 2022) https://ricepapermagazine.ca/2022/05/red-soup-by-louise-leung-fung-yee/

JOSHUA: There's an older generation for whom Singlish is reductively seen as just 'bad English' and something to be ashamed of. This generation lived through a period where English was a minority language, a means for social mobility via service with the colonial masters or as the language of international commerce, and where the accent of English itself was a definitive status symbol. For kids today, English has long taken on majority language status due to it being the first language of education, and Singlish is common—a way of life. Conversely, the Singaporeans who came of age in the 1980s butted up against the official 'Speak Good English' movement—the government's attempt to clean up Singlish with a sanitised standard English—and had to fight tooth and nail for Singlish's acceptance. Champions like Colin Goh blazed a path through government displeasure and outright censorship with websites like Talkingcock. com and the groundbreaking *Coxford Dictionary of Singlish*, whereas Singaporeans who grew up in the 2000s and beyond can take Singlish more or less for granted due to the efforts of Colin et al.[5] Nineties kids like me are a bridging generation that can remember both the 'bad English' days and today's situation where it's more accepted.

FELIX: *I understand that the government and education system have not exactly been supportive of Singlish (given the Speak Good English movement). Is this attitude changing or likely to change?*

JOSHUA: The most prominent example of this in recent years is from 2016, when Gwee Li Sui, a local poet and one of my early inspirations, wrote an op-ed in the *New York Times* trumpeting the awesomeness of Singlish, claiming that 'years of state efforts to quash it have only made it flourish', and that 'now even politicians and officials are using it.'[6] One would imagine that a small cultural coup for Singapore, with one of its definitive characteristics taking a bow on an international stage. Instead, the Prime Minister's Press Secretary felt obliged to smack him down with a petty retort,

---

5   Colin Goh, Woo, Y Y, *Coxford Dictionary of Singlish* (Angsana Books, 2009).

6   Gwee Li Sui, 'Do You Speak Singlish?', *The New York Times* (13 May 2016), https://www.nytimes.com/2016/05/14/opinion/do-you-speak-singlish.html

asserting that 'not everyone has a PhD in English Literature like Mr Gwee, who can code-switch effortlessly…and extol the virtues of Singlish in an op-ed written in flawless standard English.'[7] Points for rhetorical jujitsu, but minus points for missing the lesson on the Streisand effect in How-(Not)-To-Press-Secretary 101.

That said, I think over the past few years, the attitude of the government has softened, as wiser minds have come around to the fact that Singapore needs everything it can get to define itself. An immigrant nation with denizens thrown together from cultures with thousands of years of history has to exploit every ground-up narrative available if it wants to be more than a transit hotel, and Singlish is the most ground-up of them all. As such, various government bodies have begun to actively use Singlish in campaigns to feel more relatable, and to better communicate to a public that continues to live and breathe Singlish.

FELIX: *What is the relationship between Singlish and class? Is it predominantly used by (as Ann Ang puts it) the 'Anglophone elite'?*[8]

JOSHUA: That's an odd quote to come from Ann, a Singlish champion in her own right, and I'd be interested to hear the context of it. Singlish is certainly not exclusively used by the Anglophone elite. There may be some degree of truth to what the Press Secretary asserted to the *New York Times*—that Anglophones are the ones who can flawlessly code-switch between acrolectal/mesolectal/basilectal Singapore English, with Singlish occupying the basilectal layer, whereas the wider population would only be able to switch between the mesolectal or basilectal.

Instead, a true marker of eliteness would be the inability to speak Singlish at all (or only being able to feign an affected version of

---

7   Chang Li Lin, 'The Reality Behind Singlish', *The New York Times* (23 May 2016), https://www.nytimes.com/2016/05/23/opinion/the-reality-behind-singlish.html

8   Ann Ang, 'Literature in Singlish: Reading Joshua Ip and Hamid Roslan', *Sing Lit Station* (25 March 2022) http://www.singlitstation.com/calendar/2022/3/25/lecture-literature-in-singlish-reading-joshua-ip-and-hamid-roslan-ann-ang

it picked up via TV or YouTube) due to being effectively closeted —via an ecosystem of nannies, drivers, delivery apps, tutors, and international schools, then Ivy League universities and internships— from ever coming into contact with anything less than acrolectal Singapore English.

FELIX: *When was Singlish first used in a literary sense?*

JOSHUA: Singlish has popped in and out of Sing Lit for longer than Singapore has existed as a nation—the instant Raffles landed in 1819 with his ungainly Queen's English, various people with common sense have been trying to whittle it down into a more efficient language, viz. Singlish pieces like Yin C.H.'s 'Small Town Romance' from 1959 liberally employ Singlish for comic effect. There was an early effort by Goh Poh Seng to create a literary language for Malaya by merging English, Malay and Chinese into EngMalChin, but the effort was eventually abandoned. Arthur Yap managed to employ Singlish with dexterity to reflect on social class rather than just for comedy in the 1970s and 1980s, with poems like '2 mothers in a hdb playground'. Then in the 1990s, we begin to see works written fully in Singlish, or some version of it—Ming Cher's *Spider Boys* from 1995 was notable for being written entirely in rather eccentric Singlish which retains a certain awkward charm (despite all the Singlish being stripped out of it except dialogue by linguistic ideologues in a modern reprint); in Gwee Li Sui's *Who Wants To Buy A Book of Poems*, the Singlish tongue never leaves its cheek.[9]

FELIX: *What are some must-read literary works featuring the use of Singlish (including your own works)?*

JOSHUA: Gwee and Ming Cher, certainly. Ann Ang's *Bang My Car*, which inhabits the Singlish register of a Singaporean kopitiam (coffeeshop) uncle with uncanny energy.[10] My own *sonnets from the*

---

9   Ming Cher, *Spider Boys* (Penguin, 1995); Gwee Li Sui, *Who Wants to Buy a Book of Poems* (Landmark Books, 1998).

10   Ann Ang, *Bang My Car* (Math Paper Press, 2012).

singlish is not exactly in Singlish(!) but is a riff on Browning's *Sonnets from the Portuguese*, with the Portuguese/Singlish being the author, not the language.[11] I do have a handful of poems in Singlish, and another bunch more that only scan if you read them in a Singaporean accent. Hamid Roslan's *parsetreeforestfire* is the new must-read kid on the block.[12]

FELIX: *How would you say Singlish came to be?*

JOSHUA: I alluded to it earlier, but English is really a terribly inefficient and inconsistent language. If the world had a Babel-esque reset and had to create a new language of business from scratch, it would not look like English. Probably something closer to Malay, or a non-ideogrammatic form of Chinese, with less complicated ways of rendering tense and more consistent rules of spelling. As such, whenever English via its colonial acolytes encounters a population possessed of superior languages, it naturally gets upgraded to a superior form via mapping onto the more efficient sentence structures of the higher languages, and importing loan-words to make up for its numerous inadequacies. The result is usually termed as a creole of some form, but we all know it's a drastic improvement.

FELIX: *Kongish and Singlish both feature the usage of code-switching and particles (e.g. la, liao, sia). How are these linguistic elements used in Singlish poetry?*

JOSHUA: Whenever I hear of Victorian times and the secret language of hand fans (or parasols, or gloves or whatnot), I think of the humble 'lah'. Sentences consisting of the same words are transformed and elevated by a single end-syllable, imbued with fresh meaning discernible only to those in the know. This smacks both of drastic efficiency as well as the evolution of a high culture that can convey multiple layers of meaning not only through the addition of a syllable but by specific intonations and/or elongations of that syllable. Lah, leh and lor are the grace notes of Singlish, unnoticeable to the

---

11   Joshua Ip, *sonnets from the singlish* (Math Paper Press, 2022).
12   Hamid Roslan, *parsetreeforestfire* (Ethos Books, 2019).

unschooled, but secretly conveying the higher social status of the speaker. Oh, was I supposed to talk about poetry?

FELIX: *One limitation that writers who attempt to write in Kongish have discussed is that Kongish work can easily take on a colloquial and even joking tone. Does Singlish poetry share the same problem? Do you have problems with Singlish not being taken seriously?*

JOSHUA: Yes, there was a time where the invocation of Singlish was purely for comic effect—its abruptness, directness and intimacy drive straight to the hard-to-define core of comedy. In this it excels, but it does become a problem where Singlish cannot be used without eliciting immediate laughter. Arthur Yap conveyed one way out of this problem by using different levels of English/Singlish and code-switching between the two to centre on a class-based commentary. Fully Singlish works like Ann Ang's and Ming Cher's still elicit a chuckle every few lines or so, but once the reader is immersed in the lexicon and register, the comic effect dwindles and we are able to read further into the text. Hamid's *parsetreeforestfire* takes a radically different approach, tearing apart and iterating various Singlishes to the point of unrecognisability—literally Language poetry, centring the use of language and languages within the poem, found to be both familiar and unfamiliar, rather than meaning alone. In that, I think it is the most Singlish book I have ever read, despite large parts of it being unreadable by the average speaker of Singlish. No one can take that book anything less than seriously—though that statement in itself asserts that the unserious is somehow 'less' than the serious, something I challenge in my own work.

FELIX: *Why do you think writers choose to write in Singlish and not in standard English? What are the lyrical or poetic possibilities allowed by Singlish?*

JOSHUA: Why do people choose to speak in Singlish and not in standard English? In my ear, the ghost of the Press Secretary intones: 'Most people cannot choose, you know.' Shushing her, I would say that those of us who can, simply wish to exploit the possibilities of every tool available to us—it need not be consciously a political gesture (though there are other ghosts who would rise up at that murmuring 'all language is political.')

As a formalist, I will say that Singlish allows me many options to wriggle into the strictures of my chosen formal straitjackets—the condensation of grammar and tense, the efficiency of particles, and the convenient way a Singlish accent places equal stress on almost every syllable, allowing extreme contortions to match the demands of iambic scansion. And perhaps that is a political statement in and of itself—writing poetry in iambic pentameter, that most English of forms, that only counts as iambic pentameter if you read it as a Singaporean would.

I once had the mentality that Singlish was for Singaporeans, and that I wrote only for them. But the poet Alvin Pang dislodged those thoughts some time ago, when I saw him read a poem called 'Candles' at StAnza Poetry Festival in St Andrews, Scotland, before an audience exclusively of middle-aged white people. It was entirely in Singlish; a dialogue between two brothers about stealing candles from the church to study at night. The audience was rolling in laughter throughout the entire poem. I began to realise that I had more in common with this lot than I thought—a community that might not really look on the stiff-upper-lip Westminster accent that fondly, and who recognised the clear signs of a linguistic upgrade when they saw one—I've been told Scots is quite an elevated language of its own. Since that reading, I've been much more comfortable with reading out poems that feature Singlish to international audiences, and I've reaped the same rewards of uncanny recognition time and time again.

*

A poem in Singlish by Joshua Ip

What is Coasting

landshop is where ppl go to play land, do land party. pah land.

sand? you want to be sand? go sit on the mountain and meditate lor. cannot eat meat must eat vegetable only, wait long long, maybe you can zor sand. eh sands ah. sands is that one like ancestral tablet then go bai bai that one lah. marina see bay sands that one lor.

clam is gong gong or la la sometimes i also not sure. oh claim ah? claim is small claim big claim petty claim that kind. reclaim is after your claim kena reject then you reclaim lor, but then bo bao they maybe still rereject you.

beach can don anyhow call ppl beach can or not. or son of a beach. sekali they beach you next time. next time you play land and you think u like sand but actually ppl think you beach, but clam that you not.

history is the historical that one, when they scream scream very loud like woodbridge liedat. go into historics.

erosion is some sex thing issit?

coast? this one is millenial term lo. is when you close your handphone and u ignore someone when u dowan to date them la. that is called coasting. only beach then do these kind. if you land me your handphone i show you how to b beach. don sand any message. don be historical. just coasting can already. coasting.

A poem in Kongish by Felix Chow

Dear (Representations of) Hong Kong

'Why is it so hard to tell our own stories?' — *P.K. Leung*

1.

Our ancestors thought the five elements could explain everything.
As if life could be grouped into patterns. Okay, I try try.

金	as in *golden days*
木	as in *wooden horse*
水	as in *flowing water*
火	as in *fire magic*
土	as in *scorched earth*

2.

Okay, now I talk. 講經 , 港經.
What do we know of Hong Kong?
'Egg tarts, fishballs and ferries.'

Sik dak ga? An urban buffet of clichés.

The first cock-tail bun was made by a man
wanting to save up more money.

3.

'If China is *Ah Yeh*, shouldn't Hong Kong be Mum?'
Well we all know what *Ah Yeh* will say.

'Now that the city has *dai ma* makeup,
Let's Meitu those slogans on walls.
The place needs a facelift to make people remember,

"Hong Kong is Asia's world city".'

4.

Some people love the breathtaking photos of open umbrellas
more than those who wielded them as shields.

Flowing water parted waves, so that
fire magic could make scorched earth.
They say 畫面唔靚? Sor9ry wor.

5.

There's an Apple in Central, a Xiaomi in Mongkok
but the city can't text us back.
Snapshots of neon shop signs at night—
We fucking love Hong Kong.

The photos, not the city.

6.

What if the city's trajectory is designed
like a bus route?

My coping mechanism: read the news, share the news,
surrender (to) the news.

7.

When buildings are falling apart, take nice photos
of them—a way to preserve.

Neon signs fade. Streets disappear.
Our children will never walk here.

If pretty visuals could explain everything,
do we try to get used to the view?

***

VOICES OF A POET

Jinhao Xie and Will Harris

Jinhao Xie and Will Harris discuss how a poet's voice can convey a multitude of selves.

Hi Will,

Last night, listening to you read your new poems brought so much excitement out of me. The poems are the results of the work of a poet and, sometimes, it is hard to see the work—in the sense of how the poem came about, what sort of life a poet must live to reach out with those words, what kind of verbal inventions poets must come up with, to affirm their own existence, even if that means creating a brother to talk to that childlike truth of wanting!

Lately, I have been thinking about what it means to understand each other. In this supposed community of writers, there is so little we know about one another—because sometimes the types of questions are limited by the kinds of events or spaces we find ourselves attending.

Lots of love,

Jinhao Xie

*

Jinhao,

What a beautiful message, thank you. I started writing to you after we saw Lee Hyemi and Soje. Didn't Hyemi say something about the body being a disposable cup and the soul a warm drink, and that to feel the soul's warmth, the cup of the body has to be held by others?

It makes me think about 'reaching out'. The paradox, for me, is that in my writing I'm creating an internal other to talk to (even when the addressee does exist outside in the 'real world'), so reaching out is also reaching inwards.

I've found that paradox hard. In my childhood and young adulthood, I would often feel very lonely. I wrote to communicate with others; I wrote because I didn't know how to communicate with others. But we are talking, and maybe there's something in poetry and its 'chanced' encounters that allows the possibility of really communicating, of breaking out of our disposable cups for a moment.

I'm now writing to you on the way to work on Boxing Day. I stayed at my parents' home for a couple of nights over the weekend. Before then, I was ill for a week, and I was working non-stop. Now I'm back to work again at the care home. But I feel better, and am glad to be boarding a near-empty Tube train to see the residents again. I missed them. You said you wanted to talk about voice? I've been thinking about it too. Here are two entangled thoughts:

1) The *Mission:Impossible* franchise has been going for about 25 years now (excluding the original TV show; I just mean *M:I* with Tom Cruise). Spanning seven films so far, but especially in the first four, the 'character' of Ethan Hunt (Tom Cruise) changes almost constantly. He's a normal guy who just wants to settle down, a gambler and near sociopath, a master of human psychology. His hair is long and short. He can disguise himself as anyone and learn their mannerisms almost immediately. He climbs without crampons. He gets married. He goes off-grid for months at a time. The point is, if the same actor wasn't playing him the whole time, it would just be a succession of different characters. Maybe Tom Cruise in the *M:I* films is what we talk about when we talk about voice?

2) Aside from Tom Cruise in the *M:I* films, there are two competing versions of language I've been thinking about:

a) In Annie Ernaux's *The Years*, she talks about the language of school (of the grammar book) and of the language of home ('the language that clung to you, that was a slap'); one is of the mind and one of the body.

I feel like I grew up with that binary instilled in me. My parents each have different non-standard languages of home, formed out of their own particular backgrounds and experiences; I couldn't (and can't) speak like either of them. The language I found in books was my refuge; poetry, in particular, was freedom. Books released me from the various assimilative pressures of home. But maybe I never felt language in my body.

Another view of language:

b) Anthony Vahni Capildeo has a prose poem in which they say: 'Language is my home. It is alive other than in speech.'[1] If Ernaux's attitude suggests the dichotomy of language vs home, for Capildeo, language *is* (=) home. It cannot be reduced to the body (it makes sense I wouldn't want a language reduced to the body / home). Capildeo writes: 'It is beyond a thing to be carried with me.' Ernaux writes that it 'clung to me'. For Capildeo, even though language is like the world serpent of Norse myth, 'girding the oceanic earth' and shaping 'our territories of habitation and voyage', it is also the case that 'thought is not bounded by language.'

Words are 'variegated' and 'muscular' (Capildeo) but they are separate from us. A singular language which defines and shapes us is an illusion. How many different language communities do we move through each day, or do we ingest language like an unseen microbial system? And when I think of voice I don't think of a particular 'language/voice/dialect' expressing itself—because I have none or too many—but millions of unknown shadows expressing themselves through the words.

How does any of this sound to you?

Much love,

Will

*

---

1   Anthony Vahni Capildeo, 'Five Measures of Expatriation', *Measures of Expatriation* (Carcanet, 2016).

Hi Will,

I wanted to talk about voices because they are entangled with identities, especially for writers like us. And to have a voice means that there is a route to have that voice heard. Somehow, the idea of trying to pin down a voice and gain a voice with clarity doesn't sit right with me. I believe that humans are always in flux with their surrounding environment (and this environment is always linked to nature and earth and, by extension, the universe itself). Therefore, I think the desire for clarity is not something I aspire to. Perhaps, that is one of the reasons I am so drawn to poetry—the space for ambiguity, anti-clarity, and anti-voices.

What I am trying to say is that language or literature sometimes doesn't allow mess to happen, if it is indeed about mess. It has to make sense. Like this conversation—the starting point of my thought is actually from thinking about you being sick, how I imagine your vocal cords would be inflamed and how your voice may be distorted and sandy and rough, and the pain there might be when you try to pass air in between and make sounds.

The voice you make would be different from the one I hear on the podcast—*Literary Friction*—where you spoke about the 'He' in your poems. I particularly like the idea of you talking about the voice or the persona of 'He'. You treat it as a puppet version of you, where you are manipulating it so that it performs the way you want. Previously, you talked about Tom Cruise and how he played the same character across seven *Mission:Impossible* films. I've only watched a few of them. I wouldn't call myself a fan of Tom Cruise or the idea of (White) American Heroism where in the film the chosen one gets to save the world somehow. Rather, I find a stronger resonance in the film *Everything Everywhere All at Once* ('*EEAAO*') featuring Michelle Yeoh. I like this multitude of personas that we have as people, humans, or homo sapiens. I like the idea of a multiverse where we are all one, even in this universe, where Will and Jinhao are poets exchanging ideas and having a conversation on the idea of the multiverse, though in another universe we are complete strangers. What I am trying to say is that in *EEAAO*, Michelle Yeoh played so many versions of herself—the film even included clips of her in the real world. There she is a mum, a martial artist, an actor, and more. I think beneath the skin, each one of us is a space that contains a multiverse.

Our bodies contain multiple tiny universes. The one we let ourselves live in is the reality and the other infinite universes are our imaginations.

I often think about who gets to speak and who gets to be read. Recently, I was reading *How to Read Now* by Elaine Castillo.[2] I was really struck by the fact that in her writing she tried to expand the inherently elitist art or literary worlds by including the working classes, the less educated people. That made me think of my mother and her generation, of how the intersectionality of her gender, her class, her family history, and the era she grew up in has stunted her ability to read and write. This means she had to learn in the real world of work, outside of educational institutions. She had to open her mouth to ask. And oh she learned fast and well. She told me how she spent a lot of time reading newspapers, magazines, and going to places where people are telling stories to entertain audiences of tea drinkers. But she only learned to write and read so she could work. Not to realise her own ability to create and to tell her own stories.

Not until recently did she begin to write her autobiography. That's when she felt the sense of existing.

You talked about how both your parents have their own languages of home. This is very much true in my own case as well. My dad speaks Cantonese and my mother speaks Sichuanese. I grew up with mixed languages. My mother always reminds my brother and me that we are not like other kids in school because our dad is from Kaiping. Like, I can't take the same level of spice as others, or our lips are thicker than others, or that we are more likely to tan in summer.

Just now, I thought about how my father married in Sichuan, how he had to learn Chengdunese (a dialect of Sichuanese) but how no

2   Elaine Castillo, *How To Read Now* (Atlantic Books, 2022).

matter hard he tried, his Cantonese twang is still detectable and how my mother had to abandon her village dialect and acquire the city language in Sichuan. Code-switching in Chinese languages is little-known.

I am aware that this response is very illogical. Hope you find this understandable.

Lots of love,

Jinhao xx

*

Dear Jinhao,

Your message didn't read as illogical to me at all, or it felt entirely understandable whether logical or not!

Thank you for homing in so sympathetically on the image of my vocal cords. It was actually more of a head cold, though I feel like my vocal cords have been through the flu-wringer these last few months too. This time it was a headache, a strange shoulder spasm, a nauseating shivery feeling—and the worst thing was I couldn't even read or watch anything in my sickbed! But I'm better now. I've just been carrying this tired sense of lag (be-lagged laggerdy laggardness) over into the Lunar New Year—an exhausted *why*—which I'm hoping will lessen as the days get longer.

I'm writing this on the Tube to work as well. Severe delays. People barging into the carriage, squeezing others further down. Lots of shady looks. Lots of people trying—like me—to dissociate.

I love what you say about the multiverse in our bodies. It makes me think of the people I spend time with in care homes, people whose experiences of the world have been warped—in some cases, wildly expanded—by dementia and other cognitive impairments. One woman is barely verbal but loves music; it takes her back to different specific points (places; spots of time) in her life: she'll be a child waiting for her parents to pick her up from music class, and then she'll start crying because she's working as a secretary and misses her husband.

After my last email, I went to see my parents for dinner. They had two friends over and I had to whisper in my mum's ear several times to explain what people were saying (*no, it's a TV show... they're Catholic*). I tried to explain to her that I didn't have a hotmail address, so even if she correctly put in the first part of my email address it still wouldn't reach me. I felt the bizarreness of the words coming out of my mouth. I was repeating myself and it still wasn't getting through. It was my mouth but not my voice. Yesterday, at the care home, a similar thing happened: I was struggling to understand what a 95-year-old man was telling me—something about rubbing cream on his leg at two in the morning—so I steered the conversation towards football, which he loves (he played a lot when he was stationed in Gibraltar after the war). But he couldn't understand me, and the more I flailed about—telling him stories from his own life (*the orange buoy, the porpoises!*)—the less we seemed able to communicate. But in both cases, despite the breach in communication, there was a surprising feeling of warmth, of intimacy.

There's this idea with poems (especially in how they're taught) that they should have an 'explanation'. 'Explanation' as a wind to clear away the fog of *language* leaving behind a small hard object called *meaning*. And maybe the terror with cognitive impairment is that you might lose access to meaning, that you'll be wandering around in ever-deepening fog. Maybe this sounds glib—I'm conscious of the very painful (also ironising) inadequacy of the analogy—but I feel like poems keep me habituated to the fog—as in, they keep me far from *meaning*, in a space where everything is charged with *meaning*. And there's so much familiarity there. I learn not to fear being lost or adrift in words—like I was as a child shuttling between languages, trying to understand my parents—but happy in the fog.

Before disappearing (like a fog) from your inbox I remembered something I wanted to share last time, also to do with *language*: the Algerian poet Habib Tengour says that 'the language of the mother is also the language of the teacher... it's the job of the poet to discover an incantatory spontaneity from *inside* the servitude of words' (Pierre Joris's translation; my italics).[3] What I like about how Tengour puts it is the sense that there's no outside (what exists outside? the static bludgeons of race and nation). Inside, our freedom may be restricted but there's also collectivity and floating strangeness and so many words with which to still—in spite of everything—sing spontaneously.

Much love,

Will

*

Hi Will,

Apologies for the delayed reply. I am still recovering from the Lunar New Year celebrations a few weeks back, having spent a weekend with friends in London—good food and great company. There is an indescribable feeling of celebrating the Lunar New Year in the UK. Because for most people here, the year had already started. Somehow, people who don't celebrate Lunar New Year still care. I would have colleagues and friends asking *what is the Chinese Zodiac animal this year? What does it mean?* Even in this supposed secular society, people would like to believe in the mystical power from the 'East'.

Before I knew it was called 'Lunar' New Year, I was taught in school that it was 'Chinese' New Year; before that, it was just 'New Year' and then always followed by the Spring Festival. It was about the spring-cleaning on New Year's Eve. It was about smoked meats, sausages shared amongst friends and families. It was about visiting relatives. Firecrackers and fireworks. It was loud and scary at the same time. But that's all changed, you know; firecrackers and fireworks are banned in cities because they contribute to air pollution and are fire hazards.

I meant to reply to you immediately, but the idea of having to write with a deadline filled me with dread and was kind of debilitating.

---

3   Habib Tengour, *Exile is My Trade: A Habib Tengour Reader*, ed. and tr. Pierre Joris (Black Widow Press, 2021).

Again, I am writing my reply on the train to work. Today, I decided to come into London for work after realising that fewer people are taking the train since hybrid working is more common for office workers now, since the pandemic. I still wear my mask on the train (I wouldn't want to risk it as my partner works with people with compromised health conditions). At times, I even feel guilty for forgetting to wear one.

[*Now I am on my way home to Ashford, the train is quiet and grumbling.*]

Whenever poetry is mentioned in this country, the most common response from people is 😩. Then, I learned how poems were taught: poems are treated as mysterious and are supposed to be incomprehensible (or a fog if you wish). The about-ness is asked and as a student you are supposed to understand exactly what this poem given to you is about and you are supposed to appreciate its greatness because you are told to do so. Personally, poems, like any other art works, don't require this universal language of appreciation. What they need is that personal connection to the writing. Even if it is by the 'greats'—whenever I hear that I question: *'great' according to whom?*

Once, I paid a visit to the National Portrait Gallery in London. I remember that I was so moved by a painting called *Mother #1*. The artist, Yunsung Jang, was from South Korea and the canvas was enormous. Even though no words were inscribed on the canvas, I remember it like a poem. To paint is to pay the utmost attention to the subject matter. The painter not only needs to paint the most eye-catching part of the subject, they also need to paint other bits: the strand of hair, the freckles and the wrinkle. But depending on the style—we know one can also be an impressionist, an abstractionist, or even a conceptualist, depending on how much the artist is willing to 'explain' via their medium. I'd rather think making a poem is like that—it is the conceptualist way of art-making. Once people are given freedom in their own way of engaging with the poem, as they do with conceptual art, I believe more people will be interested in poetry.

I can't help but dive into the etymology of 'explain'. The original meaning is 'to flatten, to make plain, to spread it out'—from *ex-* ('out') and *plano* ('flatten'). How can a poem be truly appreciated with an explanation? A table cannot be a table if it is still in its IKEA flat-pack package. It has the potential of being a table, but without assembly, it will never be a table. To explain is to disassemble the structure of a poem. And therefore, the poem is not there anymore.

Words are made up but the reality is that things exist whether or not the language has been invented for them. A thing can exist in a complete sense without any acknowledgement. It is free. But when the time is right, another thing will take notice of its movement or even collide with it. Together, a new thing is created within and without us.

Lots of love,

Jinhao

***

THE LANGUAGE OF MY BEING

Aaron Maniam

In his dialogue with the world, Aaron Maniam pays tribute to the medium of his dreams and prayers.

In Singapore, as in several Asian countries, we speak of having 'a mother tongue': not always the literal language of a female parent, but the language with which we are deemed to have the closest cultural, historical, and traditional affinity. I realised recently that I have never really questioned why language is anthropomorphised as a woman—it seems natural, even, since it is often in the prenatal roots of language that most of us form the deepest aspects of ourselves.

But I find myself resisting the assumption that there must be *a*, singular, mother tongue. Could people in general, and writers in particular, especially in the polymorphous region that is Asia, instead be seen as possessing and possessed by the gravitational pulls of multiple languages?

PROLOGUE

Part of this resistance stems from my variegated family background. Ethnically, my father is half-Tamil, half-Portuguese-Eurasian, descended from Portuguese merchants who came to Melaka in the 1500s and, later in Singapore intermarried with locals over time. My mother is part-Malay, part-Pakistani, with a smattering of Chinese from her great-grandmother, who was born to a Chinese family that could not afford to raise her, and was adopted by my mother's Pakistani great-great-grandparents.

If this ethnic mix isn't confusing enough, the family is also religiously diverse. Dad's father converted from Hinduism to Roman Catholicism when he married my grandmother; Dad was raised Catholic and became Muslim when he married Mum. Several of my Catholic aunts have married Hindu men. As a result, I have developed a deep and abiding interest in inter-religious dialogue, the theory and practice of which has given me vocabularies to understand the diversity of others, and navigate my own.

My family's cultural range raises particularly pointed questions for the assumption about having a single mother tongue. What would ours be, hopelessly hyphenated as our ethnic identities are? Mum's family stopped speaking Urdu, the lyrical, flowing language indigenous to Pakistan, a few generations ago—they all speak Malay now, as do many (but not all) Muslim families in Singapore, partly because many of them married local Malays. Dad's father did not pass down Tamil to any of his children—they still speak Kristang, a creole unique to the Eurasian communities in today's Malacca and Singapore, especially since fellow Singapore writer Kevin Martens Wong started teaching Kristang classes a few years ago.

There are simple, practical answers to the question of what our mother tongue would be. We all speak English—a pragmatic choice, given that so many others in Singapore (and globally) do. In many ways, this is also a response to a political choice, given that early in its independence, Singapore's government identified English as a 'language of administration' inherited from our colonial history under the British, but also co-opted and made our own. English is certainly the language of my mother and father, even if not of both their mothers!

Nearly all my extended family also learned Malay in school. Mandarin was not really an option; Malay was a fairly natural choice within Mum's family, and in Dad's case, it seemed the less difficult option compared to Tamil. In both cases, the decision was part of Singapore's policy that all students must study a language other than English, often named with the meaning-pregnant shorthand 'Mother Tongue', but increasingly referred to with the more neutral 'Second Language'.

But somehow these simple and practical answers don't quite cut it. I keep finding myself returning to the question—what exactly is maternal about these linguistic choices? And is there a better way to conceptualise and categorise the words and language that define the most important parts of my daily living? In this letter to the world, I wrestle with this question in three particularly seminal dimensions in my creative life—writing, dreaming, and praying.

WRITING

As a writer, a natural starting question seemed to be: what language do I write in? And the answer is almost exclusively: English. My poetry is English in both its textual content but also its subtextual and contextual underpinnings. Some of my favourite writers, and certainly my earliest influences, were part of the Anglophone tradition, even if they were not English poets by nationality: Ted Hughes, Robert Frost, T. S. Eliot, George Herbert, Wordsworth, Carol Ann Duffy, Wendy Cope, Louise Glück. I don't experiment much with form and metre, preferring the more unseen disciplines of free verse, but when I do it's often with Shakespearean or Miltonic sonnets. So far, I have spent three formative periods, as an undergraduate, Masters student, and doctoral candidate, in Oxford. It is objectively the oldest university in the English-speaking world and subjectively the most English of English universities—so I am pretty sure its influences on my thinking and writing are broad and deep.

So, is English my mother tongue? As a writer, even if not in ethno-biological terms?

The answer lies in the qualifier I included almost unconsciously two paragraphs ago: '*almost* exclusively'. There are little exceptions to the dominance of English in my life that I find increasingly interesting to explore.

A small trio of poems in my first collection[1] interrogates issues of ethnicity and language. 'Uncles Over Christmas Dinner' is in free verse and has a clearly English sensibility in its diction, exploring issues of mixed identities and ageing—but, periodically, it employs Kristang words and references to Malay and Indian food. It is followed by 'Alagappan: A Non-Speakers' Guide to Tamil Names',

---

1 Aaron Maniam, *Morning at Memory's Border* (Singapore: Firstfruits Publications, 2005).

where I explore a language many expect me to speak because of my skin colour but I don't, and how that makes me a 'marooned native'—all within the structures of an Elizabethan sonnet. The next poem is a 'Pantun for a Drink Seller at Newton Circus', one of Singapore's largest and most diverse sources of hawker food. The poem's form belies its substance, as I find that the pantun's echoing rhymes and repeated Malay line help me explore the interconnections and interdependencies in my life languages, which English alone cannot portray.

More recently, the staple writers in my life have come from outside the Anglophone world—though, admittedly, I still read them in English translations. Rainer Maria Rilke's *The Book of Hours: Love Poems to God*, Pablo Neruda's *100 Love Sonnets*, and the poetry of mystics like Rumi and St John of the Cross, have all become constant travel companions: my go-to writers on long flights and quiet hotel-room nights when my inner introvert needs tending.

I know that these are important, but in terms of my lived reality, I have to admit they are exceptions that prove the rule of English in my life. They provide subtlety and texture to what and how and why I write, but they make most sense against the anchor and bulwark provided by English. Put another way: even if my writing life oscillates, rotates and teeters into other linguistic realms, English is its centre of gravity.

DREAMING

I often think of dreaming as the private corollary of published writing: the domain of inchoate, yet-to-be-articulated thoughts and ideas that might someday find their way into expression, but for now at least are unformed and unbeen. Octavio Paz alludes to something similar when he says, 'Between what I dream and what I forget: poetry'—a line I used as an epigraph for the poem 'Words Lost' in my first collection.

As with my writing, I find I dream almost exclusively in English, which says something about the depth and degree of its hold over my life, conscious and otherwise. But also, as with my writing, certain points of nuance prompt interesting lines of inquiry. Every so often, I find myself dreaming in Malay—often after meeting friends from school or military service, with whom I speak a mix of the language and English. These experiences remind me how unobtrusively present Malay is in my life. It's there in street names and road signs, in announcements on public transport, in military commands I heard every day in the army, in the national anthem I sang every day while in school. None of this is unusual, given that Malay is Singapore's national language. It's there in the sharp accuracy of its words—where the youngest uncle or aunt on my mother's side has a different relational epithet from the oldest counterpart on my father's, or where there are multiple words for verbs like carry—to carry in the palms of the hands (tatang), to carry on one shoulder (tanggung, pikul), to carry on two shoulders (junjung), to carry a baby (dukung)…

This presence and precision are real, firm, but also gentle—like background noise I count on for familiarity and comfort, but don't always give as much attention as I should.

Even less frequently, I dream in French, a language I learned for six years in secondary and high school. This usually occurs during periods of deep immersion—a three-week stay in Nice and Avignon as an undergraduate, where I was the unofficial translator for our group of travelling friends; a six-week stay in Estonia, where broken and halting French was the only common language I had with the owner of the AirBnB where I lived. As with Malay, there are things French can do with a brevity and depth that English sometimes lacks: when I was fifteen, I remember reading a passage describing a character's eyes being 'un bleu aussi profond que l'océan'—a phrase technically translated as 'a blue as deep as the ocean', but without some of the music and melancholy of the original.

These dreams pique my curiosity because in them my Malay and French fluency is far greater than in real life. The dream-conversations always have a fluidity to them, without the two-second pauses I need to think and translate, before I speak. Like my literary life, my dream life seems to have a centre of gravity, in that most of it is apprehended (even if not fully comprehended!) in English.

But the periodic forays outside English suggest a yearning for the possibilities of other linguistic structures and paradigms, for new explorations, even as I acknowledge the foundations English continues to give me.

PRAYER

English is similarly central in my prayer life, when I talk to God. I articulate my deepest spiritual thoughts in English, and I interpret God's responses—through books, conversations with others, nature and signs of the times—through the medium of English.

Growing up Muslim in Singapore was an intriguing test case of this role for English. During my 1980s childhood, most religious instruction for young Muslims—whether learning to read the Quran in the original Arabic, or learning about the dogmas and doctrines of Islam—were in Malay. I understood the material intellectually, but something felt missing when I prayed in Malay, as if I was speaking to God in a language that was curiously liminal—more than borrowed, but still not fully mine. I wasn't unhappy, but I found myself periodically confused when I felt more spiritually at home in a church with my cousins, than in a mosque. The words of Christian hymns—especially those that praised God the Father and did not foray into theological debates about Trinitarianism and the divinity of Jesus—felt like they could easily be part of Muslim prayer.

It was only many years later that I finally teased out why I felt this way. As a graduate student at Yale, when I heard Friday sermons and read books about Islam in English, the words finally felt like they were my own, and I could feel myself beginning to develop a more direct relationship with God. Around the time I finished at Yale (2002), a new bookstore was being set up in Singapore, specialising in English-language material on Islam and a few issues of interest to its owner, the wonderfully erudite and personable Ibrahim Tahir: interfaith dialogue, multiculturalism, environmental activism. Wardah Books has been a powerful shot in the arm for my spiritual life, building on the English-language exposure started at Yale, and helping me to feel like I had found a linguistic home in Islam.

But as with my writing and dream life, exceptions persist, forcing me to avoid reductive simplicity. The more I explored interfaith dialogue, for instance, the more I found that I needed more than English for the complexity, range, and intricacy of spiritual experience. Where English speaks of 'death' and 'the afterlife', for instance, Malay has both the literal word 'mati' (to die) as well as the more evocatively metaphorical 'semadi', meaning to pass into a state of new and transcendent consciousness, similar to its Sanskrit root 'samadhi'. There are certainly efforts to articulate this in English—entering into 'eternal life', for instance—though I find that many lack the simultaneous economy and expressiveness of the Malay/Sanskrit. The Malay translation of the Christian Lord's Prayer is similarly deceptive in its brevity: the line 'Hallowed be Thy name' is translated as 'dimuliakanlah namaMu', where the mix of prefixes, suffixes and abbreviations ('Mu' for 'Kamu' or 'Thy') make for a remarkably compact, but no less substantively meaningful, articulation.

The more I explore this interfaith (and by extension, inter-language) space, the more I find that we need multiple vernaculars to make sense of the richness and range of the divine. Arabic hymns to the Virgin Mary from the Maronite and Coptic traditions, for instance, which use the term 'salam', helped me to see new facets of the word in Islam, including how it is both plural and singular, verb and noun, bringing together peace and submission, choice and receptivity to grace, all at the same time.

Increasingly, I find myself concerned with how, sometimes, we need to go even further: moving beyond language to locate the primal pulse of articulation underneath all our words: 'Silence', one of the prose poems in my second book[2], describes a space

> in, outside, beyond time: that reverberating womb in which all our words, all our names for ourselves are kindled, and echo, and rhyme.

Rereading that poem and a few others while writing this letter also highlighted that I have been concerned with the language of silence

---

2   Aaron Maniam, *Second Person* (Singapore: Firstfruits Publications, 2018).

for a while, even if I wasn't fully aware of the preoccupation while it was developing. 'Standing Still', the final poem in my first book, for instance, ends by examining how

> ... in otherworldly silence
> There is some whisper of what we seek
> When, freed of the world's static
> God's word grows loud
> And the silences - His, mine - speak.

English is the medium through which I name this silence, however incompletely and imperfectly. But as all writers know, the message is far more than the medium or the messenger.

EPILOGUE

So what is English then? Clearly not my mother tongue, or even one of several mother tongues, given the deep limitations of that term. But it is certainly the language of my writing, my dreaming, my prayer—and my silences. I settled on the phrase 'language of my being' in the end, which I think captures how defining English can be in all those domains—it is my language, for better and worse, with all its opportunities, pitfalls, and vagaries.

But it is also, irrevocably and undeniably, inadequate when it comes to the ultimate heavy lifting of conveying complexity, intensity, and dynamism. We are all perpetual drafts after all, perennially 'becoming' something and not just 'being' in a static way. I am realising that no single language, English or otherwise, can be the language of all our becomings. Occasionally, however, in pieces of poetic magic, these languages of our being can connect to other languages, shining new light onto old words, or refracting old light through new lenses. Sometimes they even open tempting but transient doors to the larger place outside language, with paths toward the Word under all words: that pulsing common grammar that beats through all our languages, our language, and our lives.

***

HOME

NOT AS A NOUN BUT AS A VERB

Alvin Pang and Laura Jane Lee

Alvin Pang and Laura Jane Lee discuss home and restlessness.

ALVIN

16 August 2022 | Umbria, Italy

As I write this, I am making a sort of home out of a room in Civitella Ranieri, a 15th century castle in central Italy that hosts a long-standing creative residency programme. The air is sweet with hay, summer vegetables, garden herbs, and the olivine air of the Umbrian mineral hills that surround us. Unlike my home city of Singapore, with its hyper-urban clamour and equatorial swelter, the castle offers comforting affordances of quiet, cool, vista, clean air, stretch space, and, most of all, free time. The good people behind this residency work hard to make a home for artists, writers, and musicians here. They tend to our needs and then leave us be, to tend to our own processes. They know they cannot do our work for us, but what we experience is their love for the land, for the place, and for the mysterious and fickle weather of creativity under which we labour and seek nourishment.

A restless spirit such as myself can sometimes wonder why it is that my creative energies are always pulling me elsewhere than home (meaning my legal, long-term place of residence, my domicile, my permanent address). A fellow resident artist here asked whether I do most of my work at home. I replied that, apart from differences in quantity and quality of time and attention spent, some part of my creative process always involves being outdoors, or elsewhere, than my usual desk at home; that I find the tension between staying and going, the familiar settled here and the fluid there, stimulating. One of the definitions of home in the *Oxford English Dictionary* is a place or condition in which something thrives. In that sense, my creative spirit calls that electric gradient home.

My physical body, another kind of home, needs rest, but it also needs movement. It craves comfort but is also curious for sensory input. Intimacy, to me, is a puncturing of aloneness through encounter with an other; it is the gift of vulnerability, which can otherwise evoke terror.

In the same way a castle's primary purpose is fortification against pregnability, this is home as keep: keeping out and keeping in. When these parameters are defined to a satisfactory balance, trade and traffic become possible. A castle that is absolutely impermeable—that lacks doors and windows; that disallows the passage of water, air, sustenance, occupants, visitors—is lethal and lifeless. What I mean by home might be a kind of managed and manageable permissiveness; a translucency; a filtering; an open well, not a closed urn.

Robert Frost has written, somewhat sardonically, '[h]ome is the place where, when you have to go there, / They have to take you in.' Home in this sense is that which is permeable to us; that lets us in, even as so many structures in the world are about filtering us out in various ways: borders, standards, categories, labels, qualifications, genres, genders, institutions, proprieties, budgets, disciplines… At the same time, there are also situations that shake what we know; that crack our sense of home; that are impenetrable in their ineffability: the death of a loved one, for instance. Or, for many these days, war. The spit of steel against a neck. But it could also be the birth of a child; the discovery of a secret; the burn of a touch, long missed, after a spell of denial or absence.

It is not our place in the world but the world's place in us that I want to think about during my stay here. In *Wanderlust*, Rebecca Solnit writes of Kierkegaard as an example of a thinker as solitary walker, who as a class of people are 'unsettled, between places, drawn forth into action by desire and lack, having the detachment of the traveller rather than the ties of the worker, the dweller, the member of a group'.[1] I ask myself:

Can one abide, learn to inhabit, a state not of homelessness but of home-loose-ness?

---

1   Rebecca Solnit, *Wanderlust* (Granta, 2014).

Do our walls walk with us always?

Is it the distinctive trait of the artist to be nomadic in disposition; to seek sail over shore, even if we might be stemmed in one ground or another?

Are we the ones for whom a window is always open, a door unlatched, springing leaks to and from the unhomed world?

LAURA JANE

26 August 2022 | Singapore

Where?

I think I understand what you mean when you say that your writing lulls you elsewhere than home. In that sense, your restless energy is not so different from my own restless bones, though the chief difference here is that home is first and foremost a prerequisite for exploring the wide world which lies beyond. Now, after being hastily uprooted from home soil, I think that to be safely nomadic is to always have somewhere to return to permanently. To be home-loose is, as you said, to have somewhere they'll have to take you in.

Lately, I have returned to your city after an extended stay in the UK, and have been stirred at how simple home is to many. Having left some clothes in my parents' house, my mother told me to 'come home often', which deeply irked me, because it is not my home, though she might maintain that it is 'her house with my room in it'. I said something to the effect of 'my home is the one I will pay for myself', though now, having become engaged, I wonder if I would be a 'houseowner' or a 'homeowner'.

What is the difference between owning a home and having one?

I am deeply aware of my legal status in this country as a 'Long-Term Pass Holder' rather than a Permanent Resident, and the perhaps pragmatic desire to be able to permanently reside here. Yet I keep contemplating the morality of becoming absorbed into the country.

Having been ejected from my city, Hong Kong, where I was born and raised, and unable to return, home feels like an unfinished matter.

Do I dare think about sinking roots?

Perhaps for now, home is having an anchor in a safe harbour, a permanent mooring. Home is a very heavy stone. Paperweight. Carabiner. Though part of me wishes to engage in the act of burying, of burrowing, of belonging, I know that nothing of me can stop my being uprooted, dug up, and sent away.

Yes, this seventh month, I am thinking of Hungry Ghosts and their restlessness.

This summer, I visited Oxford, and found that I did not need a map to get around. I visited my favourite haunts with my fiancé and for a moment or two felt something almost adjacent to home, though perhaps more in the person that tethered me like a point of light to the wide, dark world.

Do you think somebody could be home?

Often I have asked him where home is, and he would motion towards a point to the left of his chest, saying 'here'.

I must confess I do not know how much of home is 'place' and how much is 'person', and that I am afraid to even think of wandering the world without first having somewhere to return to. So for now I will let my thoughts wander for me, while I write myself (a) home.

I do not think I could ever be nomadic. Migratory, perhaps, like birds, or wild geese. Yes, if I ever had a home I never lost it would be the Mary Oliver poem that held me together.

ALVIN

26 August 2022 | Umbria, Italy

Your reply makes me think of home not as a noun but as a verb. To home: to adopt, house, give shelter to, take in. To home in on: to seek out and approach with clarity, focus and commitment. So a question for me is *how?* rather than where?

In reading Rebecca Solnit's *A Field Guide to Getting Lost*, I am reminded that nomadic peoples traditionally have a stable relationship to their routes and landscapes.[2] They move more like seasonally migratory birds than wanderers. But I am also thinking about those who wayfare (in Tim Ingold's sense of wayfaring)—who have honed their senses and skills to read the terrain wherever they are and to proceed from there; they do not drift but ride the waves: they are, in a sense, always at home because they always know where they are relative to their circumstances, and know how to find their way and keep going. This is, to me, a kind of taking oneself in: and it calls for both an awareness of self and its relations to and in the world, as well as a kindness to oneself.

Perhaps one learns this awareness and this kindness through practice: by relating to others, navigating forms of kinship. Kin / ship: nearby vessels on the seas of human connection.

I too moved out of my parental home, by way of marriage (as is the Singaporean wont), soon after returning from studies abroad. I had become too accustomed to a different way of being in the world and moving through it, and the familiar harbour of my old, childhood life felt confining, at odds with new rhythms, understandings, and movements. This expressed itself in various resentments and tensions that only settled somewhat once I had a place to call my own, an apartment apart from my parents. I suppose that safe distancing allowed our relations to become what we might now term a new normal: to be safely rehomed.

---

2   Rebecca Solnit, *A Field Guide to Getting Lost* (Canongate, 2006).

Home may be a story in the telling. Solnit writes that 'a relationship is a story you construct together and take up residence in, a story as sheltering as a house.' To me, this idea of home as an ongoing, confluent narrative marries both place and person; geography and history. To make a home together is to co-navigate life's fluidities. This does not guarantee security or stability (nothing does); instead, it is the reassurance that any inevitable challenges will not have to be faced alone. Over time, a map accrues—memories, desires, routes taken, deserts crossed and mountains traversed—a togethering that I regard as home. This may or may not take place at a certain fixed address. In the past two decades I have moved house several times: each time to a different sort of residential setup (including two rented premises). Each of them have imparted a different sense of living; each added something to my idea of what I would like from a dwelling; none quite fulfilling all my criteria. In Singapore, at any rate, most of us find ourselves in leasehold properties, ours to occupy only for 99 years or less. Temporality is built into the system: all we can keep is the family story. Of course, I have the security of my nationality—but as we see in the world today, that too is a story that can be disrupted. Singapore itself is the outcome of such a rupture—Singapore-as-home, which began as a traumatic, caesarean excision from Malaysia-as-home, was never expected to survive on its own. It took decades for the home-becoming to take place; for the inhabitants of the island to feel at home in their own city-state. Some perhaps have never quite made that journey; the story has not stuck for them.

Yet, when and how do we know home (whether noun or verb)? What qualities of light or mood or material presence convey that sense of being at home or approaching it? It cannot only be that sense of familiarity, comfort or assurance, for it is not always thus, and we know we long to stir from it. And as you say, at times we find a certain adjacency to that feeling of home in various elsewheres: what exactly is that feeling (apart from confidence in one's sense of a locale). What signals it? And what interrupts it?

And how does writing home us?

*

LAURA JANE

3 October 2022 | Singapore

Sorry that it has taken a while for me to write. But your question on how one homes has followed me around this past month, tapping on my shoulder like the incessant chirping of a small bird as I begin to make and navigate plans for a home of my own, or perhaps with this home of my own.

How indeed?

If we all as wayfarers are wading through the tide of life, perhaps home and kin are simultaneously blessed Polaris and sacred songline. It is what thrusts the salmon towards its natal river to spawn and die, because it must.

Home, because it must.

And if home is a story in the telling, it is told because it must. This telling and togethering is a necessary huddle for some light and reprieve in a world which, as you said, tends towards brevity. This too is true of the city from which I have been excised, so I should hope that my own home-as-story is a bulwark of remembering, a deposit of experiences I chose, with the one I chose. As J.M. Coetzee so rightly ponders in *Foe*:[3]

> 'Is that the secret meaning of the word story, do you think:
> a storing place of memories?'

Having thought long and hard about how we know home, I have started to wonder if we are not so different from our mammalian counterparts who use echolocation. We know home and its shape by what is reflected off it, navigating towards and around it—and at times away from it. We can know home by whispering into the void and listening for its echo. To know home, you must put something out into the world: a sound, a thought, a pebble skipping across the lake.

---

3   J.M. Coetzee, *Foe* (Penguin, 2010).

Do you think that is why I've been writing about home so much?

I am determined to disturb the quietness of this surface, to send a boomerang out into this haze, hunting for home. Perhaps I should find it, or something quite adjacent, have to wander out into the haze to retrieve this reality. And should I chance upon the home-adjacent in realising the home, all the more should I take joy in it—the comfort and connection of neighbour and community just beyond the frontier of home. Somewhere to stop for a while. Maybe I am thinking about Ray Oldenburg's 'third places'. It is, after all, home away from home.

I must admit that I am slightly jealous. Singapore has the kopitiam and the hawker centre. With the way things are going, and the direction rent is going (up) I'd be hard pressed to name a third place in my natal city nowadays. Cafes are for influencers and Instagram, and it's hard to find a cha chaan teng not taken over by a chain. The surviving independent ones ask you to clear out once you've finished your meal. For good reason: they do need the next customer's purchase to keep the business afloat.

I dream of opening a bookstore-cafe one of these days, where customers are free to browse, read, work, talk, write. And I'd be in the corner with my poems or behind the counter making (affordable) coffee or a grilled cheese. Perhaps it's a shophouse, and I live in a flat-above-shop situation.

I have dreamt this very specific dream before, it is not a metaphor. In my dream I even had a baby strapped on my back. But for now, mostly, dreams of affording a roof over my head or having my application for permanent residency go through on the first try have very much crowded it out.

Living in Singapore has made me an increasingly pragmatic person. Or maybe it's trauma. Perhaps both.

Do you think I'm bowing to what everyone here thinks is safe, what everyone thinks 'home' is supposed to be?

Having 'lost home' once, is it wrong of me to choose stability over whatever the alternative is?

ALVIN

28 November 2022 | Singapore

In correspondence, a friend I met during my residency, an American artist and scholar who had moved to and set up home in Umbria decades ago, shares a reflection that one's sense of home begins with the self, but at the same time one's sense of self extends to the material reality one inhabits. So when we move places, to what extent can we move our full selves, bound as we are to places we have had profound material relations to in ways we cannot fully know or control? Or is it that what we know as our 'selves' is a network, really—not just the ant colony nor its queen but the city they carve out underground in the course of their affairs, and where we have spent time becomes our mark on the world and also sustains us?

I do not believe any specific or enduring material trappings can give us that home-sense with certainty, although there are probably common hygiene factors: such as whatever offers us basic physical and psychological safety and security. I cannot help but consider that our species, in pursuing these notions of comfort and stability, may have already made the world too much our own, in ways both personal and public, remarkable and tragic, driving our native planet to exhaustion and fever.

But by now you are married—as evinced by the photographs on your Instagram account—and I have been several weeks home from my residency abroad and other travels. I'd like to think we have both experienced home as the gravitational pull of a 'must' (as you put it); the musk of necessity. Home as choosing to make of something a compulsion that we take upon ourselves: a vow, a quest, a decision to return that we imagine not to be a decision at all, but the way things are.

Thinking about home and homing as willed, and in a sense arbitrary, makes it no less powerful in practice. Home is that which in us tells us we must, we are. Perhaps that is what writing does when we pursue it: it is a way of defining, by encircling, our core values, beliefs, dreams, insistences. Even if these change (and all mortal creatures who participate in time change—it is the home state of being), we imagine there is a that-which-changes: an identifiable zone of flux; or perhaps it is the need to imagine such a thing that home is.

An early poem of mine, written in my twenties, claims that:

> We resort to words
> the comfort of them
> testing the silence for echoes

These lines now feel uncannily akin to your reflection that 'We can know home by whispering into the void and listening for its echo'. It suggests writing as a form of echolocating not our place exactly but our felt sense of home, by seeking familiarity and pushing against the contours of what isn't home-feeling.

What draws me back to writing is that nagging sense that there is one more mysterious door to my inner idea of home: something always not fully opened, an incompleteness to things. It could be my idea of home is of a life always in the making and never quite done (since doneness is a figure of death), because the very foundation, upon which we who home in time must travel, is fluid. It could be that we ourselves billow and fray with the years, and if we are to be home to others as we are to ourselves, then we must close our windows with the coming rain and watch for spills in the kitchen.

To be home, and to be home to another, calls for us to flex and sway; to find our footing in a churning world, when we too are of churn. I think of the back and forth rhythm of writing, a rocking, a rowing that not only propels us forward but also keeps us upright, and tells us, like the practised knowledge one can acquire through friction and tug upon the oars, where and how we are, and that we are.

Perhaps home is choosing not to let go of the oars and sink to the sunless depths in which no specificities are any longer demanded of us. Home is the constant risk of loss and courage in the face of that risk. Home may then be the active work of being, and writing a way of home seeking and home making, and a form of inhabiting.

It also comforts me to think of writing as a shepherding, giving purpose, meaning, cohesion, and shelter to the wayward and the lost within ourselves: finding space in our mind and making room in our hearts for particular ideas, feelings, reflections or imaginings that could one day embed themselves and become part of our landscape, our place.

I wish you all the very best in your married life, your new home-building journey. May this be the beginning of a story that steadies and comforts you, and may your writing lend oars and wings to your continual homecoming.

LAURA JANE

20 December 2022 | Singapore

Did you know that the largest organism in the world is a fungus in eastern Oregon whose mycelium spans hundreds of square miles? Most of it is largely invisible, its thread-like hyphae yearning and stretching through the earth in a network which connects this singular fungus to other fungi and plants as far as it can grow. Some are like it, and some are not.

I think this is what it means to be truly at home in the world.

This organism in and of the earth is not so different to our 'selves', on and of the earth. I am no scientist, but the idea of the mycelium internet, of a fundamental interconnectedness across place, species, and history intrigues me. It intrigues me perhaps because—as you have also countered—it is not so foreign.

Having pondered your question, I now wonder if I have left my mark on the places I have spent time in, and the people and words I have spent time with. There is a trend going around on the internet where people share moments that have 'altered their brain chemistry'. I am certain there are places I've lived, people who have passed through my life, the poems I've written, which for better or worse have fundamentally altered who I am.

It's comforting, isn't it? To know you'll always be thus linked to other souls, other narratives, other geographies. I tell myself: at the very least you'll always be home in *your* world, your chosen net of linking threads.

I like your proposition that home is a choice we do not choose. The pull of a magnetic field. There is no explanation for what is inevitable. We can spend a life writing of it, on it, around it and yet find no tidy answer, no need for an answer other than to heed this compulsive pull in an increasingly confuddled world.

Yet still, after all, I find myself writing about home. In her memoir *The Writing Life*, Annie Dillard declares that 'A writer looking for subjects inquires not after what he loves best, but after what he alone loves at all'.[4]

Perhaps in seeking my shape and sense of home I can indeed recognise it not by what it is, but by what it is not. A process of home-searching, by elimination, through writing. Perpetual, yes, but dare I say, healing? Holistic. More comprehensive. Thankfully not 'done'. I think that the matter of home is one of an imperfect pilgrimage, and one beyond the mere physical plane. At least for now, though it will, as you have forewarned, most certainly and happily change.

I have never been a big letter-writer, but thank you for writing to and with me. Thank you for sharing the wisdom of your years and experience with a young writer puzzling out a more complete idea of home, a sense of something we will continually tend towards throughout the course of this human life but perplexingly—somewhat relievingly—never fully arrive at.

***

---

4   Annie Dillard, *The Writing Life* (Harper Perennial; Reprint edition, 2013).

HOW IT FEELS ON MY SKIN

L Kiew and Khairani Barokka

L Kiew and Khairani Barokka discuss how home feels on the body and in poetry.

L KIEW

2 October 2022 | South London, UK

In the weeks when London hits its summer highs and the air becomes heavy with humidity, I dream of home. What can I tell you about how home feels on my skin? It's the temperature around 27°C, humidity around 80%, and the air agitated by electric fans. It's seeking shade on the street and when indoors lying on cool concrete or stone-composite floors. It's longing for late afternoon rainstorms clearing the heat haze, water rushing down monsoon drains and flooding the roads. It's grille-fronted rooms open to catch any breeze and the greetings you would shout through the grillework when you visited your aunts and uncles. I dream that I am visiting again, feeling that joy of recognition, and waking crumpled like the blue aerogrammes I used to write home. Royal Mail ceased selling aerogrammes in 2012, the year I moved back to London from Scotland. My parents stopped writing letters long before that when we all got email. Is my body being nostalgic when it revives that equatorial skin-sense? The climate is changing everywhere, as people remake the environment. There are flyovers and new roads cutting through the old neighbourhoods where my family live; rubber plantations overwrote the rainforest, and are in turn overwritten by oil palm plantations, housing estates, and highways.

When I look for home, it's in glimpses like an ornamental banana tree seen briefly behind a garden wall. I am standing streetside and trying to find my way. A London gardener told me that in the twenty years he's been working, the public planting schemes have become increasingly subtropical. Perhaps I'm following those seedings, dispersed, uprooted and re-rooted. When I write, am I collecting seeds and putting them in envelopes to send to new homes?

2 August 2022 | North London, UK

Firstly, thank you for beginning our correspondence of homing; we are birds of flight with our criss-crossing migratory patterns. 'Skin-sense' is a wonderful way of putting it. When you write, how is it directed towards where you come from?

Just before I read this, I was kneeling on my floor, looking at a bookshelf and choosing what next from the TBR pile, and noticed my chest reverberating with echoes. Having just calmed the mind by reading, I found myself in that stillness, that calmness that brings the ever-present subconscious to the fore. In this case, it was voices: the throats of family members both alive and gone, cooing and soothing me as if I was a baby.

My bodymind was telling me it missed being surrounded by my language, and these ties. The sonic leaves grooves in our bodies, ready for an impetus resembling vinyl's needle, to be able to replay memory-soundloops. I'm grateful for what countless Jakarta street sounds have carved in our flesh, the casual attunement to car sounds like chatter, or the quiet reverence for travelling street food vendors' tunes—each singing and/or broadcasting via speaker their own little ditties for fried tofu, fresh bread, sate padang, and ever more. Ambient mosque azaans, mall cacophony blighted by marketing drills, the sounds of spoons tinkling against a bowl holding cendol. These and many more sounds, if kept in the audio equivalent of a singing bowl, would hold the ability to soothe a keening for home upon breakage.

It has been comforting, as well as filled with saudade, to imagine all the homesounds we each carry in our bodies as ever-present.

L KIEW

6 November 2022 | South London, UK

When I write, how is it directed towards where I come from? If my fingerprints were read by the stylus on a record player and the bodycharge transferred to an amplifier, those signals conducted to the speakers are always homesounds.

Like soundwaves resulting from the back-and-forth vibrations of the particles of the medium through which they are moving, my writing oscillates with the common chirrup of sparrows, humhiss of cars along wet tarmac, Doppler effect of sirens, that particular crowing of kampung chickens, a stray dog barking and rain running in rivulets off a corrugated tin roof. It attunes to vibrations from back then and back there, with here and today.

Have you ever pressed your ear to the bark of a tree? There's a xylem thrum of sap and water, and it's as if you are a stethoscope touched to the skin of a landscape, hearing what stirs below. I imagine my reader in that posture, feeling today's weather on their skin and looking out from their place in the landscape, my homesounds drawing in and perhaps roosting with them.

What will the reader do with the signals I transcribe? Will their imagined flight become another homing, a windborne bird, a seed lifted through air?

K. BAROKKA

22 November 2022 | North London, UK

Imagining your homesounds roosting now, as I'm sure they do. Thinking of an ear to a tree as akin to a needle on a gramophone, and feeling us all pulsing to different grooves in the daily sonic atmosphere. Grooves that are echoes of each other, that form part of the same song without knowing.

I can't remember whether or not I've listened to a tree so intimately, skin on its trunk, but I likely did—as a child, I remember speaking to trees. Addressing them all as 'Mr Tree' (patriarchal gender programming in action, gladly now reversed!) When alone, I thought that they, surely, are all-seeing, all-knowing, all-understanding. These days I remind myself that palm oil plantations contain trees

239

that are harmful, that are built after the destruction of old-growth rainforest trees, and I imagine even palm oil trees containing a selfless knowledge that they should not have.

Foliage fills a room with gentleness. Rain on leaves, as well as their rivulets off roofs, define the monsoon season for me. Rain on all the green, the thundering of it, is a curtain of continuity, a dampening of human sound, an enveloping of us all in a mighty power. Yet one that still retains all that gentleness.

Perhaps that is what I write to, and what I hope to write towards, to approximate—a soft curtain of emotion that envelops, calms, and reflects our heartbeats back to us. Acknowledges how loudly the pulse pounds and protects us, like the undulations of dry-rainy-dry season. Climate change has shifted rain to more of a dry season in Jakarta, and dryness to more of a rainy season. Still, a torrent in monsoon season retains its indelible mark, giving to the soil, a sea coming for its thirst.

L KIEW

27 November 2022 | South London, UK

Thinking of foliage filling rooms, I remember seeing abandoned houseshells where the speculator-developer ran out of funds, and I reflect how disruption can stimulate growth, opening the ground to light. Isn't it a hopeful happenstance that there are many plants tolerant to high temperatures, direct hard sunshine and nutrient-poor soil, that pioneer species tend to be fast-growing? I think of resilient bamboo, wild bananas, rampant gingers, climbing vines that enshroud the canopy of logged forest, the ubiquitous resam fern which covers red earth along disturbed fringes. While trees that regrow after logging may have curved-kinked trunks as a result of struggling up through dense thickets of climbers, they still grow upwards.

I believe trees and their spirits have no intentions towards us. If you are careless brushing against a rengas tree, its black sap burns blisters on exposed skin. Mango and cashew trees are related to rengas; sweetness stings and salt tenderises; daun kentut salves. I think of the stories of hantu hutan I heard as a child, and am more horrified now by people and what we can do.

Can we truly describe what we have lost, pawprints and blood dissolving in rain? Some horrors continue to coat the back of our skulls and sometimes that is what I write to. Then I remember that the forest can return leaf by leaf, with the thrum of insects and macaques travelling the treeways. That is what I write towards, even as I feel the air heavy with humidity and the clouds ready to split into thunderous storm.

I have been thinking this week about a work colleague who heard that I write poetry and then found some of my poems online. She asked why my work was so nostalgic and I was cross in responding. Why is it that some writers are celebrated for mourning what is lost and others told to forget and move onto another subject? It seems fine to be nostalgic when visiting country houses to gaze at the ephemera of upper class privilege and their status symbols showing off wealth made out in the colonies; it's fine to buy heritage jams, printed tea towels and visit tearooms on a sleepy Sunday afternoon; it's fine to to remain oblivious to historic conditions and labour which made the apolitical visiting experience possible. When I write back and towards where I come from, I can't easily forget how it once was; that the Portuguese, Dutch and British settled, partitioned and plundered. How we feel, and how we felt—we know certain things that we are told repeatedly to forget—it is geothermally heated groundwater emerging onto the skin of the Earth. A channel of hot water runs through my centre, memories sulphurous and recurring. As I write, I see the beams of sunlight cutting through steam, stirring tree leaves.

K. BAROKKA

UK winter | North London, UK

What your work colleague called nostalgia is also—apart from the blissful unawareness you write of, with regards to how indelible colonial labour and environmental extraction contributes to western 'nostalgia'—a denial of how present and current pangs of remembrance are. As you say, it is felt in the bodymind, our blood and neurons keen towards, home in on, and this is physiological, immediate, in the now, and shapes our future movements.

In Indonesian and Malay, we have no tenses. Past, present, and future are always there, always a possibility, in every sentence. I like to say that, because of this, every translation of Indonesian into English is science fictioning, for it fixes just one temporal possibility out of potentially infinite ones. What is 'normal' to me is the commingling of timelines that are outside linear constructs of Gregorian calendars. These possibilities speak to cosmological sophistications that are not easily made apparent in the English language, are not 'native' to it.

Our ancestral approach to time, and language, is a throughline of kin and place-making that connects all we've done, all we will do, to how we are in the now. Colonial theft in the present, through multinational corporations, and aligned 'structural adjustment programs' for 'the third world' imposed by Bretton Woods institutions—programmes that gut public services and mandate debt on a gargantuan scale—is always present when I think of home in the grey, buzzy cloud of anxiety that lingers over my heartbeat. I read somewhere that constant anxiety in a world of continuous colonial theft is only natural. This does not ease it, nor make it comfortable.

However, our clues for calming are also found in the past. In my case, the acupressure point my grandmother taught me to apply two fingers to, when nausea and headaches persist. The secret safe place she told my father she would imagine herself in, to settle her nerves; a place he told me about, and that I have inherited in and for my own mind.

I recently got married in a dress I designed to illustrate this imaginary place from my grandmother's mind, and how bodyminds interact with this place. I wanted to cover myself in safety and calm, and I wanted my grandmother to be present, for her place of calm to be manifested in our world in some external way. I also wore her Javanese batik sarung from the 1920s on that day, and I felt all our soil-and-tree histories on my body. On a cool day in London,

I wanted to simultaneously be home: to be in my East Javanese, West Sumatran, and Jakarta homes. In some small way, I hope I was also able to feel the homes of the Arab, South Asian, and Chinese travellers that intermingled with indigenous islanders, and shaped my family's cultures, and the angles of our faces.

The soils and waters they traversed. The continual threads they wove, literal and haemoglobic, the food cooked every day in the face of colonial brutalities, and the truths of multiple tenses at once existing in all of our bodies. I am thinking of your resilient bamboos, bananas, and gingers, and I am smiling.

L KIEW

8 January 2023 | Recently returned from Kuala Lumpur | South London, UK

Thank you for your words which console and uplift me as the dark pressures of this winter press down. While I largely live and write within the English language, it strikes me that perhaps it is a language particularly suited to a scarcity mindset; the public discourse in the UK has for the best part of a decade laid bare an underpinning English narrative entirely obsessed with a lack of something—usually money or prestige—so that public figures can't seem to focus on anything else, not that they even seen to seem to try. This scarcity narrative seems to have limited any ability to collectively plan, focus or seek equitable solutions to the socio-economic challenges we are experiencing. As the days shorten, it feels like I am trapped within someone's constricting tunnel, their thoughts reverberating harshly off walls running with damp and mould, the shouts again and again about the somethings they don't have until all vision is reduced to a pinprick of light, winking in and out as the tunnel twists and turns to impulses that no one thinks to control.

For those of us with bodyminds marked by legacies of continuous colonial theft, what can we carry with us as we come to sit alone in a stranger's garden, on opposite and uncomfortable benches? I think of Li-Young Lee's *The Winged Seed* and what we cradle in the folds of fabric, the pockets of coats.[1] In seeds—however tiny they may be—I sense the past, the present, and the future continuing, possibilities interleaving and interweaving.

I am revived, too, thinking of your happy news and am sending you all my best wishes. No matter the times we live in and the journeys we are on, each union of love reaffirms all; the ceremonies held to mark these comminglings celebrate pasts, presents and hold out the promise of futures. I think about what we wear on our backs and over our skins as we move towards and away from home; your dress sounds powerful, and I think of how batik carries the colours of departure and return on its surface, its patterns formed through a wax-resist dyeing and layering process. An elder once told me that the word 'batik' has a shared root with the words for 'drawing' or 'writing'; I am no etymologist and perhaps no one can really trace a true linguistic root upstream against the rushing rapids of time. Tongues intermingle in the poems I write, my skin is porous as the clothes I wear. I write partly to restore colour against the fading effect of time, to unlace the corset of English tense(s). I am filled with joy at the thought of all our soil-and-tree histories alive and sensed on our skins.

In closing our correspondence of homing, I return to your question about how writing is directed towards where we come from. It is directed towards the borders we have crossed and back again; it both translates and leaves untranslated, slipping along the edge of languages. It brings our readers the canopies of trees, the forest floor, the lak-krak of frogs after heavy rain, the sound of something in the dark leaping between branches, the wind lifting the flight of bats and the putt-grunt of a motorbike in the far distance.

I am grateful to have been heard and to have heard you, to have seen and been seen, to have travelled and returned to homes, lit by many moons and damp with rains.

**

---

1   Li-Young Lee, *The Winged Seed: A Remembrance* (Reissue: BOA Editions, 2013).

BELONGING AND ELSEWHERE

Leong Liew Geok and Shirley Geok-lin Lim

Leong Liew Geok and Shirley Geok-lin Lim's conversation ranges from their shared sense of nomadism that includes living in the US, Malaysia, Singapore, and elsewhere, to the very first time they started writing seriously.

SHIRLEY GEOK-LIN LIM: In 2019, my lecture for City University of Hong Kong Gold Leaf Seminar Series included an analysis of your poem 'Forever Singlish' which you recorded for the event. 'Forever Singlish' was a crucial part of my lecture's focus: the relationship between sound and sensibility in post-colonial literature. I wish to shine a light on your voice, a unique contribution to Anglophone Singapore, Southeast Asian, and World Literature. I view your work through a retrospective perspective, of my own 'road not taken'.

LEONG LIEW GEOK: Although we are both migrants, you, far more so than I was or am, there was only one road for me—home, eventually. You have lived in the US since you went to Brandeis in 1969 as a graduate student. I received my primary and secondary education in Penang, then in 1967 went to university in Australia. After graduation, I taught school in Kedah for one and a half years before proceeding to Leicester for an MA in Modern English and American Literature (1972–73). Then I got married in Oxford and, with my husband, left for Washington DC in the summer of '75. It was Kok Peng who put me through the PhD programme at George Washington University, a stone's throw from the World Bank where he had secured a job as a Young Professional. Two of our three children were born in the United States. In 1981, we returned to this part of the world—to Singapore rather than Malaysia, for obvious reasons—because his parents were getting old, his four siblings were living abroad, and he was the eldest son. I became an Assistant Professor in the Department of English Language and Literature, National University of Singapore (NUS).

SHIRLEY GEOK-LIN LIM: Your trajectory is also 'migratory'. We have similar beginnings—Straits Settlements born and raised, Penang and Malacca. My Fulbright and Wien Fellowships at Brandeis, Massachusetts, were hugely anxiety-provoking. It's odd with your international mobility that you view yourself as 'a frog in a well' in contrast to me!

The choice I made in my twenties of career over marriage reads as an analogue to Robert Frost's lines in 'The Road Not Taken': 'I took the one less traveled by, and that has made all the difference.' I rejected invitations for Singapore academic positions, after my First Class BA at the University of Malaya in 1966, then an English Department lectureship, with a guarantee of Permanent Resident status; and, lastly, an ISEAS Research Fellow position in 1986. The 'what if' question haunts me. What if I had chosen to (re)turn to this city state, this non-sceptered isle that is forever capitalist?

In contrast, despite thirteen plus years spent abroad before settling in Singapore, your 'nomadism' is absent in your poems. Is this 'aporia' a deliberate, conscious or unconscious choice?

LEONG LIEW GEOK: Although I spent five years in Australia, two in England, and six in the US, living in one English-speaking country after another, I never took to writing poetry seriously until I returned to my part of the world. The reason is *rootedness*: a home-base to be grounded in to launch myself. I never felt I belonged to any of the three host countries even though I enjoyed the freedom of living and studying there. I was just too busy keeping up with my reading, with the submission of essays, and the grading of student assignments as a teaching assistant!

I'd written poetry sporadically in secondary school, but only resumed writing it when I came back after thirteen years abroad! You could say that I felt, and feel, a sense of familiarity and belonging in Singapore. A native environment was a confidence-booster. I was, moreover, encouraged by NUS colleagues like Edwin Thumboo, Koh Tai Ann, Arthur Yap, Kirpal Singh and the Filipino writer F. Sionil José, who asked for poems they could publish in journals or anthologies they were guest-editing or editing. By the time we came to Singapore in 1981, I was well past 33 and a mother with two young children. Our youngest child was born in Singapore in 1985.

SHIRLEY GEOK-LIN LIM: I knew by the time I was ten or younger that I wanted to be a poet. I began writing poems, almost all rhymed and in formal stanzas, and had a few published in my secondary and sixth form school journals and as prize-winning poems in *Malacca Times*. For me then (as now), imagination gave me subjects for my child's poems. Imagination made the quotidian, every object, thought, sight, subjects for poems. Rootedness, loss of roots, rootlessness, air roots, decayed roots of teeth, whatever: writing poetry (and later, fiction and creative non-fiction) was my identity as subject/person/woman/human.

In my first graduate semester at Brandeis, 1969, I registered for my only creative writing course ever (offered to undergraduates). Professor J.V. Cunningham asked us to explain why we were at his seminar. I said because I had 'a sense of destiny.' What a naïve statement to make before a bunch of strangers! What could such a pretentious, presumptuous phrase mean? Yet I knew even then that writing poetry was not about ambition, career, profession, money, or even vocation. It was a vision of my future as a Malaysian writer, contributing to a national literary history. I don't recall Cunningham looking askance at this 'foreign' student's proclamation. Perhaps that sentiment was commonplace then in the US. Bob Dylan's 'The Times They Are A'Changin'' sums up the zeitgeist of those years when many activist Americans marched and wrote protest poetry.

LEONG LIEW GEOK: I never came across a single creative writing class in the universities I attended. Like numerous poets, I taught myself through practice, and through reading the work of others, including yours. I drifted into writing poetry and preferred it to fiction, not having the time or the space to delve into the latter. Temperamentally, too, I am more suited to poeticising.

SHIRLEY GEOK-LIN LIM: You became a 'serious' poet only after you felt you 'belonged' to a place. If that had been the case with me, I would probably have stopped writing poetry. 'Belonging' is a quest, a question, something to be made with much difficulty, and that is easily unmade. Writing from a self-domestic-rooted place is also what I admire about your poems. You are like Jane Austen, carving a whole world in a small piece of ivory, while I am more like a wild Brontë sister, wandering in the Yorkshire heaths…

LEONG LIEW GEOK: Unlike you, I was a late starter. I consider myself a Singaporean/Malaysian poet. And, unlike me with my need for a home-base, there is an admirable ease with which your 'transnational' poems absorb your environment. In your travels to different countries in the course of your academic career, your changing environment melds into the imagery of your poetic output. Thus, countries where you have spent time as a visiting poet, scholar or academic, have yielded poems—based in Singapore, Malaysia, Hong Kong. Your chapbook, *Embracing the Angel: Hong Kong Poems*, is explicit in reference.[1] You did spend time in Australia, but I've come across only one from Australia, 'Kangaroo'. You write in *In Praise of Limes*, 'Everywhere is full of poems'.[2] No other Australian poems?

SHIRLEY GEOK-LIN LIM: My 2010 collection, *Walking Backwards*, has a sub-section, 'Past Danger and Drowning', composed when I was a writer resident in the Newcastle Lock-Up, a historical jail for drunken sailors and petty criminals, now a museum, with a studio on the upper floor for the resident poet.[3] I was utterly isolated for about a month, to write or not. I spent hours walking on the miles-long beach, wrote journal entries, and published three poems, spatially identified, e. g. Bogey Hole, the ocean rock pool hand-hewn by convicts for the Newcastle British Commandant, and Nobbys Beach, a Pacific strip popular with surfers and sharks. Many poems were composed while I was visiting faculty in Western Australia, Perth, and Flinders University, Adelaide, still waiting for retrieval in my journals. As this Australian digression underscores, my academic,

---

1   Shirley Geok-lin Lim, *Embracing the Angel: Hong Kong Poems* (City University of Hong Kong, 2014).

2   Shirley Geok-lin Lim, *In Praise of Limes* (Sungold Editions, 2022).

3   Shirley Geok-lin Lim, *Walking Backwards* (West End Press, 2010).

teaching life experiences have been richly productive for my poetry.

Is NUS your only teaching institution? As with your thirteen years abroad, you have written little of your 21 years at NUS. Why have you not shared these 'life writing' subjects in your poems?

LEONG LIEW GEOK: Rather than explicit writing, my observations as a teacher and academic in NUS have instead filtered into and infiltrated poems about students, texts, writers (e.g. 'After Listening to a Student's Grief', 'Meditation over a Tecnogas Cooker', 'Beckett and Lawrence', 'Student, Photo, Docket, Glue', 'Free Spirits', 'Graffiti Conversations', 'After the Conference'). Obliquely, unnamed academics feature in 'Vignette', 'Narratives', 'Old Story'. Some of these will appear in my next collection.

As an academic, I did not go out of my way to develop an academic network or to secure visiting positions abroad. As a result, I was never offered a stint as a visiting fellow. My several sabbaticals were spent in Singapore, excepting one month attached to the Australian Defence Force Academy, Canberra, to do research on the Literature of the Pacific War, and another in London, much of it poring through the holdings at the Imperial War Museum. The foreign-centred poems I have written are few and far between: 'inter alia, inter alios'; 'At Sissinghurst'; 'Liquidamber in the Chinese Garden, Sydney'.

Why have I stayed put in NUS? Children; schools; logistics. Some (female) academics in NUS moved with their entire families abroad for their sabbatical year. Not me. Too disruptive for the children; too stressful for me. And the ease with which male academics got going, bags packed, flying abroad to spend their sabbaticals—while their wives presumably handled matters at home—filled me with envy—and rage. My sabbaticals abroad amounted to one month in Canberra, and another in London. Abbreviations symbolic of putting family over career.

You, on the other hand, have taught in Australia, Spain, and Hong Kong, and stayed for longer periods in Singapore to research and write. I see you as a giant; myself as an ant, or the frog under a coconut shell (*Saperti katak di-bawah tempurong*).

SHIRLEY GEOK-LIN LIM: Unlike your modest self-evaluation, I admire what you have achieved within those constraining consequences. I wish to explore the kind of feminist poetry you have produced with the public voice you have created in Singapore, the 'womanist' oeuvre that is your unique contribution to fin-de-siecle 20–21st century Singapore literature.

LEONG LIEW GEOK: Feminist poetry, or quasi-feminist poetry, yes. Do I write as a poet or as a woman poet or a feminist poet? All three. I write whatever appeals to me. My family; gardening; flora and fauna; observations of people and scenes. I like to challenge myself with inherited forms like the sonnet, ballad, villanelle, etc. I enjoy playing with acrostics. I don't know about the analogy you draw with Jane Austen. For one, I'm not that civilised, poetically! Whom do you write for?

SHIRLEY GEOK-LIN LIM: I was asked that question in the 1980s by New Zealand scholar Norman Simms and I recall being stumped by his simple, direct query. After 13 May 1969, which Malaysians were reading English literature, not to say poetry, and written by a fellow Malaysian? How could I evoke such a non-existent native reader as my audience? Lloyd Fernando, Professor and Chair of English at the University of Malaya, professed Bahasa was the nation's language, English the language of colonisers, not even a second language. Yet I was also not writing for an American audience. Living in Brooklyn, not a citizen, how could my concerns—unsettled, uprooted, Southeast Asian-émigré-oriented—resonate with New York cosmopolitans? My persistence has everything to do with an internalised audience—clearly, an 'ideal' reader, reading *sub specie aeternitatis*, under the eye of Eternity, curious, receptive, always waiting for the next poem to surprise, perhaps delight, often failing her demanding eye and ear. I usually address her in shorthand as 'Muse'.

LEONG LIEW GEOK: I have always regarded myself as a compromised feminist, in my life as well as in my poetry. The activism is actually directed towards my family, particularly my children, who know (I made sure that they did!) that I gave up my career, so to speak, for my family. Have I regretted this? At times, yes. On the whole, no.

SHIRLEY GEOK-LIN LIM: 'Compromised feminist' suggests a self-criticism against a benchmark of 'activist feminist'. To my mind, every feminist has to make decisions that take into account community and social pressures, values, and anxieties. I am not sure you 'gave up your career' for your family. You made certain choices (as I did), and each has lived with the consequences of those choices.

Despite the desire for ideological purity, to live in society, women have to negotiate relationships fraught with conflict, contradiction, ambivalence, and contesting values. Your poems are deeply oral, almost always composed in a woman's voice. They feature gendered personae; deploy coded devices, such as re-telling well-known myths; satirical stances; irony; humour; zany comic-rhetoric-like puns and dialect plays as in code-switching and linguistic registers for social criticism. Many poems call for close readings to unpack their layered, multiple twists and turns.

Some poems dramatise troubling womanist themes by ventriloquizing personae, as in your epistolary poem, 'Madam, My Time is Past'. Epistolary poems are rarely deployed, and the Sri Lankan maid's letter with its misspellings ('marriage Propasal'), fractured grammar, and digressive passages gives voice to an underclass of foreign female domestics that is a particularly Singaporean social phenomenon. The letter writer, her employment contract ended, is abject, reporting on unexpected expenses and challenges on returning to her poorer country, with little future prospect. The chief tone is her wrenching attachment (emotional and economic) to the children and parents she had served for years. The speaker/poet's relationship with her female subject is empathetic, and socially differentiated. The ex-housemaid's pathos is strongly represented, while the authorial reserve underscores a dissonance between the maid's distress and the speaker/poet's emotional absence.

However, in 'Farewell to Sumana', the Singaporean mother who has employed Sumana speaks directly to the housemaid as she is driving her to the airport to fly home to her Sri Lankan family, hence forming a paired dialogical narrative. Both women's distress at the wrenching apart of female domestic intimacy and looming separation are foregrounded. In the last stanza, the Singaporean employer rebukes the housemaid: 'You're not going to start again, are you?/ You don't want us all crying to the airport'. The power differential between the two structures the eight-stanzaic monologue. Employed for six years, Sumana is not yet forty. The values imparted as Sumana is weeping are wholly patriarchal capitalist: 'Go home and find a good man to marry.' 'Look after your savings./ Don't lend any people.' 'It's your money—you work hard. / Keep it for yourself.' The poem bluntly states the socio-cultural difference between a successful Singapore state where women possess work equity and Sri Lanka where women are vassals subordinated to men's desires for youth, beauty, or 'one million rupees' dowry.

The economic rationale is unequivocal. In another ten years (at age near fifty) Sumana will be too old to work. She is therefore of 'no use'; the human rights to decent wages, food and shelter, the social contract between citizen and government, does not include subordinate non-citizen 'guest' workers like Sumana, who at fifty may 'fall sick, die in house.' This ghastly prospect for the employer is also the prospect of responsibility for her worker's life: 'Then how?'

These ironies undergird a 'compromised feminism.' The paired narrative-poems vividly, bluntly, and viscerally treat the problematic employment and power relations between Singapore liberated professional women and foreign female domestics they contractually employ, whose services in fact may be what makes it possible for Singapore professional women to engage in successful careers while still enjoying a full life as wife and mother.

LEONG LIEW GEOK: Not all my poems are 'deeply oral', as you put it. Some are, others are not necessarily written so that their meanings are fully apparent when read aloud. And there are others which are clearly 'literary'. I'm not sure I understand what you mean by 'public voice'. I'm not aware that I've created a public voice. Why would I need a public voice when in large part, I write for myself? But some of my poems take on personae ('A Chauvinist Pig Speaks'; 'Dramatic Monologue'; 'Microwave Cooking Class'; the Gardener poems) to enlarge and diversify the poetic territory.

SHIRLEY GEOK-LIN LIM: I used the term 'public voice' while fully conscious of how private a literary figure and person you are. Many of your poems are in the tradition of Arthur Yap's poems which are written in a public voice, even though Arthur was famously noted for his very private, modest presence. He and his cultural productions, short fiction, poetry, and paintings, are now highly esteemed by the younger generation of Singaporeans and by political figures. He was the first Singaporean poet to use Singlish, for socio-cultural satires, and to mock puffed-up elitist personages, albeit through somewhat coded means. These poems were not appreciated by most Singaporeans during his lifetime, yet he is currently lauded as the singular poet of his generation. Many of your poems similarly deploy Singlish (which Arthur clearly used as the social identity marker for the national community he was both representing and critiquing).

LEONG LIEW GEOK: The colloquial voice(s) in 'Farewell to Sumana' and 'Microwave Cooking Class' seemed right for the subjects I wanted then to address. The two poems wouldn't have sounded 'spot-on' otherwise. I make deliberate use of personae to give different points of view. It's a means of extending my range, to give representation to other voices or perspectives, as in 'Penelope's Theme', where the voice and point-of-view are the wife's, waiting for an absent husband's return, fobbing off suitors 'who'd seize his kingdom for my dowry' and guarding Ithaca for Telemachus, son and heir. I don't see these as poems written in a public voice. It would be more accurate to view these speakers as my *dramatis personae*. Insofar as a part of me is reflected in my persona(e), or alter ego(s), as in the various Gardener poems, the inclusion is deliberate. When I write, I'm not conscious of using a public voice, although I may be using satire and tongue-in-cheek irony. 'Women Drivers' is one such poem. It satirises stereotypical perceptions of women drivers. Similarly, 'The Obligatory Nude Scene' anatomises the nudity that is now a given in filmic versions of Henry James, Charles Dickens or Jane Austen. I'd rather say that these poems exist in the public domain, compared to, say, 'A Middle-Aged Woman Dissuades a Potential Lover' or 'Sometimes I Work in Natural Light', both more personal poems. Once a poem is written, no matter how public, private or confessional, it belongs to the public domain and becomes public property. I don't write with a poetics in mind or with a conscious distinction between public, private or in between. My primary consideration is the creation of a workable, effective piece.

SHIRLEY GEOK-LIN LIM: On Singlish poetics, framed as a dialogue, the two poems I discussed represent a specific cultural-economic society that echoes Arthur Yap's now-canonical poem '2 mothers in a hdb playground'. Yap's poem uses the colloquial English register of local characters, watching their sons at play while their conversation underscores socio-economic competitiveness in their humble-brag of school grades, expensive furniture, and new cars. However, Yap's satirical voice in '2 mothers…' can in no way be confused with the speakers, while your paired poems, composed in a register of colloquial oral English, necessitate further contextualisation to clarify the satirical drama narrated by your compromised feminist voice.

Your Singlish poetics is brilliantly and profoundly authentic Singaporean. Given space constraints, I will focus on your genius poem, appropriately titled 'Forever Singlish'. This Singlish poem is both an oral and aural masterpiece. The compression of registers, ranging from Standard English (as in the use of perfect grammar—colons, semi-colons, idiomatic syntax, etc.) to various dialect Chinese and race/ethnic tags (leh, lor, hor, lah; Ah Lian, Ah Beng, Mamak, Goondu); intermixing of Malay and Tamil words; common Hokkien scatological phrases ('kana-sai'/like shit; 'chau si'/deadly stink); and their syncopation through rhythm and rhyme (e.g. 'Why they care? Hard core kaypoh – / Bo dai chi cho') is exemplified in the first two stanzas. The propulsive opening rhythms ('It got rhythm'; 'It got reason'; 'We say sorrysorrysorry'; 'No lubang, so teruk'; 'Vegetable, Animal, Mineral, Abstract'; 'No class Singlish here to stay'), various Chinese dialect spellings, the five-line stanzas with breath line breaks, caesuras, rhetorical turns and sequential witty closures: this short poem in an Anglophone poetic form is absolutely, absurdly zany and original. It is a self-deprecating satire, mocking Singapore's dense urbanscape, whose inhabitants piss in the elevators, and abuse their multiracial neighbours, elitist proper English speakers, and high society and bureaucratic regulators. The satire celebrates the resistance voiced by a hodge-podge unruly citizenry whose identity is emblematised in their Singlish speech. I have admitted to my lack of confidence in using Manglish as a creative register in my poems and fiction, despite my life-long admiration of Amos Tutuola's *The Palm-Wine Drinkard*; and I admire in your poem a similar genius at play with a local dialect English.

LEONG LIEW GEOK: In 'Forever Singlish', I had wanted to test the potential of Singlish as a medium of poetic expression. I had a fun time writing it! It was a matter of putting together the cadences and colloquial expressions familiar to my ears. Oral and aural plagiarism of a kind!

How do you write? I find your productivity impressive and inspiring. The domestic; and the untamed, or, should I say, the unrelenting vividness of metaphor and image in your work, the assurance in voice and tone, the range in locales, subjects and forms. That arresting imagination is omnipresent in your latest volume, *In Praise of Limes*, as in 'Farmers' Market', 'No Rain Sonnet', or the forest fires in California which have created 'Sunrise in the West'.

SHIRLEY GEOK-LIN LIM: I write in multiple genres—formal and free verse, short fiction, the novella and novel, memoir, creative non-fiction, academic and scholarly writing, etc. I began with poetry around the age of nine or ten, enthralled by British children's literature, reading as escapism from childhood traumas of maternal abandonment, paternal violence, homelessness, hunger, poverty, social shame and misery. I fell in love with the chanting musicality of Walter de la Mare's 'The Listeners', John Keats' 'La Belle Dame sans Merci', Tennyson's 'The Lady of Shalott', Christina Rossetti's 'Goblin Market' and more. These poems, as with prose works, told enchanting stories in language that penetrated my mind as 'immortal' art because the lines imprinted almost indelibly, effortlessly, worded in memory. Prose sentences did not sing as poems do. I've remained a formalist poet, fixed on rhythm, rhymes, word play, and more. My shift to longer prose forms underlines that I am a writer, but as I began my life-work with poems, in my senior years I am returning to poetry: 'In the beginning is my end.' How do you write?

LEONG LIEW GEOK: How do I write? It depends on the subject, the inspiration and the impetus. Some drafts are filed away for years before I remember them and turn them into finished poems! An example is 'Looking In,' a poem about two cockatoos (this poem will be in my next collection). One poem may lead into another poem because of the momentum which the earlier poem has set in motion, though the poems may not be related in material or theme.

An interesting feature of your work are your allusions to the canon (then) which you (and I) probably read and imbibed as undergraduates: you make references to the Romantics (Keats, Wordsworth, Coleridge, Shelley), Hopkins, Yeats, Eliot, Auden, Marianne Moore and Whitman. I'm wondering if they might be a fruitful hangover for you. But there are also at least half a dozen prose poems ('A Wet Market in Hong Kong', 'Morning Walking', 'Firefly', 'Dating', 'Notes from an Open Mic Poetry Reading' to name five) in your oeuvre. What is their relationship to 'rhythm, rhymes, word play and more'? Were you looking for more space for what you wanted to capture or express?

SHIRLEY GEOK-LIN LIM: I love your phrase 'fruitful hangover'. Yes, the Romantics/British Lit/US poetics undergirded my work for many years. Prose narratives, fiction and creative non-fiction, gave room to stretch my subjects, grow voices other than those associated with lyrical and formalist poetry, and push Imagination's boundaries, so the prose poem was a parallel organic development. Often, the published prose poems began as blank verse. The final drafts bear the stylistics of my formal poems—internal and half rhymes, alliteration, assonance, rhetorical play, etc. I am struggling with completing my twelfth collection, because the poems I am writing now are quite radically different in voice and style, which means these poems are, for me, new, new, new.

LEONG LIEW GEOK: We have both been attracted to poetry as an art form, to the fact that free verse is not free (to quote T. S. Eliot), but requires aesthetic control. One may be a confessional poet, but poetry is not freewheeling confessionalism at all. We are both fond of lyric forms. I admire your villanelle, 'Family Album', 'Pantoun for Chinese Women' and 'Mother's Song' with its rhyming tercets. All three use form to create the tensions between what is, and what may or will come to be, between mother and a child too young to be aware of the future. 'She knew the guarded yards outside, crazy/ Dogs and hearts, mind locked behind sigh./ He knew as none did what it was to be'. Then you use the pantoun with its repetitive rhymes to move an imminent infanticide to which both parents are party, because the newborn is a girl, towards the inevitable. 'They say a child with two mouths is no good...We had saved ashes for a hundred days, / Knowing, if the time came, that we would.' I am a sucker for form! As well as stringent, unforgiving forms (to quote Yeats, 'the fascination of what's difficult'), I enjoy challenging myself with acrostics, sometimes merging the sonnet and acrostic.

SHIRLEY GEOK-LIN LIM: That feature is what drew me initially to your poems. With so many English-language poems coming out of Singapore-Malaysia in our generation, almost all in 'free verse', what you term 'aesthetic control' is seldom present. I prefer 'aesthetic play'. I view that play as intrinsically, vitally present in lyric forms. I confess to manifesting, even if in coded ways, a confessional poetic sensibility. The best of confessional poetry in 20th century US literature is always shaped by what you term 'aesthetic control'. Robert Lowell's *Life Studies* comes to mind; how poetic forms and stylistics were the anvil that crafted poems out of such mental messiness, as with the confessional poems of Sylvia Plath, Anne Sexton and now into the 21st century, with confessional poetry on every other page!

How have you dodged that modernist bullet?

LEONG LIEW GEOK: It's very boring to be continually confessional! I consciously strive for diversity and extension—in voice, subject, environment. Your domestic and family poems, portraits of your mother, grandparents, father, which are arranged in sequence in

Listening to the Singer, are deeply confessional, and unflinching in their honesty.[4] But your work is not wholly confessional either. Far from it! There's more to poetry than the autobiographical. One needs to look out, as you do—for other subjects, scenes, possibilities. Yours is a multi-track sensibility.

Subordinating our commonalities, we have differing attitudes towards the English and Chinese languages. English was your adoptive, but now naturalised language, just as America is now your country. This is the direction your work has taken. You've crossed country and ocean to California and embraced it as your home. I find a recognition of place and home in *In Praise of Limes*, published significantly in Santa Barbara where you live. The poems here speak to the landscapes of California, from its wildfires to its beaches and surf, to coyotes, owls, bees and lizards. But in an earlier phase, you were writing angst-ridden poems about estrangement, as if searching for an identity. English is not your native tongue; Chinese should have been, but it is not, by virtue of your being Peranakan, and the medium in which you were educated. You felt guilty, compelled to read Li Poh 'in a stranger's tongue' because 'I cannot speak your tongue with ease'. My parents felt that prospects were better for the English-educated than the Chinese-educated. My father was half Peranakan and lived during a time when the Peranakans were known for their Anglophile loyalties. I feel that my illiteracy in written Chinese and spoken Mandarin, also because (like you) I was educated in English—after one year in a Chinese school when I was five or so—is one of the tragedies of my life. Correspondingly, Chinese poetry has to be read, and lost, in translation. But I have not written a single poem about the disjunction between 'should' and 'is'. Given the inescapable conditions of one's life, one moves on.

***

---

4   Shirley Geok-lin Lim, *Listening to the Singer* (Maya Press, 2007).

I MADE YOUR SOUP

Sean Wai Keung

A response to 'War Soup' by Jihyun Yun

i couldnt find american cheese
so instead i substituted extra

tofu - i also
used packets

of imported hongkong delivery ramen
instead of ramyun

even though my korean friends
offered to give me some

in some ways it felt wrong
to change the recipe as you wrote it

but i was raised on hongkong delivery ramen
so to not use that would also feel

disrespectful to my mum
and po po (who raised me)

you understand dont you
its less about your recipe

and more about whats inside
of me - and what i feel in my stomach

i talked about it at a food-writing workshop the other day
how hunger could be what unites us

(by us i either mean we of eastasian descent
or we as people of different diasporas)

and how historically hunger has been what inspires us to change
our recipes as we learn more about the world around us

just like how we (whoever we are) moved from eating grass
and bones to ramen and ramyun to injeera and staffordshire

oatcakes - you see unfortunately none of my personal history
involves american cheese though

so hopefully you dont mind that i didnt use it
because to me the soup was still so delicious

it made my belly swell with warmth
and my palms as hot as coals

***

CONTRIBUTORS

Eddie Tay is an Associate Professor at the Department of English, Chinese University of Hong Kong, where he teaches courses on creative writing and poetry. His bilingual poetry collection, *The Mental Life of Cities*, is a winner of the 2012 Singapore Literature Prize. *Dreaming Cities* is a collection featuring both poetry and street photography set in Singapore and Hong Kong. His most recent work, *Hong Kong as Creative Practice*, blends creative documentary writing with street photography. He is currently completing a draft of an autoethnography of creative practices.

Jennifer Wong was born and raised in Hong Kong and now lives in the UK. She earned a creative writing PhD from Oxford Brookes University. Wong is the author of three poetry collections including 回家 *Letters Home* (Nine Arches Press, 2020) and of *Identity, Home & Writing Elsewhere in Contemporary Chinese Diaspora Poetry* (Bloomsbury, 2023). She was the writer-in-residence with *Wasafiri* in 2021 and a visiting fellow at Oxford TORCH for 2022. Together with Jason EH Lee and Tim Tim Cheng, she co-edited *Where Else: An International Hong Kong Poetry Anthology* (Verve Poetry Press, 2023). She is also an advisor to the Leeds Centre for New Chinese Writing.

*

Romalyn Ante FRSL is a Filipino-British poet, essayist, and editor. She was born and bred in Batangas, Philippines and migrated to her second home, Wolverhampton, at sixteen. She is co-founding editor of *harana poetry*, a magazine for poets who write in English as a second or parallel language, and the founder of *Tsaá with Roma*, an online interview series with poets and other creatives. Her debut collection is *Antiemetic for Homesickness* (Chatto & Windus). She was awarded the Jerwood Compton Poetry Fellowship. She was recently elected as a board member of *Poetry London* and as a Royal Society of Literature Fellow.

Khairani Barokka is a writer and artist from Jakarta, and Editor of *Modern Poetry in Translation*. Among her honours, she has been *Modern Poetry in Translation*'s Inaugural Poet-in-Residence, a UNFPA Indonesian Young Leader Driving Social Change, an

Artforum Must-See, UK Associate Artist at Delfina Foundation, and Associate Artist at the National Centre for Writing (UK). Okka's work includes being author-illustrator of *Indigenous Species* (Tilted Axis, 2016), author of *Rope* (Nine Arches Press, 2017), and co-editor of *Stairs and Whispers: D/deaf and Disabled Poets Write Back* (Nine Arches Press, 2017). Her latest book is *Ultimatum Orangutan* (Nine Arches Press, 2021), shortlisted for the Barbellion Prize.

Natalie Linh Bolderston is a Vietnamese-Chinese-British poet. Her poems have appeared in *The Poetry Review*, *Poetry London*, *The Rialto*, *Magma* and elsewhere. In 2020, she received an Eric Gregory Award and co-won the Rebecca Swift Women Poets' Prize. Her poem 'Middle Name with Diacritics' came third in the 2019 National Poetry Competition and was shortlisted for the 2021 Forward Prize for Best Single Poem. She is an alumna of the Roundhouse Poetry Collective, the London Library Emerging Writers Programme and the VanThanh Productions Development Programme. Her pamphlet, *The Protection of Ghosts*, was published by V. Press in 2019. She is now working on her first full-length collection.

Troy Cabida is a Filipino poet from south-west London. His recent work appears in *Outspoken*, *fourteen poems*, *bath magg*, and *100 Queer Poems* (Vintage, 2022). His poem 'How to wear a Love Bracelet' was shortlisted for The Bridport Prize for Poetry 2022. His debut pamphlet is *War Dove* (Bad Betty Press, 2020). Troy is an alum of the Barbican Young Poets and has produced for the London open mic night Poetry and Shaah. He currently works for the National Poetry Library, Southbank Centre.

Mary Jean Chan is the author of *Flèche* (Faber, 2019) and *Bright Fear* (Faber, 2023). *Flèche* won the Costa Book Award for Poetry and was shortlisted for the International Dylan Thomas Prize and the Seamus Heaney Centre First Collection Poetry Prize, among others. In 2021, *Flèche* was a Lambda Literary Award Finalist. *Bright Fear* is a Poetry Book Society Recommendation and is currently shortlisted for the 2023 Forward Prize for Best Collection. Chan edited the anthology *100 Queer Poems* (Vintage, 2022) with Andrew McMillan, and is a judge for the 2023 Booker Prize. Born and raised in Hong Kong, Chan lives in Oxford.

Victoria Chang's forthcoming poetry collection, *With My Back to the World*, will be published in 2024 by Farrar, Straus & Giroux and Corsair Books in the UK. Her most recent book of poetry, *The Trees Witness Everything* was published by Copper Canyon Press and Corsair Books in the UK in 2022. It was named one of the Best Books of 2022 by the *New Yorker* and *The Guardian*. She currently lives in Los Angeles. She is the Bourne Chair of Poetry at Georgia Tech.

Chen Chen is the author of two books of poetry, *Your Emergency Contact Has Experienced an Emergency* (BOA Editions and Bloodaxe Books, 2022) and *When I Grow Up I Want to Be a List of Further Possibilities* (BOA Editions, 2017; Bloodaxe Books, 2019), which was longlisted for the National Book Award and won the Thom Gunn Award, among other honours. A 2022 United States Artists Fellow, he currently teaches for the low-residency MFA programs at New England College and Stonecoast.

Tim Tim Cheng is a poet and a teacher from Hong Kong, currently based between Edinburgh and London. Her pamphlet *Tapping At Glass* (Verve Poetry Press, 2023) explores womanhood, multilingualism, and psychogeography. Her poems are published or anthologised in *POETRY*, *The Rialto*, *Poetry London*, and elsewhere. Her latest appearances include the StAnza Festival, Hidden Door festival, Singapore Writers Festival, and BBC Scotland. She is a WrICE fellow, an Ignite fellow, a member of Southbank Centre's New Poets Collective 2022/23, and a mentee under the Roddy Lumsden Memorial Mentorship scheme. She edits, translates between Chinese and English, and writes lyrics.

Felix Chow Yue Ching is a poet from Hong Kong and works as an English tutor. He is the winner of the The HKBU Century Club Citywide English Poetry Competition 2020 and The Maisie Choa English Poetry Prize. His poems are published/forthcoming in *Voice and Verse* and *CHA: An Asian Literary Journal*. He is also working as a part-time research assistant at MU and is interested in Hong Kong and its representations in Hong Kong English-language writing.

Kit Fan's third poetry collection *The Ink Cloud Reader* is shortlisted for the Forward Prize Best Collection 2023. He is the author of two books of poems, *As Slow As Possible* (2018) and *Paper Scissors Stone* (2011). His first novel is *Diamond Hill* (2021). He was elected a Fellow of the Royal Society of Literature in 2022 and appointed as a Non-Executive Director of the Author's Licensing and Collecting Society (ALCS) in 2023.

Jay Gao is a poet from Edinburgh, Scotland. His debut poetry collection *Imperium* (Carcanet, 2022) is a winner of an Eric Gregory Award and a Somerset Maugham Award. He is also the author of three poetry pamphlets. He earned his MFA in Literary Arts (Poetry) from Brown University. He is a Contributing Editor at *The White Review* and a reader for *POETRY* magazine. Currently, he lives in New York and is a PhD student in English and Comparative Literature at Columbia University where he researches experimental poetics and race.

Will Harris is a London-based writer. He is the author of the poetry books *RENDANG* (2020) and *Brother Poem* (2023), both published by Granta in the UK and by Wesleyan University Press in the US. He has been shortlisted for the T.S. Eliot Prize and won the Forward Prize for Best First Collection. He helps facilitate the Southbank New Poets Collective with Vanessa Kisuule, and co-translated Habib Tengour's *Consolatio* with Delaina Haslam in 2022. He currently works in extra-care homes and is a Visiting Poetry Fellow at UEA working towards a community-led archive of poets' work.

Sarah Howe is a Hong Kong-born poet, academic, and editor. Her first book, *Loop of Jade* (Chatto & Windus, 2015), won the T. S. Eliot Prize. She is the founding editor of *Prac Crit*, an online journal of poetry and criticism, and teaches poetry at King's College London in England.

Antony Huen is an academic based in his home city, Hong Kong. He holds a PhD in English from the University of York. As a literary critic, he won the 2021 Wasafiri Essay Prize and came second for the Women Poetry Prize, awarded to a critical essay on the poetry of women of colour. As a poet, he was shortlisted for the inaugural

Poetry London Pamphlet Prize. His poems appear in *The Dark Horse*, *Poetry Wales*, *PN Review*, and elsewhere.

Joshua Ip is a Singaporean poet, editor and literary organiser. He has published six-ish poetry collections, edited eleven anthologies, and co-founded Sing Lit Station, an over-active literary charity. His latest book, *translations to the tanglish* (Math Paper Press, 2021) gathers contemporary and anachronistic translations of classical Tang/Song Dynasty poetry.

L Kiew is a Chinese-Malaysian living in London. She works as a charity sector leader and accountant. She holds a MSc in Creative Writing and Literary Studies from Edinburgh University. Her debut pamphlet *The Unquiet* was published by Offord Road Books in 2019. Her debut collection, *More Than Weeds*, was published by Nine Arches Press in 2023. Her poetry has been anthologised in *Living with other people: an anthology for indefinite times* (Corrupted Editions, 2022), *From the Silence of the Stacks: New Voices Rise* (London Library, 2021), *Crossing Lines: an anthology of immigrant poetry* (Broken Sleep Books, 2021) and *Footprints: an anthology of new ecopoetry* (Broken Sleep Books, 2022).

Li-Young Lee is the author of *The Undressing* (W. W. Norton, 2018); *Behind My Eyes* (W. W. Norton, 2008); *Book of My Nights* (BOA Editions, 2001), which won the 2002 William Carlos Williams Award; *The City in Which I Love You* (BOA Editions, 1990), which was the 1990 Lamont Poetry Selection; and *Rose* (BOA Editions, 1986), which won the Delmore Schwartz Memorial Poetry Award. His other work includes *Breaking the Alabaster Jar: Conversations with Li-Young Lee* (Edited by Earl G. Ingersoll, BOA Editions, 2006) and *The Winged Seed: A Remembrance* (Simon and Schuster, 1995), a memoir which received an American Book Award from the Before Columbus Foundation. He has two books forthcoming from W.W. Norton in 2024: *The Invention of the Darling*, a collection of poems, and a co-translation (with Yun Wang) of *The Dao De Jing*.

Laura Jane Lee is a Hong Kong-born, Singapore-based poet. She is a winner of the Sir Roger Newdigate Prize and various international poetry competitions. Her work has been featured in *The Straits Times*, *Tatler Asia*, *Poetry London*, *Ambit*, *QLRS*, and the 52nd

Poetry International Festival in Rotterdam. Laura Jane also works with the Asia Creative Writing Programme, and is Poetry Editor at *SPLOOSH*. She is also part of the poetry.sg team. Her most recent pamphlet *flinch & air* was published with Out-Spoken Press in 2021. Much of her writing and poetic practice is informed by the work of Mary Oliver and Naomi Shihab Nye.

Louise Leung Fung Yee is a Hong Kong English-language poet. Their usually rebellious works engage with social and cultural politics, Hong Kong's everyday life, subject to their confessional whimsies. Their poems have been featured in *Voice & Verse Poetry Magazine*, *Cha: An Asian Literary Journal*, *Canto Cutie* and others. They are part of a growing body of Kongish literature.

Leong Liew Geok received her primary and secondary education in Penang, Malaysia, and studied in universities in Australia, England and the United States. She taught in the Department of English Language and Literature, National University of Singapore, from 1981–2002. She is the author of two collections of poetry, *Love is Not Enough* (Times Books International, 1991) and *Women without Men* (Times Books International, 2000), and edited, among other publications, *More than Half the Sky: Creative Writings by Thirty Singaporean Women* (Times Books International, 1998). Her poetry has been anthologised and has appeared in various journals. She is finalising her third collection of poems.

Dong Li is a multilingual author who translates from Chinese, English, French, and German. Born and raised in China, he was educated at Deep Springs College and Brown University. His works have been published by *Conjunctions*, *FENCE*, *Kenyon Review*, *POETRY*, *The New York Times* and elsewhere. His full-length English translations from Chinese include Zhu Zhu's *The Wild Great Wall* (Deep Vellum, 2018) and Song Lin's *The Gleaner Song* (Giramondo & Deep Vellum, 2021). He has received fellowships from Akademie Schloss Solitude, Camargo and Humboldt Foundations, MacDowell, PEN/Heim Translation Fund, Yaddo, and others. His debut poetry collection *The Orange Tree* (The University of Chicago Press, March 2023) is the inaugural winner of the Phoenix Emerging Poet Book Prize.

Shirley Geok-lin Lim's (PhD, Brandeis; Professor Emerita, UCSB; Visiting Professorships, MIT, NUS, NIE, National Sun-yet Sen University, CityUHK, Chair Professor Hong Kong University, UCSB Women's Studies Chair) poetry has been widely anthologized; published in *The Hudson Review*, *Feminist Studies*, *Virginia Quarterly Review*, etc., featured by Bill Moyers, Tracey K. Smith's Slowdown, and set to music as libretto for various scores. Recipient of the Commonwealth Poetry Prize, two American Book Awards, MELUS and Feminist Press Lifetime Achievement Awards, and the University of California Santa Barbara's Research Lecturer Award she's authored 11 poetry collections, 3 novels, *The Shirley Lim Collection*, 3 story collections, 2 critical studies, and is editor/co-editor of over 18 anthologies and journal special issues.

Mukahang Limbu is a Nepalese writer based in Oxford. A three-time Foyle Young Poet, winner of the First Story National competition and the Out-Spoken Prize, and has been longlisted in the National Poetry Competition and the Forward Prizes. His poems have been published in *England: Poems from a School* (Picador, 2018), *bath magg*, *Oxford Poetry*, *The Sunday Times*, *The Kindling Journal*, and *Tell Me the Truth About Life* edited by Cerys Matthews. His debut pamphlet *Mother of Flip-Flops* (Out-Spoken Press, 2022) was chosen as the Poetry Book Society's Pamphlet Choice. He is a recipient of an Eric Gregory Award and the Harper Wood Award. For this project he was granted the Hawley Fund by The Queen's College, Oxford, and is grateful for their generous support.

Aaron Maniam is the author of two collections of poetry, *Morning at Memory's Border* (one of three books shortlisted for the 2007 Singapore Literature Prize) and *Second Persons* (2018). He is a regular editor of *The Birthday Book*, an annual collection of essays on, of, and for Singapore, and writes regularly on public policy, futures thinking and the use of metaphors in large, complex organisations.

Theresa Muñoz was born in Vancouver, Canada and lives in Edinburgh. She is Research Associate at Newcastle University and Director of the Newcastle Poetry Festival. She has also managed several literary initiatives through the Newcastle Centre for Literary Arts, including the James Berry Poetry Prize, the first prize in the

UK to offer mentoring and debut publication to emerging writers of colour. In 2022 she shortlisted for the Royal Society of Literature Sky Arts Prize for her creative non-fiction. She has published one collection of poetry, *Settle*, which shortlisted for the Melita Hume Poetry Prize. Her work has appeared on BBC Radio Scotland and in several international journals including *Arc* magazine, *Canadian Literature*, *The Poetry Review*, *Southward*, *The Scores* and elsewhere. She has won the Robert Louis Stevenson Fellowship, Muriel Spark Centenary Award and a Creative Scotland Award. Her second collection will be published in 2025.

Alvin Pang, PhD, is a poet, writer, editor and translator whose broad creative practice spans three decades of literary and related activities in Singapore and elsewhere. Featured in the *Oxford Companion to Modern Poetry in English* and the *Penguin Book of the Prose Poem*, his writing has been translated into more than twenty languages, including Swedish, Croatian, Macedonian, Chinese, Malay and French. A 2022 Civitella Ranieri Fellow, he has received Singapore's Young Artist of the Year Award, the Singapore Youth Award and the JCCI Education Award. Among other engagements, he is an honorary Adjunct Professor of RMIT University, serves on several editorial advisory boards, and was a judge of the 2022 Dublin Literary Award and the 2023 Society of Authors Travelling Scholarships. His recent books include *What Happened: Poems 1997–2017* (2017), *Uninterrupted time* (2019), *Det som ger oss våra namn* (2022), and *Diaphanous*, co-written with George Szirtes.

Nina Mingya Powles is a writer, zinemaker and librarian from Aotearoa New Zealand, currently living in London. She is the author of several pamphlets, zines and poetry books, most recently *Magnolia* 木蘭 and a collection of essays, *Small Bodies of Water*. She is a pamphlet selector for the Poetry Book Society and writes an occasional e-newsletter about food and memory called *Comfort Food*.

Helen Quah is a British poet and writer whose work has appeared in journals such as *The Rialto*, *bath magg* and *The Poetry Review*. *Dog Woman* (2022) her debut pamphlet, was published by Out-Spoken Press and received an Eric Gregory Award from the Society of Authors. She currently lives and works as a doctor in London.

Sean Wai Keung is a writer and performance maker based in Glasgow. His work often uses food as a starting point for explorations of identity, migration and communities. His pamphlet *you are mistaken* won the Rialto Open Pamphlet Competition 2016 and he has also released short-length works *how to cook* (2017) and *be happy* (2018) with Speculative Books. His first full length poetry collection, *sikfan glaschu,* was published by Verve Poetry Press in April 2021, and was described as 'joyful, earnest and offering unexpected poignancies from everyday life' by the *Scotsman.*

Lora Supandi (they/she) is a writer of Hakka-Indonesian descent and student at Stanford University. Through the diaristic and the imagined, her poetry experiments with the possibilities of radical futurism, postcolonial landscapes, and unseen intimacies. In their writing, she explores what it means to grieve and dream during the apocalypse. Outside of her personal art practice, she works as a prison abolitionist alongside formerly incarcerated folks.

Arthur Sze has published eleven books of poetry, including *The Glass Constellation: New and Collected Poems* (Copper Canyon Press, 2021); *Sight Lines*, which won the 2019 USA National Book Award for Poetry; *Compass Rose*, a Pulitzer Prize finalist; *The Ginkgo Light*; *Quipu*; and *The Redshifting Web: Poems 1970-1998*. A new collection, *The Silk Dragon II: Translations of Chinese Poetry*, will be published by Copper Canyon Press in the spring of 2024. Sze is the recipient of many honors, including a 2022 Ruth Lilly Poetry Prize for Lifetime Achievement from the Poetry Foundation, the 2021 Shelley Memorial Award from the Poetry Society of America, the Jackson Poetry Prize, and a Guggenheim Fellowship. A fellow of the American Academy of Arts and Sciences, and a Chancellor Emeritus of the Academy of American Poets, he is a professor emeritus at the Institute of American Indian Arts and lives in Santa Fe, New Mexico.

Marylyn Tan is a large-beasted, supple, queer, female Chinese Singaporean writer-artist whose proclivities are promiscuous and appetites indiscriminate. Her work aims to subvert, revert and pervert, and works to disrespect respectability and reclaim power. Her first child, *GAZE BACK*, is the lesbo trans-genre grimoire you

269

never knew you needed, and made her the first woman poet (woet) to clinch the Singapore Literature Prize.

Jennifer Lee Tsai is a poet, editor, critic and teacher. She was born in Bebington and grew up in Liverpool. She is a fellow of The Complete Works programme for diversity and innovation and a Ledbury Poetry Critic. Her poetry and criticism are widely published in magazines and journals including *Poetry London*, *The Poetry Review*, *The Telegraph*, *The TLS*, *The White Review*. Her debut poetry pamphlet is *Kismet* (ignitionpress, 2019). In 2019, she was awarded an AHRC scholarship to undertake doctoral research in Creative Writing at the University of Liverpool. Jennifer received a Northern Writers Award for Poetry in 2020. She is a winner of the 2022 Women Poets' Prize. Her second poetry pamphlet *La Mystérique* (2022) is published by Guillemot Press.

R.A. Villanueva is the author of *Reliquaria*, winner of the Prairie Schooner Book Prize. New work has been featured by the Academy of American Poets and on National Public Radio—and his writing appears widely in literary publications such as *POETRY*, *Ploughshares*, and *Poetry London*. His honours include commendations from the Forward Prizes and fellowships from the Constance Saltonstall Foundation for the Arts, the Sewanee Writers' Conference, and Kundiman. He lives in Brooklyn, New York.

Jenny Xie is the author of the poetry collections *Eye Level* and The *Rupture Tense*, finalists for the National Book Award. She has received fellowships and recognition from the New York Foundation of the Arts, the Vilcek Foundation, and the Jerome Foundation. Xie lives in New York City and teaches at Bard College.

Jinhao Xie is an alumnus of Barbican Young Poets and Southbank Centre New Poets Collective. They are currently creating their first pamphlet collection. Their work is in *POETRY*, *The Poetry Review*, *Harana*, *bath magg*, *Gutter Magazine* and *fourteen poems* and anthologies, including *Articulations for Keeping the Light In*, *Slam! You're Gonna Wanna Hear This* edited by Nikita Gill, *Instagram Poems for Every Day* by National Poetry Library, and *Re. Creation*. They are interested in nature, the mundane, and the interpersonal. They love to cook for their beloved.

Yanyi is the author of *Dream of the Divided Field* (One World 2022), finalist for the 2022 New England Independent Booksellers Association Award for Poetry, and *The Year of Blue Water* (Yale, 2019), winner of the 2018 Yale Series of Younger Poets Prize, finalist for the 2020 Lambda Literary Award in Transgender Poetry, and one of 2019's Best Poetry Books by New York Public Library. Most recently, he is the recipient of a 2023 Vermont Arts Council Grant and a 2022 Tanne Foundation Award. He teaches poetry at large.

Eric Yip was born and raised in Hong Kong. His work appears or is forthcoming in *The Poetry Review*, *Magma*, *The Adroit Journal*, *Best New Poets*, and elsewhere. His poem, 'Fricatives', was the 2021 winner of The Poetry Society's National Poetry Competition selected from a pool of more than 16,000 entries, and has been shortlisted for the Forward Prize for Best Single Poem in 2023. He was also a Poetry Society Young Critic with reviews forthcoming in *Poetry London* and *Magma* and is a co-host of *Ying Si Hak Yi*, a Cantonese podcast on global Anglophone poetry. He is currently an undergraduate studying economics at the University of Cambridge.

Monica Youn is the author of four poetry collections, most recently *FROM FROM*, which was published by Graywolf Press in the US and Carcanet Press in the UK in 2023. She has been awarded the Levinson Prize from the Poetry Foundation, the William Carlos Williams Award of the Poetry Society of America, a Guggenheim Fellowship, a Witter Bytter Fellowship from the Library of Congress, and a Stegner Fellowship. Her books have been shortlisted for the National Book Award, the National Book Critics Circle Award and the Kingsley Tufts Award. A former constitutional lawyer, she is a member of the curatorial collective the Racial Imaginary Institute and is an associate professor of English at UC Irvine.

Ethan Yu lives in Sacramento, California, with his family and works at the community college library. He majored in Philosophy from University of California Santa Barbara and will work on his Master's degree in Theology there next year. His poetry has appeared in *Liminal Transit Review* and *Where Else: An International Hong Kong Poetry Anthology* (Verve Poetry Press, 2023), and his poetry manuscript was longlisted for Palette Poetry Chapbook Prize in 2022.

NOTES

Selected other titles by Out-Spoken Press

Email: press@outspokenldn.com